FOUNDATIONS:
STRATEGIES FOR THE FUTURE OF COLLEGIATE HOUSING

FOUNDATIONS

Strategies for the Future of Collegiate Housing

edited by   BETH MCCUSKEY | NORB DUNKEL

Association of College and University Housing Officers - International (ACUHO-I)
941 Chatham Lane, Suite 318
Columbus, Ohio 43221 USA

To order additional copies of this book, or other titles published by ACUHO-I, please visit our Web site at www.acuho-i.org.

Publishers Cataloging-in-Publication Data

Dunkel, Norbert W. 1956-
McCuskey, Beth M. 1966-
      Foundations: strategies for the future of collegiate housing
          p. cm.
      Includes bibliographical references
      ISBN 0-945109-11-3 (pbk.)
      1. College students—Housing—United States. 2. Residence and Education—United States. I. Title.

      LB3227.5 2006
      378.198 710973

The information contained in the table on page 25 ("Characteristics of Millennial Students" and "Generation NeXt Model Select Traits") is re-printed with the permission of the authors and the publisher, respectively. ACUHO-I and the editors thank them for their cooperation.

Cover photo subjects include the students and buildings of Massachusetts Institute of Technology, University of Florida, The Ohio State University, Roanoke College (Virginia), Baylor University (Texas), Valparaiso University (Indiana), Appalachian State University (North Carolina), St. Edwards University (Texas), University of Oregon, University of Southern California, Case Western Reserve University (Ohio), University of South Carolina, and Syracuse University (New York). All photos used with permission.

Baylor photo courtesy of Hanbury, Evans, Wright & Vlattas.
Appalachian State University and University of South Carolina photos courtesy of Little Diversified Architectural Consulting.
University of Southern California photo courtesy of Cannon Design.

Additional photos obtained via photos.com.

Cover design by James A. Baumann

Printed by Thomson-Shore, Inc.

The paper used in this publication meets the minimum requirements of the American National Standard for Information Sciences—Permanence of Paper for Printed Library Materials. ANSI Z39.48–1992.

9 8 7 6 5 4 3 2 1

This book is dedicated to

Mr. James C. Grimm
1932 – 2004

"Find the Money. Protect the Money. Protect the Money."

CONTENTS

Part III: The Politics, Budget, and Accountability of Housing Operations

ACKNOWLEDGMENTS

We want to thank the chapter authors. By providing your time, expertise, and experiences, others will have the opportunity to "see over the horizon" to better plan and prepare for the future of their housing operations. We also want to thank James Baumann, ACUHO-I Director of Communications and Marketing, for coordinating the editing, cover design, printing, and marketing of this book.

Beth McCuskey: I wish to thank my co-workers at the University of Wyoming for their dedication, patience, and support. They are truly an amazing group of colleagues and day after day, make me proud! I would also like to thank my co-editor, Norb Dunkel, for the opportunity to work with him to make this project a reality. Norb's expertise in the area of writing and publication is remarkable and I have learned so much by having the opportunity to work with him. I am also grateful to Jim Grimm who saw the potential for this project and pointed me in Norb's direction as a possible co-editor. Jim's mentoring was undoubtedly the impetus for this book. Finally, to my husband Brad and children Chris and Allison, my thanks for your undying love and support.

Norb Dunkel: I thank my wife, Kim, and son, Nicholas, for their continued support of my writing and traveling. I would also like to thank the staff of the University of Florida Department of Housing and Residence Education. These staff members continue to amaze me with their talent, dedication, and loyalty to both students and parents. I also thank Mr. Jim Grimm, the former Director of Housing at the University of Florida. I will miss our great lunch conversations but at least I know that, with his mentoring of the many housing professionals he came into contact with, the future of the housing profession is in good hands.

Introduction

magine the world of collegiate housing if we could definitively see the future. How might we make decisions differently? How might we intentionally alter the outcomes of our work?

This was the foremost question in our minds as we began to assemble the work you now hold in your hand. It seemed a fitting time for a book that explored the central aspects of housing and residence life that are being buffeted by shifting forces, particularly because those forces are gaining strength. These include demographic shifts, external dynamics such as changing expectations for higher education's roles, and internal considerations such as aging facilities. The interplay of these and other issues require housing officers to be visionary, employing a variety of strategies to plan and lead effectively during these transformational times.

The basis and topics for the book came out of the doctoral research Beth M. McCuskey, Ed.D. conducted in 2002 to identify future events most likely to happen and influence the housing profession. A panel of 30 practitioners and faculty members identified 35 high-impact items that they believe will be prevelant during the next 20 years. Grouping those into 12 categories (and later, three general themes), the chapters of this book emerged (see study methodology).

The authors for this book were selected based on their expertise within each of the content areas. Although the dissertation provided the basic foundation for the book, authors had wide latitude to address topics in ways they deemed most appropriate. The authors were challenged to think beyond their day-to-day dealings to envision scenarios of the future. In each chapter, they discuss how the profession has adapted to change in the past and, when predictions had basis, they identified current and future trends that are likely to affect housing operations. Drawing on their experiences of today and their intuition for what tomorrow holds, the authors establish the foundation upon which the future of collegiate housing will be built.

Utilizing the Information

This book is intended to be a useful tool for change. It was our intent to collect information, insight, and points of view from a variety of different authors and experts regarding the different facets of collegiate housing. While each chapter in this book focuses on a specific topic of collegiate housing, the topics are so interrelated that it remains a book that should be read in its entirety. It also can serve as a stepping off point for assignments or exercises as housing operations face new initiatives, programs, job duties, and relationships.

For instance, a number of housing operations have developed professional development programs that include individual reading assignments as a precursor to planning and discussions. This book can serve as fodder for a departmental book club. Also, strategic planning generally involves dissecting internal and external influences to ascertain dynamics that could precipitate changes in operations. This book can serve as an excellent resource to facilitate brainstorming and discussions surrounding a department's plans for the future.

Housing departments might also consider using this book to power a mind-mapping session. Mind mapping, developed in the late 1960s by Tony Buzan, is a technique of visually arranging ideas and their interconnections. For instance, to mind map a car, one would start with a drawing of the chassis and engine. Then a line is drawn to the next connected piece, such as the carburetor or transmission. Eventually lines would connect every nut and bolt within a car, establishing the relationships between the parts.

Using mind mapping as a process for working with this book, the group would visually break down each topic into its components. For instance, when discussing external financial pressures, the components may be the federal and state governments, as well as institutional, divisional, departmental, family, and student cohorts. The group would then break it down further into current financial contributions, future financial contributions, threats to financial contributions, etc. The completed project would be a large, visual representation of the external financial pressures and a useful tool for strategic planning.

Conclusion

Conceptualizing the future is not an easy task. For the most part, forecasting involves extrapolating current information into a hazy future, making it somewhat tenuous in the best of times and foiling everyone during an upheaval. Nonetheless, it is important for leaders to be visionary if they are to stay ahead of change. This book is designed as a resource for anyone looking to the future of the housing profession. It does not purport to be a crystal ball, but it does tap into the insights of forward thinkers and generates ideas to consider as we move into the future of the housing profession. We challenge readers to explore these topics, see how they apply to each campus's unique situations, and blend your own predictions into the fray.

Beth M. McCuskey and Norbert W. Dunkel ~ April, 2006

Research Methodology for The Future of the University Housing Profession and Implications for Practitioners: A Delphi Study

Beth M. McCuskey, Ed.D.

The research for the dissertation underlying this book (McCuskey, 2003) employed the Delphi Technique, designed in the 1950s as an approach to derive a consensus decision on a complex topic using an expert panel (Dalkey & Helmer, 1962-63). "The Delphi process is distinguished by four key factors: identification of an 'expert' panel, anonymity of the experts' responses, iterations of responses facilitated by the researcher, and feedback to the panelists demonstrating their individual responses vis à vis the mean response of the group" (McCuskey, 2003, p. 8).

To identify experts for this study, a nominating panel of six individuals were each asked to nominate as many as 20 individuals who:

- Contributed significantly to the university housing profession
- Served at least five years as a chief housing officer (or equivalent) at a Carnegie Doctoral Extensive institution
- Served as faculty members noted for their contribution to student affairs and/or student housing

However, a caveat instructed nominators to use the criteria as a means to narrow the field not to exclude individuals who have made significant contributions. A total of 83 individuals were nominated. All 22 who received more than one nomination were invited to participate on the panel. Choosing names randomly filled the remaining slots. A total of 30 panelists completed the study.

The study comprised three rounds. In the first round, panelists were asked to "briefly describe the events that are likely to impact the University Housing Profession and have at least a 50% chance of occurring during the next 20 years" (McCuskey, 2003, p. 71). These responses were then synthesized into a questionnaire that was administered to the same panelists in the second round. The questionnaire comprised 101 items. Panelists were asked to establish a timeline for each item—never, immediately (1-3 years), mid-range (4-10 years), long-term (11-20 years), and beyond 20 years. Panelists also were asked to assign an impact rating to each item on a seven-point Likert scale, where one was *very low impact* and seven was *very high impact*.

Compiling the second round surveys involved determining the "median consensus range" or the range in which 68% of the responses occurred. Panelists
whose answers fell outside of the range were given the opportunity in Round
Three to either change their response to the median or defend their response in
writing.

The study results were determined by analyzing the responses from Round
Three. Items that achieved consensus and had an impact rating of at least five on
a seven point Likert scale were considered high-impact and included in the
study's findings. Of the 101 items on the survey, 35 were determined to be high-
impact. These items were grouped into 13 categories for final discussion within
the dissertation. This reasearch was completed in 2003.

A presentation at the Chief Housing Officer's Institute in 2004 opened the
door to the possibility of a book project. The editors used the findings of the dissertation to develop the concepts for the chapters. Authors were then selected to
write each chapter based on their expertise in the area.

References

Dalkey, N. & Helmer, O. (1962-63). An experimental application of the Delphi
    Method to the use of experts. *Management Science, 9,* 458-467.
McCuskey, B. M. (2003). The future of the university housing profession and
    implications for practitioners: A Delphi study. (Doctoral dissertation, West
    Virginia University, 2003). *Dissertation Abstracts International* 64(06), 1999
    (UMI No. 3094591).

Part I

The Education and Demographics of Students in the Campus Community

Students are the *raison d'être* of any residence life operation. Just as many a shopkeeper has been reminded "the customer is always right," so have student needs and behaviors influenced the mission and direction of housing departments.

What might the students of tomorrow bring to their colleges? How will the demographics of age, race, gender, and nationality change in the coming years, and how will those changes influence the halls in which they live? And how much of a role will the campus housing profession play in supporting these changes? These questions and many others form the foundation for Part I.

Programmatic Philosophies in Residence Life

Phyllis McCluskey-Titus, Ed.D.

Budget cuts and deficits have become an annual ritual in higher education. They are forcing a greater level of accountability for all student service programs, and housing is no exception. Suddenly campus administrators are taking a careful look at the differences between dorms that provide a place to sleep and residence halls that contribute to the institution's overall mission. It becomes increasingly important for housing professionals to understand, apply, and assess results from sound theoretic models that guide the structure, function, and outcomes of facilities, operations, staffing, and programming.

A variety of philosophical models and theories from student development, business, economics, and student learning disciplines can serve as a basis for establishing or restructuring a housing program. In isolation, these philosophies or theories may not provide an inclusive enough framework for a comprehensive housing operation with many different functional areas. On the other hand, certain theories may appear to be at odds with one other if put together. An institution's goals, philosophies, mission, and unique circumstances will dictate which frameworks serve up an optimal mix.

Student Development Philosophy: A Basis of Solid Practice

Many current housing professionals' training is grounded in student development theories, which examine how campus programs and services do or do not contribute to students' personal growth. Of all the theoretic foundations, student development philosophies are the most comfortable for housing professionals. Additionally, housing professionals can significantly impact student development simply because of the opportunities for extended, substantive contact with students where they live. A number of specific developmental theories provide housing professionals with a theoretical basis for developing more effective programs, facilities, services, and staffing to meet student needs. These theories include those of Abraham Maslow, Alexander Astin, and George Kuh.

Most people in student housing are familiar with Maslow's hierarchy of needs but perhaps never considered it a theory of student development. In many ways, it is a fit. Students move through the five original stages of Maslow's hierarchy in a progression from lower-level basic needs, to safety needs, to affiliation and belonging needs, to self-esteem needs, and finally work toward the ultimate (although nearly unattainable for most) level of self-actualization (Maslow, 1970).

From the perspective of a housing operation, a student's basic needs for shelter, food, water, and clothing would be met by providing a furnished room and either cooking or dining facilities. Safety comes through providing trained housing staff, safety systems, routine facility maintenance and upgrades, and policies and procedures directed toward maintaining safe environments. Affiliation needs are addressed through such elements as roommate matching, developmental programming, student run organizations, living-learning groupings that cluster students with similarities on some level, and one-on-one attention from trained staff. Self-esteem is bolstered through meaningful student involvement on task forces, committees, or programming boards; participation in employment with developmental potential; and intentional recognition and leadership development programs. To move students toward attaining self-actualization, housing staff can support and challenge students' career aspirations, serve as mentors and role models, and otherwise help students realize their full potential as high functioning, independent adults.

Maslow believed that students grow and change as they progress through the hierarchy toward higher order needs. His theory is situational; anytime students face new circumstance, they may need to satisfy their lower level basic needs before addressing affiliation or self-esteem needs. In any given day, students may move in and through Maslow's hierarchy at different need levels. This consistent working through unmet needs requires supports and challenges, and housing professionals are in an ideal position to have an influence.

Basic needs are not that difficult for housing professionals to address. According to strategist Peter Senge, author of the *Fifth Discipline* (1990), however, traditional organizations such as campuses aren't structured as well for meeting higher order needs. This may become even more true in the future as housing programs downsize and require only first-year students to live in residence halls. First-year students are not always ready to work toward higher order needs, focusing instead on simply getting established on campus, learning to live on their own, and acquiring new relationships in an unfamiliar setting.

Alexander Astin, a professor and member of the Higher Education Research

Institute based at the University of California, Los Angeles, wrote in an article for the *Journal of College Student Personnel,* "student involvement refers to the amount of physical and psychological energy that the student devotes to the academic experience" (1984 p. 297). Astin's theory of student involvement broadly considered the academic experience to include all aspects of college life, including curricular and cocurricular activities, relationships with peers and faculty and other activities that keep a student connected to the college or university, such as working on-campus. Astin's theory contends that the more time and effort a student puts into a program, class, or activity, the better that program will be, the more the student will gain, and theoretically, the more academically successful the student will be. This theory provides rationale for giving students opportunities to become positively involved in the development of new programs or services in their living units. "The effectiveness of any educational policy or practice is directly related to the capacity of that policy or practice to increase student involvement," Astin writes (1984, p. 298).

George Kuh (2001) takes the concept of involvement a bit further. He believes students should be involved in educationally purposeful activities, connect with "right-minded peers," and make meaningful connections to faculty outside the classroom. Engagement should be purposeful and intentional, requiring a campus to make a commitment that activities, programs, and services be designed with developmental outcomes in mind, which will contribute to an effective education.

Astin and Kuh believe that students learn by doing, and Maslow held that students needed to meet specific needs in order to become more whole. Another theorist, B.B. Crookston, saw what he called the *intentional democratic community* as a way to give students extensive opportunities to explore their sense of self within a supportive community environment.

Believing that residence halls were an untapped educational resource Crookston (1974) took concepts from social psychology theory and pioneered the model of an intentional democratic community (IDC). Drawing particularly from Maslow—and what is now identified as current leadership, involvement, and engagement theories—Crookston envisioned a group-centered residential community that focused on building a collective of members who governed themselves based on shared ideas and values (Crookston, 1974).

Crookston (1974) identified 10 elements essential for the development of an IDC:

1. *A social contract* that outlines the principles and conditions necessary for community-oriented living;
2. *A primary group* that serves as a family and functions as a relational center of operations for the community
3. Shared *goals and values* among members to hold the group together
4. Group-established *boundaries* within which members agree to function

5. Agreed-upon use of *power* within the group and with various outside constituencies

6. Type and amount of *work* required to keep the community living space maintained at the agreed-upon standard

7. A system of *processes* to maintain the community membership, communication, leadership and follower positions, problem-solving, decision-making models, and community evaluation

8. *Commitment* to the group outside of self

9. *Transcendence* that is awareness beyond the self

10. *Communion* that is sharing beyond the self.

The final three elements of the effective IDC are more spiritual, designed to encourage the community to work for the collective good. These 10 elements lead the group toward self-actualization according to Crookston (1974). "Students and staff now know that it takes far more than people, a place, idealism, and good will to make a democratic community work" (Crookston, 1974, p. 383).

In spite of the age of the IDC model, and perhaps a shift away from the '70s communal ethics, Crookston's model has some interesting concepts that might work, for instance, in a living-learning community focused on academic-major themes, such as public administration, anthropology, communication, or sociology. Along with appropriate support from the department or program concentration, these themes lend themselves easily to Crookston's democratic and community concepts. Students might even "live out" the theoretical concepts of their specific discipline, giving the connection between theory and application new meaning for faculty and students.

Student development philosophy will continue to provide valuable insights for residential programs in the future. Being able to use developmental theory to link other theories and philosophies in this chapter and drawing from ideas such as Crookston's IDC will allow housing practitioners to keep an eye on the future needs and wants of students.

Business/Management Philosophy: Lessons from the Corporate World

In light of recent calls for fiscal accountability and stronger management principles, housing professionals should be familiar with current and future-focused business and corporate philosophies. Two predominant models are conventional, hierarchical bureaucratic leadership and an alternative, more recently recognized model involving systemic leadership. Both offer theoretical approaches that have relevance for housing operations but require a new leadership paradigm that campuses potentially are not accustomed to.

Housing operations are more inclined to adopt the first, more traditional business "top-down" structured, bureaucratic model of leadership. In this model, a leader is ultimately responsible for making decisions, initiating communication that filters down to staff members at various levels, and managing in a predictable pattern of organization that dictates how an organization's work is accomplished and problems are solved. Within this structural model, change takes time because the system or structure drives the organization rather than people being responsible for the necessary change (Allen & Cherrey, 2000).

Bolman and Deal (1991) describe a few core assumptions that make bureaucratic organization effective. The model gives leadership control and a framework for working toward organizational goals. It has a problem-solving structure that is rational and particular to each circumstance, ensuring that staff members have specific functions in which they specialize. The model also calls for standard operating procedures that can maximize effectiveness.

To achieve success, bureaucratic organizations focus on systems and structures, reorganizing or restructuring rather than retraining staff members, who typically have little effect or control over the end results. Such hierarchical organizations are comfortable with the status quo are rule oriented, and value competence (Barr, Desler & Associates, 2000).

In contrast, an office organized systemically or networked tends to employ circular, nonlinear patterns of communication, which require staff members to provide information as they have or obtain it. Using the systemic leadership model (Allen & Cherrey, 2000), management uses all the information it can obtain through existing means and networks, and work is accomplished by teams of people who might come together only to complete one task. Problem solving is seen as a process and an ongoing opportunity to make decisions that serve the best interest of the office or the clients at any particular time.

In a networked organization, boundaries are not clearly defined. Collaboration is critical to completing tasks, and change is constant and expected. The focus is on the whole big picture rather than on discrete tasks or goal completion. Using systemic management or leadership practices requires organizations to develop new ways of communicating, to share resources, to manage and embrace change, to emphasize learning, and to allow many to share leadership roles (Allen & Cherrey, 2000).

In the future, housing professionals will need to be able to use information as it is available to make the best possible decisions. Traditional structural communication patterns and hierarchical decision-making models will need to be, in some instances, modified.

Author Peter Senge (1990) called systematic thinking the "fifth discipline," the fundamental principle of his innovative leadership and management approach. According to Senge, a learning organization exists when "people continually expand their capacity to create the results they truly desire, where new and expansive patterns of thinking are nurtured, where collective aspiration is set free, and where people are continually learning to see the whole together." This model of applied leadership theory calls for an organization to be flexible, adaptable, and poised for change (Peter Senge, 2005). As individuals learn and grow, an organization likewise can continue growing and can benefit by constant review and revision of the organization's function and purpose. "Traditional organizations require management systems that control people's behavior, learning organizations invest in improving the quality of thinking, the capacity for reflection and team learning, and the ability to develop shared visions and shared understandings of complex business issues" (Senge, 1990, p. 289). A learning organization can be created, says Senge, by a visionary leader who has the ability and foresight to put his five concepts, or disciplines, to work: systems thinking, personal mastery, mental models, shared vision, and team learning.

Systems thinking requires a different approach to problem solving, planning, communication patterns, and level of control than does bureaucratic thinking. "Systems thinking is a discipline for seeing wholes. It is a framework for seeing interrelationships rather than things, for seeing patterns of change rather than static snapshots" (Senge, 1990, p. 68). The entire learning organization concept is grounded in the establishment of a systems-thinking perspective.

Although a learning organization is a group of people, individuals who are committed to learning through personal mastery are a necessary part. Personal mastery is an engaged process of ongoing reflection and anticipation of change (Senge, 1990).

Each of us carries assumptions and perceptions that are rigid and grounded in our own realities. This is what Senge (1990) refers to as mental models. Systems thinking requires that members of a learning organization be able to disconnect from those mental models and think freely about what will allow for the organization to move toward a common vision.

Building shared vision is important in Senge's model. Often the vision of the organization is the leader's, but other members of the team do not understand or share that same idea or purpose. Senge believes shared vision helps people break away from simply following commands, instead feeling invested in the organization's success. He also contends that learning organizations are about team learning with people acting as a single unit, communicating meaningfully, and thinking critically together without relying on old assumptions or beliefs (1990).

Implementing a learning-organization concept in housing and residential life could prove useful for the future housing operation that aims to become a living-learning environment. It could start with involving all staff members in developing a training session on the fifth-discipline model and creating a common vision-and-goals statement for the office or department based on the five disciplines. A true learning organization would go further to reframe its structural or bureaucratic leadership model. This could break down "silos" that invariably develop and polarize thinking in housing and residential life operations and beyond (maintenance, budget/finance, programming, judicial affairs, administration, conferences, family housing, and academic affairs) because every person who would be involved in decisions and outcomes would be included in the process, and visioning would not be an exercise for an annual administrative retreat or simply for when goals or missions are under review.

Student as Consumer Philosophy: Meeting Needs to What End?

A recent change in language and philosophy that will continue into the future is the concept of students as consumers of goods and services. As a result, consumer, economic, or production theories are beginning to have new relevance to housing professionals, whose sense of what constitutes consumer needs comes more from popular culture sources such as the media or commercial publications.

Even if student consumerism is not a primary construct guiding housing operations, an understanding of consumer economics is certainly beneficial to housing staff in decision-making roles. Thinking about student consumer needs or wants over the projected lifetime of a newly constructed housing facility, for example, requires research into the needs of students not yet born. This brief overview gives insights into the theories as a future trend worth watching.

Demand

In economics, the basic theory of demand states, among other things, that when all things are equal, higher price will cause people to buy a lower quantity of a product or service. Traditional demand theory focuses attention on the value of the product offered, the usefulness of the product to the consumer, and the caution of the consumer in acquiring the product (Roth 1998). Students and parents certainly scrutinize costs associated with on-campus housing expenses relative to other options or housing costs of one institution versus another. Some students or parents will see new facilities or ones with updated amenities to have more relevance or value.

Demand at many institutions is artificially created by a mandate that certain students must reside in campus-owned or operated housing facilities. Perceived values will also drive decisions. Demand also comes into play when housing operations offer a variety of housing choices with a range of services, amenities, and pricing options.

This difference in student desires or preferences leads to a consideration of what choices may be available or offered to the student consumers of the future.

Product choice

Redman (1979) emphasizes the need to take into consideration consumer preferences, familiarity with other local market options for consumers, and awareness of what consumers are able and willing to pay for services. This is certainly important for housing professionals, who should consider these three issues when designing and marketing types of room(s), the range of amenities, how today's and future students might use their living spaces, trends in décor and furnishings, and appropriate balance between functionality and appearance in living units.

At a 2005 regional conference of the Student Affairs Administrators in Higher Education, Performa, an architectural and engineering firm that specializes in high-performance campus environments, presented their vision for renovating and building student housing that would be designed to stage students' steps toward independence (Langdon, 2005). First-year students live in a traditional residence hall with double rooms and community baths. Sophomore students have the option of living in residential suites with fewer students, sharing a bath and access to a common study area. Upperclass students can choose an on-campus apartment facility with cooking areas and private baths. Accordingly, rental agreements and food plan choices are structured for more flexibility and choice as students' developmental readiness increases. This example offers student consumers different choices but is grounded in developmental theory. To consider students as consumers, "emphasis must be placed upon a systematic characterization of the consumer's decision process...(that is) to explore and simulate the actual decision-making process of the individual consumer" (Roth, 1998, pp. 109–10).

Being able to assess what students are able and willing to pay for housing while enrolled in college, now and in the future, demands that housing professionals understand the demographics and backgrounds of their student bodies and the family structures and backgrounds from which they come. They must understand student motivations. They must forecast these various considerations for as many as 10 years into the future if they are to stay competitive, particularly on those campuses where there are no parietal rules for some or all students.

Motivation to acquire

Factors influencing preferences or motivation to acquire products can be grouped into two categories: customer personality and social influences (Redman, 1979; Mowen, 1987). Personality traits that influence consumer behavior include motivation to obtain the product (Redman, 1979), need for the product/service (Othes, 1988), self-image/worth of the consumer, and relationships with significant others involved in making the decision or learning about the decision (Mowen, 1987). Housing professionals can use this information to their advantage. Traditional-aged students would have different responses to housing types and be more influenced by, say, parental relationships than would older students. Integrating academic lifestyle or other interest-specific housing units would provide support or interest for other sorts of personality types.

Emphasis on delivering housing with stronger academic benefits would appeal to certain student behavioral needs or qualities.

Social influences related to consumerism comprise family support and structure, socioeconomic status (Forbes, 1987), ethnicity or culture (Goodman & Cohen, 2004), personal values and decision making (Roth, 1998), and response from significant others to consumer decisions (Mowen, 1987). A major social influence on students today, forecast for the future also, is their parents (Howe & Strauss, 2000). Appealing to parent needs and wants could have a significant impact on how housing professionals design or renovate facilities, market on-campus housing, plan programs and activities, or set room rental rates.

Housing staff look for ways to motivate students to choose on-campus facilities and convince these potential consumers of the social and esteem benefits. Residence life programming professionals can look to these consumer theories to market their benefits.

Product consumption

There are four stages of product consumption, including provision or acquisition, usability and durability, ongoing maintenance or control, and replacement of the product after use, wear, or destruction (Othes, 1988). Housing professionals and student customers and families are interested in these product consumption issues. Perceptions of quality and getting the best value for the money are important values associated with students in the current generation. "A consumer culture means that our central shared values have to do with consumption and a set of meanings through which individuals can relate their individual lives to larger themes" (Goodman & Cohen, 2004, p. 32). In the case of student housing, these "larger themes" might include availability of off-campus or alternate housing; location, types and prices of campus versus off-campus housing; and newer, better, or more updated choices. Types of building materials (durability, safety, aesthetics, and so forth) will be another critical part of understanding, attracting, and retaining on-campus residents in the future.

Understanding students as consumers and providing motivation for them and family members to invest in on-campus housing products is critical to responding to and meeting future campus housing demands.

There is some conflict between the consumer-driven model and student-development or student-learning theories. What students (as consumers) may want or demand can be dramatically different than what they need. On the other hand, the abiltiy of campus housing to remain competitive, particularly in some local housing markets, may require varying degrees of consumer responsiveness that does not always feel right. Finding a balance between catering to student desires and challenging students to grow is important as housing professionals move into the future, if they are to retain their role as developmental educators on campus and hold student learning as a preeminent value.

Student Learning Philosophy: A New and Important Trend

Student affairs practice changed in the early 1990s with the introduction of the Student Learning Imperative (American College Personnel Association [ACPA], 1994). This new philosophy introduced two fresh ideas. First, behind all elements of practice in the student affairs profession is the concept of student learning; and second, the purpose of student affairs organizations is to support the academic mission of the institution. The statement went on to assert that any policy or program developed or implemented by the institution should encourage or enhance student learning, and the value of institutional policies or programs would be judged according to their ability to promote a learning experience for students.

The Student Learning Imperative was a departure from established practice. It led to a newer model of student learning that has been developed by representatives from key student-affairs professional associations. In 2004, the National Association of Student Personnel Administrators (NASPA) and the American College Personnel Association (ACPA) jointly released *Learning Reconsidered* (1987), which built on the earlier work of the *Student Learning Imperative*. *Learning Reconsidered* frames student learning around seven outcomes, including cognitive complexity; knowledge acquisition, integration and application; humanitarianism; civic engagement; interpersonal and intrapersonal competence; practical competence; and persistence and academic achievement (NASPA & ACPA, 2004, pp. 18-19). Outcome goals are reflective of what a learner will be able to achieve rather than goals that merely assert what an office or operation will do to the learner. In addition, the document provides support for discussion and holistic application of "learning" on campus, encompassing everything students do while in college. It discourages labeling of activities as either in class or out of class, instead advocating for student learning to encompass curricular and co-curricular realms. Using this recommended definition for learning, every person on campus would be invested in and responsible for each student's education, resulting in strong partnerships and collaboration across many areas of campus. Learning communities provide just such a cooperative opportunity to enrich on-campus life for students.

As one method to reform general education, early educational philosophers John Dewey, Alexander Meiklejohn, and Joseph Tussman envisioned "experimental colleges" that integrate first-year students into the institutional culture and infuse the campus community with shared values (Gabelnick, MacGregor, Matthews, & Smith, 1990, p. 15). Their ideas have merit when synthesized with more recent ideas about learning in campus residential settings.

When all campus staff members understand the general education model for students, they can develop programs and services reflective and in support of the model. Residential learning communities that support a general education curriculum benefit students and other campus partners. Housing professionals can be instrumental in training staff and rethinking residence-life program models around similar themes found in the general education curriculum. For instance, while students in class are learning art appreciation, housing staff can coordinate with local or campus art galleries for an educational tour or hang a traveling exhibit in the residence hall. An even more ambitious effort would be for residence life professionals in first-year living units to develop knowledge about various areas of general education models (social sciences, applied arts, arts and sciences, and so forth) and develop strong linkages with departments or colleges. This would create a larger pool of mentors for students beyond academic faculty and provide for mentoring at more times and places.

Taking cues from these early pioneers, campuses have embraced the concept of deeper first-year student development. A good many resources are dedicated to freshmen, and a number of residential college/learning community initiatives nationally and internationally focus exclusively on the first-year student experience. These initiatives include ongoing orientation classes, special discussion groups, specialized housing programs, common readings for the entire first-year class, mentoring and tutoring programs, learning-linked service activities, and team-initiative courses and retreats of all sorts. These specialized residential experiences have improved student retention on campus and in campus housing facilities, which affords an institution additional opportunities to expand learning beyond the classroom values.

To enhance students' shared values, housing professionals can bring academic events and personnel into residential areas. Using residence halls or on-campus apartment space for teaching and learning maximizes learning experiences for students that are constrained when confined to traditional classrooms, laboratories, or auditoriums. Residential living units offer options such as conducting small group discussions by a fireplace, developing a model or map on a large table in an enclosed conference room with upholstered furnishings, or working and talking over a meal in a homey kitchen or private eating area. When housing professionals take the initiative to develop partnerships that enhance student learning and offer resources under their purview, the rest of campus might see other partnership opportunities with potential expanded student learning experiences with similar successful outcomes.

In the future, housing offices must continue partnering with others on campus to ensure that services and programs provide a number of opportunities for students to learn and reflect with other like-minded peers and trained staff in a supportive environment.

Future Directions

In the future, when housing professionals look to improve residential life operations, whether an operation chooses one model or combines related models, a strong foundation will allow them to build a successful program with core values, shared goals, and clear learning outcomes. Without this framework, however, housing organizations will not be able to effectively meet the needs of students of the future. Furthermore, these principles offer ways to develop common purpose among campus professionals and provide worthy aspirations to reach.

In anticipation of the future, housing professionals must blend the proven theoretical perspectives that have guided good practice over generations with future trends and ideas. This will ensure that housing and residential life services, facilities, and personnel are proactive campus partners in the education of students.

References

Allen, K.E., & Cherrey, C. (2000). *Systemic leadership.* Washington, DC: American College Personnel Association (ACPA) and National Association of Campus Activities (NACA).

American College Personnel Association (ACPA). (1994). *Student learning imperative* [Report]. Washington, DC: Author.

Astin, A.W. (1984). Student involvement: A developmental theory for higher education. *Journal of College Student Personnel, 25,* 297-308.

Barr, M.J., Desler, M.K., & Associates. (2000). *The handbook of student affairs administration* (2nd ed.). San Francisco: Jossey-Bass.

Bolman, L.G., & Deal, T.E. (1991). *Reframing organizations.* San Francisco: Jossey-Bass.

Crookston, B.B. (1974). The intentional democratic community in college residence halls. *Personnel and Guidance Journal, 52,* 382-389.

Forbes, J.D. (1987). *The consumer interest.* New York: Croom Helm.

Gabelnick, F., MacGregor, J., Matthews, R.S., & Smith, B.L. (1990). Learning communities: Creating connections among students, faculty, and disciplines. *New Directions for Teaching and Learning, 41.*

Goodman, D.J., & Cohen, M. (2004). *Consumer culture.* Santa Barbara, CA: ABC-CLIO, Inc.

Howe, N., & Strauss, W. (2000). *Millennials rising.* New York: Vintage Books.

Kuh, G. (2001). *The national survey of student engagement: Homepage.* Available online from http://www.indiana.edu/~nsse

Kuh, G. D. (2003). *The national survey of student engagement: Conceptual framework and overview of psychometric properties* [Electronic version]. http://www.indiana.edu/~nsse/pdf/conceptual_framework_2003.pdf

Langdon, E. (2005, October). *Innovations in the architecture of student affairs.* Paper presented at NASPA Region IV-E, Schaumburg, IL.

Maslow, A.H. (1970). *Motivation and personality* (2nd ed.). New York: Harper & Row.

Mowen, J.C. (1987). *Consumer behavior.* New York: MacMillan Publishing.

National Association of Student Personnel Administrators (NASPA) & American College Personnel Association (ACPA). (2004). *Learning reconsidered.* Washington, DC: Authors.

Othes, P. (1988). *The sociology of consumption.* Oslo, Norway: Solum Forlag.

Peter Senge and the learning organization. (2005). Available online at http://www.infed.org/thinkers/senge.htm#_The_learning_organization

Redman, B.J. (1979). *Consumer behavior: Theory and applications.* Westport, CT: AVI Publishing.

Roth, J.P. (1998). *The present state of consumer theory* (3rd ed.). Lanham, MD: University Press of America, Inc.

Senge, P. (1990). *The fifth discipline.* New York: Doubleday.

Southwest Airlines:
A Customer-Centered, Learning Organization

by Phyllis McCluskey-Titus, Ed.D.

So, what does the housing office in the future that subscribes to the consumer, systemic-management and learning-organization collection of philosophies look like in practice? According to Massnick (1997), "the members of the workforce must be aligned with and own the strategic direction of the business, have trust-based work relationships, and be able to build value with one another and their customers" (p. 27). One business, Southwest Airlines, has implemented different strategies considered as exemplars in the customer service and management realm (Gittell, 2003). This business emphasizes building personal relationships and communication among employees and focuses on empowering staff on the front line to make informed decisions as they assist customers. The Southwest Airlines model reflects more of the systemic leadership design. It provides examples for housing operations to apply toward the goal of offering superior service for student residents.

The systemic leadership model emphasizes communication and building relationships across a variety of constituents without regard for position or power structures. Southwest Airlines has focused on what it calls "relational coordination" (Gittell, 2003, p. 17), defined as "relationship focus(ed) . . . commitment and passion for shared goals, shared knowledge and mutual respect . . . [and] frequent, timely problem-solving communication" (Gittell, 2003, p. 17). Southwest Airlines uses 10 specific practices to provide excellent customer service, including the following:

- Developing credible and caring leadership
- Investing in front-line staff
- Hiring and training within the relational coordination model
- Using conflict to build relationships

- Bridging work and family relationships
- Creating boundary spanners
- Using broad performance measures
- Keeping flexible boundaries within jobs
- Partnering with bargaining units
- Partnering with material suppliers. (Gittell, 2003, pp. 197-207)

Take a look at how Southwest Airlines put these factors into practice and the examples of the relevance they could have for campus housing operations.

Credible and Caring Leadership

To achieve this goal, conveyed in the company's business plan, senior-level administration spend time building relationships with front-line employees in meetings, at training sessions, and face-to-face. This requires all senior-level management staff be of one mind about company goals and daily operations. Time invested by senior-level staff in team-building, honest discussion, planning, and working on the front lines with staff at all levels builds critical relationships. It creates opportunities for sharing values and ideas and for communicating the worth of every staff person while reinforcing his or her responsibilities.

In a housing operation, these same practices are easily implemented, starting with senior-level planning activities that filter down through such activities as "shared work days" (when senior leadership shadow or work directly with different housing staffers).

Investing in Front-Line Staff

Southwest Airlines achieved this by adding more supervisory-level positions. The company sees supervision not as overseeing subordinates or merely providing corrective feedback, but as an opportunity to develop stronger relationships personally and professionally, and to work side-by-side emphasizing company goals and values. This structure also opens up opportunities for promotions, while creating smaller supervisor-employee ratios that foster stronger camaraderie among work teams.

Housing could adjust this concept to create additional supervisor-level positions with additional supervisory functions and higher compensation—roles such as "lead custodian," "marketing manager," or "senior resident assistant." Training this supervisory staff and allowing them to time to develop their skills are critical component of this practice.

Hiring and Training for Relational Coordination

At Southwest Airlines this domain takes precedence. Leadership believes that specific job-related skills can be taught, but company values and interpersonal "people" skills of team-work, taking initiative, and enthusiasm for helping others cannot. The investment it takes Southwest to vet those most likely to fit the culture and preparing new hires through extensive classroom and on-the-job training reap benefits for the company.

This concept can be applied in housing offices by first clearly defining office values (work ethic, optimism, commitment to student development, team skills, or other specific identifiable factors) and hiring staff members who fit in with those values. Staff training also can be revised to include opportunities for the newcomers to take advantage of shadowing (with or by seasoned staff) and receive immediate feedback in their work, a component that is rarely implemented in training at any level.

Another part of Southwest's training program includes cross-training to build relationships and allow everyone in the company to gain appreciation for the work other staffers perform. This is a model that might help housing professionals develop stronger staff teams and build respect across functional areas of the housing operation.

Using Conflict

When conflicts arise, they can either be treated as problems or opportunities. At Southwest Airlines, supervisors are trained in conflict resolution and immediately bring together parties with the differences for a face-to-face resolution, with the supervisor(s) as mediators. This occurs regardless of which parties are in conflict or what positions they hold within the organization.

Housing staff can use this technique by having all supervisor-level staff trained in conflict mediation and communication skills and by recognizing the value of timely face-to-face discussion of differences. In addition, conflict can be presented as an opportunity rather than a problem, and a positive emphasis can be placed on the growth value of the mediation phase.

Bridging Work and Family

Employee stress over balance between work and family relationships in endemic everywhere. At Southwest Airlines, the company is committed to working like a family in which people look out for each other, celebrate accomplishments, share difficult times, and come together to support community causes. This organization also values employee individuality and expects that staff not have to change their personality to fit in at work. Flexible scheduling and sensitivity to family commitments is also part of company policy and is actively promoted.

Housing operations provide more than ample fodder for family life to conflict with work. Offices may consider enacting flexible scheduling, including four-day weeks, regular weekend hours, or later start times than typically required. Housing operations may include family members in regular celebrations such as holiday events or birthday dinners. Perhaps the entire office could participate in a service project, such as repairing a home for one of the staff members or retirees or collecting food and clothing for a staff person who lost everything in a fire.

Boundary Spanners

Organizations need someone who serves as the coordinator for many different types of work or systems. At Southwest Airlines, the person who coordinates all the aspects of airline boarding is called a *boundary spanner*. This person knows each function associated with getting an aircraft ready for take off and understands problems that can surface between aircraft arrival and departure.

In housing, there are a variety of different processes that require coordination among different functional sides of the entire office. Fall check-in is one large-scale example. Perhaps professional staff selection is a smaller example. In either case, one person needs to serve as the overall coordinator or boundary spanner, linking staff from various areas, ensuring that everyone knows who is responsible for what duties and attending to relationships required for a seamless process. This boundary spanner knows exactly what tasks need to be done, who is responsible for carrying out duties, how each task relates to the successful completion of other tasks, and how to problem-solve across areas responsible for the various tasks. Sometimes in housing offices this person is the director, but perhaps there are opportunities for other levels of staff to serve in this leadership role as chairperson, coordinator, adviser, or manager for different programs or projects.

Broad Performance Measures

Southwest Airlines uses performance measures to motivate its staff toward excellent performance. In the airline industry, flight delays are a major problem, and typically airlines assign blame to individuals or a work section (such as flight crews or the baggage handlers). At Southwest Airlines, once the problem behind the delay is identified, supervisors from the various sections work together with all their employees to avert a similar problem in the future. They use a team problem-solving approach rather than assigning blame to one particular sector, because rarely is the problem so simple.

By using a similar team problem-solving method in housing, leaders can track down a problem's genesis and resolve it using the collective wisdom of a group of committed staff. As an example, one common concern that many housing operations confront is lowered occupancy after the fall term. There are many reasons that students do not return to campus housing the remaining terms, and blame can become a habit. Maintenance staffers get blamed for deferred repairs or unclean spaces. Residential-life staff members are tagged if halls are too noisy or not welcoming. Assignment areas hear it if they aren't quick with room or apartment changes or if they underestimate demand. Food service is often a scapegoat. Or cost, poor planning, or even unforeseen circumstances get assigned as someone's fault. In many cases, a combination of factors and influences that go beyond housing's control can turn away students after one term. For this reason, a group problem-solving approach that enlists representatives from each functional area—and maybe beyond housing, such as to admissions—to discuss, conduct research, or get creative with solutions.

Flexible Job Boundaries

Southwest Airlines encourages flexible boundaries within jobs. Even in the highly unionized airline industry, Southwest does not establish rigid position descriptions. This goes back to the relational aspect of the company philosophy, which encourages team work. Each employee does have a job description with specific assigned duties, but it also encourages everyone to help out when needed. Thus, employees learn other functions without spreading too thin, and additional help at certain times is there when it's needed. The benefits of using flexible boundaries has resulted in greater communication across job functions, increased productivity, fewer consumer complaints, and an awareness of other employees' challenges and competencies.

This service orientation and cooperative team spirit is a good fit in housing operations. There are times of the year when other parts of the housing operation desperately need assistance. Housing lottery or reapplication periods are traditionally very busy for a short time period, and the few staff who handle this area full-time are swamped. This is not a function that needs a full-time person who cross-trained in assignments; rather, student employees or other staff volunteers could help temporarily. Likewise, this could work for summer orientation programs or conferences that require short-term but intense bursts of activity.

Partnerships

The final two practices that set Southwest Airlines apart from others in the industry are its partnerships with bargaining units and suppliers. Keeping the relationships open between union representatives and senior management includes daily communication and building relationships of mutual trust and respect. Southwest also goes against standard practice by not outsourcing. Other airlines farm out catering, fueling, maintenance, customer service, and ramp functions. Southwest handles these functions in-house but focuses on building relationships with airports, security personnel, air traffic controllers, and airplane manufacturers that supply goods and complementary services.

Housing professionals might benefit from providing more services and outsourcing fewer. Services such as cleaning, food service, linens, conferences, routine maintenance, staff selection, and others might improve if they are provided by and coordinated through employees.

Also, working with union leaders as partners to better serve students will lead to more congenial work environments for everyone, and certainly more cooperation can be counted on in times of dispute. Even in a bargaining unit environment, the quality of relationships developed between labor and management can make a big difference in the level of service and assistance we offer.

References

Gittell, J.H. (2003). *The Southwest Airlines way.* New York: McGraw-Hill.
Massnick, F. (1997). *The customer is CEO.* New York: American Management Association.

□2□

Understanding Students Today and Tomorrow

Cynthia M. Anderson, Ed.D. and Richard W. Payne, Ed.D.

W hat do we really know about the 17 million students enrolled in public and private two- and four-year institutions of higher education in the United States?

Demographically speaking, there are more females (56.6%) than males and more full-time (59.9%) than part-time students. U.S. ethnic minority students comprise about 25% of the total enrollment (U.S. Department of Education, 2002, as cited in "Enrollment highlights," 2005, p. 2). Of these students, 46% receive some form of federal financial aid, 15.6% get state aid, and 18.8% obtain institutionally sponsored financial aid (p. 12).

The majority (80%) of freshmen who graduated from high school in the previous year attended colleges in their home states ("Enrollment highlights," p. 2), and most (62.2%) college students are still considered of traditional age (18-24; U.S. Census Bureau, October 2003, as cited in "Enrollment highlights," 2005, p. 10). Men out-perform women on both the ACT and SAT entrance exams, but women graduate at higher rates (57.2% vs. 51.0% for men) after six years from their first enrollment (ACT, 2005; College Board, 2004, as cited in "Enrollment highlights," 2005, p.12).

There also are discernible shifts to the pattern of enrollment in U. S. colleges and universities with "almost half (45%) of all seniors [reporting that they] took at least one course from another postsecondary institution prior to enrolling at their current institution" (National Survey of Student Engagement [NSSE], 2005, p. 12).

In terms of societal influence on entering students, undergraduates have grown up in a country where the main business has become business, and where terrorism . . . has built up slowly but surely to become the threat it is today. Cable channels have become as mainstream as the "Big 3" used to be, formality in dress has become more quaint than ever, and Aretha Franklin, Kermit the Frog and Jimmy Carter have become old-timers. (Beloit College, 2005 p. 1).

Current Enrollments

"Higher education is on the cusp of a new enrollment boom. It is estimated that by 2012 total college enrollment will exceed 15.8 million students, an increase of more than 12 percent over 2003 enrollment levels" (U.S. Department of Education, 2002, as cited in Coomes & DeBard, 2004, p. 1). The current percentage of college attendance by those who have finished high school (nearly 65%) is striking when one considers not only the proportionate growth within the cohort of those with college plans (compared to 16% of the same cohort in 1940; U.S. Department of Education, 2002, as cited in Nathan, 2005 p. 148), but also the size of the cohort itself (Howe & Strauss, 2000).

Much has been written about the present generation of traditional-age students (Howe & Strauss, 2000, 2003; Levine & Cureton, 1998; Sacks, 1996; Taylor, 2005), with some overlapping themes but little agreement about the central "truths" manifested in behavioral explanation and prediction for their future. Are our present "traditional" undergraduate students to be understood as Millennials (Howe & Strauss, 2000, 2003), marked by their historical capture of the new millennium for their high school class? Or are they better viewed in terms of the complex and weighty societal predilections heralded during their adolescence, defining them as a generation where *"hope and fear* collide" (Levine & Cureton, 1998)? Or are our current students "the predictable product of our consumer-driven postmodern society" (Taylor, 2005) and named in honor of the generation (X) they succeeded (*Generation NeXt*), or to be named *Generation Why* (Chester, 2005)?

The Generational Lens

The *Generational Lens* is one of several models or theories advanced to expand our understanding of groups of students (Coomes & DeBard, 2004). Other models frequently used to describe student groups include student peer group typologies (Astin, 1993; Clark & Trow, 1966; and Kuh, Hu, & Vesper, 2000, as cited in Coomes & DeBard, 2004) and human aggregate or trait models such as those discussed by Holland (1973), Myers (1980), and Strange and Banning (2001, as cited in Coomes & Debard [2004, p. 6]). Cohort models track similarly aged population groups across time within the context of national and international events, trends, and patterns to describe, explain, and predict attitudes and behaviors of group members. Howe and Strauss (2000, 2003), Levine and Cureton (1998), Sacks (1996), and Taylor (2005) all seek to describe the current generation of college students via a cohort model but with distinctive yet complementary conclusions.

Most models that seek to describe the current cohort in U.S. colleges and universities note the following common aspects for students:

- They were born in or after 1982, with the first high school class graduating in 2000. The final birth year for this cohort is 2002.
- The cohort is the most populous in U.S. history, with an estimated 80 million members and the potential to surpass 100 million via immigration. That makes them nearly one-third larger than the baby boomer group of 1943 to 1960 (Howe & Strauss, 2003).
- They are more ethnically diverse than previous generations and increasingly bifurcated in terms of economic status or class (Howe & Strauss 2001, 2003; Levine & Cureton, 1998; Taylor, 2005; Nathan, 2005).
- They are stressed, pressured, and, at times, distressed (Kadison & DiGeronimo, 2004; Taylor, 2005; Howe & Strauss, 2003; Seaman, 2005; Sax et al., 2005).
- They are comfortable and proficient with emerging technologies (Howe & Strauss, 2003; Sax et al., 2005; Taylor, 2005).

Perhaps the most divergent views on this generational cohort are the optimistic assessments of Howe and Strauss (2001, 2003), who view millennials as the "next great generation," as opposed to the dour, postmodern evaluation of Sacks (1996) and Taylor (2005). Both models refer to findings from the Higher Education Research Institute's annual American freshman survey, but the authors create dissimilar logic-chains.

Howe and Strauss have a longer record of distinguished research on generational identity, personality, and influential events, but their conclusions could be influenced by their acknowledged life-roles as "Boomer parents of Millennial children" (DeBard in Coomes & DeBard, 2004, p. 34). As postmodernists, Sacks and Taylor have a perspective that "tends to be more pessimistic, sees 'truth' as individually created, to value opinion and preference over truth, experiences over science or reason, and to foster a deligitimation of authority" (Anderson, 1990; Lyotard, 1988; and Sacks, 1996, as cited in Taylor, 2005, p. 2). The table on the following page contrasts the dissimilar traits or characteristics associated with Millennial and Generation NeXt cohort models in a stark, if not slightly contrived, fashion.

Emerging Issues for Today's Students

A central theme of nearly all generational cohort models and the nascent research

Characteristics of Millennial Students (Howe & Strauss, 2003)	Generation NeXt Model Select Traits (Taylor, 2005)
Special: From precious-baby movies of the early '80s to the effusive rhetoric surrounding the high school class of 2000, older generations have inculcated in Millennials the sense that they are, collectively, vital to the nation and to their parents' sense of purpose.	**Entitlement:** Generation NeXters combine a consumerist perspective with previous easy returns (GPA in high) for relatively limited effort. As college students, they feel they deserve the credit or grade simply because they paid their tuition.
Sheltered: Starting with the early '80s child-abuse frenzy, continuing through the explosion of kid safety rules and devices, and now climaxing with a post-Columbine lockdown of public schools, Millennials are the focus of the most sweeping youth safety movement in American history.	**Safety Issues:** Violence against students by dysfunctional adults and disenfranchised peers has taught Generation NeXters that the world is not a safe place. Generation NeXters don't assume that the campus is a safe place, nor do they take responsibility for their own safety.
Confident: With high levels of trust and optimism – and a newly felt connection to parents and future – Millennial teens are beginning to equate good news for themselves with good news for their country. They often boast about their generation's power and potential.	**Skepticism:** Many factors have contributed to the delegitimation of authority and the prioritization of subjective and personal experience. Didactic and content-based instruction methods do not address the learner needs of NeXter students.
	Cynicism: Abuse of public trust by self-serving individuals and institutions has forged feelings of cynicism and mistrust by NeXters.
Team-Oriented: From Barney and soccer to school uniforms and a new classroom emphasis on group learning, Millennials are developing strong team instincts and tight peer bonds.	**Self-Interested:** Whether as a product of assuming self-care at an early age due to parental absence or due to excessive parental involvement fueling their sense of self-importance, today's students have a high level of self-interest.
	Relationships: Products of impermanent and non-traditional relationships, NeXters experiment with relationships, at times adopting negative models of attention (bullying and hazing) for expression and affirmation. Peer groups are not always safe, so the attraction of online and virtual relationships seems natural.
Achieving: With accountability and higher school standards rising to the very top of America's political agenda, Millennials are on track to become the best educated and best behaved adults in the nation's history.	**Excellence:** A product of a childhood where every sport team participant gets a trophy and from schools that value effort over excellence, NeXters expect academic success with little effort.
	Intellectually Disengaged: NeXters have more information available to them but are disinterested in distinguishing between the meaningful and meaningless unless it has a direct impact on their earning or grade-specific goals.
Pressured: Pushed to study hard, avoid personal risks, and take full advantage of the collective opportunities adults are offering them, Millennials feel a "trophy kid" pressure to excel.	**Stressed:** While they work at masking it, pressures associated with work, money/debt, and academic demands generate significant stress for NeXters. Inadequate skills and insufficient links to traditional sources of social refuge place these young people at risk.
Conventional: Taking pride in their improving behavior and feeling more comfortable with their parents' values than any other generation in living memory, Millennials support convention – the idea that social rules can help.	**Parent Issues:** Involved and hovering parents act on behalf of their students in ways ranging from advocacy for academic accommodation and assistance to insistence that their NeXter get the best opportunity. NeXter parents have no qualms about calling the president if their expectations are not met.
	Civility/Caring Issues: In an era where the "squeaky wheel" gets attention and incivility is considered "cool," NeXters work to show that they don't care.
	Value Free: NeXters are tolerant of a wide range of perspectives and ideologies but have difficulty in distinguishing what is most important or even recogniazing the impact of their own behavior. Post 9-11, some NeXters are seeking more conservative values models.

based upon them is an inventory of projected issues, trends, and endeavors a generation will experience as it matures from adolescence through adulthood. Most of what is anticipated is based on observations of the generation as children, although the leading edge of the cohort (starting with the high school class of 2000/ college class of 2004) provides researchers the opportunity to further substantiate their claims by referencing them against captured data on the cohort as enrolled college students. Emerging issues addressed here reflect predicted trends that have initial substantiation from sources other than the original researchers.

Academic effort versus achievement

Entrance credentials of college freshmen are on an upward trend in terms of high school GPAs and scores on college aptitude tests. Forty seven percent of freshmen entering higher education in 2004 reported earning an "A" average in high school (Sax et al., 2005); and national scores on the Scholastic Aptitude Test (SAT) are at the highest levels in 30 years, even as an increasing number of high school seniors take the exam (Howe & Strauss, 2003, p. 123). Competition for admission to the "top" colleges and universities is steep, and a "B" student in high school is no longer guaranteed admission to large state public institutions (Howe & Strauss, 2003).

In contrast, "connection between effort and payoff" (ibid., p. 60) appears to change after entering college, based on observed and self-reported behaviors of students. While first-year students spent more time studying than they did before entering college (Keup & Stolzenberg, 2004), "less than one fifth of first-year students expected to spend more than 25 hours per week studying, the approximate amount of time faculty say is needed to do well in college" (National Survey, 2005, p. 12). Faculty have noticed a pattern "where students are coming in with a fixed notion of an upper limit on how much they are willing to do" (Seaman, 2005, p. 62) and "by their own admission, 3 of 10 first-year students do just enough academic work to get by" (National Survey, 2005, p. 12). While dynamics such as college grade inflation (Seaman, p. 60) confound a clear assessment of the situation, college students who are not competing for top grades are consciously controlling their academic efforts for either dispiriting ideas of academic entitlement or more amenable notions to manage one's college experience in light of increased time demands.

Busy and stressed

College students today have emerged from a childhood of 37% less (33 vs. 52 hours a week) unstructured or free time than students entering college 25 years ago (Howe & Strauss, 2003, p. 45). The leading claim on a pre-collegiate's schedule is an increase in time spent in academically enriching activities. Transitioning from notoriously over-programmed childhoods, new college students are faced with accommodating diverse and often conflicting demands on their time. Following encouragement to participate in relevant cocurricular clubs and programs together with an increasing expectation to work during college (Sax et al., 2005) and the highest educational attainment goals ever surveyed (DeBard in Coomes & Debard, 2004, p.42), it is easy to understand why reported stress levels of college students are on the rise (Sax et al., 2005; Kadison & DiGeronimo, 2004). Balancing these "legitimized" demands with a desire for an enjoyable social life, Nathan (2005) observed that college students have morphed the idea of time management into an active practice of "college management," where they "shape schedules, *tame their* professors and *limit their* workload" (p. 113) to fit college into their schedule of work and other personal and pre-professional activities.

A new idea of community

Long associated with the residential collegiate experience is the establishment of a core friendship group that supplants the high school peer group. Often stemming from physical (same floor or hall) or associational (student organization, activity, or class) proximity, collegiate friendship groups were regarded as fairly distinct from earlier affiliations. Nathan (2005) found that 8 of 14 students interviewed had one or more people they knew from their home town or high school in their collegiate social network, reinforcing assertions from Howe and Strauss (2003) of the degree of connection between this generation of students. Emerging and extant technology such as cell phones and instant and text messaging serve to reinforce the tightness of a circle of friends (including nonlocal peers; Howe & Strauss, p 93) by facilitating on-demand and nearly unlimited real time communication. Today's students may find it difficult to fully develop the potential of their collegiate friendships when they are dedicating a sizable portion of their socio-emotional energy to sustain previously existing relationships.

Opportunities to create relationships and develop community are shifting in observable ways in our residence halls as well. Nathan (2005) offers a telling illustration in which she contrasts the attendance of students at a hall-sponsored Super Bowl viewing with the number of students who chose to watch the game with a group of friends in a private room. Increased student ownership of entertainment systems (TVs, stereos, DVDs, and video game players) may only partly explain the migration of student gatherings from public spaces to private rooms, leaving the community lounge as a place to "retreat from social interaction" (Nathan, p. 53).

Diversity and educational access

The increasing diversity of current college students is reflected in part within the decreasing enrollment of white students from 81.53% (1980) to 69.38% (2000)

as a percentage of total enrollment (National Center for Education Statistics, 2000, as cited in Coomes & DeBard, 2004). Despite regular gains in the diversification of the student body, cross-race relations have made little progress since Levine and Cureton's (1998) nationwide survey found that students were "more willing to tell intimate details of their sex lives than discuss race relations on campus (p. 72)." While residence halls may be fairly well integrated, other collegiate programs (pre-college bridge programs for underrepresented students, cultural fraternities, and sororities) may foster early formation of same-ethnicity friendships (Nathan, 2005). Students are critical of institutional efforts to foster relationship development across difference, and "the majority of seniors (58%) say their institution gives very little or some emphasis on encouraging contact among students from different economic, social, and racial or ethnic backgrounds" (National Survey, 2005, p. 12). The status of the university campus as a community that supports all learners comes into sharper focus when one considers that "African American and Asian American students are the least satisfied with their college experience" (p. 12).

As the percentage of high school graduates who pursue some sort of postsecondary education increases, the socioeconomic background of college students broadens to become "an increasingly less elite economic segment of society, which means that the average college student is poorer than those in the past" (Nathan, 2005, p. 150). At a time when colleges are balancing their budgets through double-digit tuition raises over the last decade, increases in student aid are essential for many students. As competition for gift aid intensifies, students with more limited financial resources face the difficult choice of initiating their college career at a local or community college, leaving the four-year university less diverse (Nathan, 2005, p. 152; National Survey, 2005, p. 19). Of some consolation is Howe and Strauss' (2003) prediction that as social activism grows among this generation, "it will increasingly target issues of class and income, rather than gender or race" (2003, p. 97).

Gender differences

Enrollment of women in U.S. colleges and universities has been increasing over the last four decades and is now more than 56% of total enrollment (National Center for Education Statistics, 2000, as cited in Coomes & DeBard, 2004, p. 33) as compared to 44% for men (U.S. Department of Education, as cited in Howe & Strauss, 2003 p. 94). With interest in alternatives to higher education such as military service, freelancing, and business startups on the rise, "coming out of high school, fewer men than women apply for college; of those, fewer men are accepted; and of those, more men drop out in their freshman and sophomore year" (Howe & Strauss, 2003, p. 95). While men outperform women on pure aptitude tests, women outperform men on nearly every measure of applied effort

(Howe & Strauss, p. 95). High school has the unintended effect of making men feel that educators regard them primarily as a problem (Howe & Strauss, p. 96). It follows that, in college, disproportionately more men violate rules and are sanctioned for violence and disruption to the community than women (Harper, Harris, & Mmeje, 2005, p. 565).

"Although women are more likely to rate their time-management skills as 'above average' or 'highest 10%' they are also twice as likely as men to indicate that they frequently feel overwhelmed by all they have to do" (Sax et al., 2005). Women continue to have lower self-confidence and rate themselves more critically on their physical and psychological health (Sax & Harper, 2005). While women outnumber men in trips to the campus counseling center, it may be due in part to "their emotional maturity," which allows them to be "more tuned into their feelings and . . . to see the connection between the stresses of college life and their feelings" (Kadison & DiGeronimo, 2004, p. 32).

Mental health issues

The introduction to Kadison and DiGeronimo's *College of the Overwhelmed* (2004) acknowledges a phenomenon with which college leaders are well-acquainted:

> If your son or daughter is in college, the chances are almost one in two that he or she will become depressed to the point of being unable to function; one in two that he or she will have regular episodes of binge drinking (with the resulting significant risk of dangerous consequences such as sexual assault and car accidents); and 1 in 10 that he or she will seriously consider suicide. In fact, since 1988, the likelihood of a college student's suffering depression has doubled, suicidal ideation has tripled, and sexual assaults have quadrupled. (p. 1)

Even the perpetually optimistic Howe and Strauss (2003) acknowledge that, despite the apparent health of this generational cohort, "there are problem areas: ADD and ADHD, asthma, athletic injuries (especially among girls), obesity, and eating disorders" (p. 82). They also concede that

> On-campus emotional and psychiatric issues will rise in importance, not because Millennials have more emotional problems than prior generations (for the first time in decades, the rate of youth suicide and self-reported depression is trending down), but because addressing any emotional problems has become a higher priority. More students seek counseling, in high school and college, and many more have psychiatric diagnoses and come to campus with prescriptions for psychotropic medications. (p. 82)

Typical college adjustment processes such as "the push and pull of dependence and independence can sometimes be overwhelming" (Kadison & DiGeronimo,

2004, p. 2), especially when considering a generational cohort that is more enmeshed with their parents than any in recent history. Emerging self-injurious behaviors, such as cutting, alarm and sometimes distance peers, administrators, and family members with limited understanding of the acts or their root causes. The uncertainty of world events adds a level of dissonance to the omnipresent stressors associated with college attendance and normative developmental processes, with the potential of overwhelming less resilient or isolated students. "Highly publicized suicides and subsequent lawsuits at schools like Massachusetts Institute of Technology and New York University" (Kadison & DeGeronimo, p. 3) have captured the attention of educational leaders on the issue of student mental health, and parental expectations will keep the topic on administrative agendas for the foreseeable future.

Parental expectations and fears

As parents and students have heightened expectations of the college experience, admissions staff know well that the job of recruiting students (and their parents) to a college or university is a challenging one (Coburn & Treeger, 1997). The amount of information available to a college recruit is massive. While a growing number of parents have attended college themselves, there are many parents who do not have a firsthand experience upon which to draw (Howe and Strauss, 2000). The expectations and demands of both groups of parents vary greatly.

Campus safety and security

One characteristic common to members of this Millennial generation is that they have been sheltered by their parents. Coomes (2005) notes

> The quintessential symbol of this generation was the "Baby on Board" sign on the minivans in the 1980s and '90s. The desire to protect and shelter this generation is evident in such signs as the post-Columbine school lockdowns, the concerns of Security Moms (the swing demographic of the 2004 presidential elections) and programs to protect youth from the nastiness of life such as Drug Awareness and Education Programs (DARE), parental warning labels on products, and blocking software for the Internet. (p. 34)

Campus safety is a critical concern for parents of today's college student (Coomes & DeBard, 2004). Information is readily available on almost any aspect of college life – from backgrounds of college professors to the number of alcohol incidents in residence halls. Parents are bombarded with newspaper and television reports depicting life-threatening meningitis, fraternity hazing, student rape, ecstasy parties, and residence hall fires. The passage of federal legislation has forced colleges and universities to make their crime statistics conveniently available to prospective students and their families. Parents want to know that the facilities themselves are safe and what steps the college is taking to ensure the safety of their children.

The demands on the college housing administrator relative to safety are many. With the large number of facilities constructed in the 1960s, numerous retrofits have been necessary to modify the buildings with requisite safety elements such as deadbolt locks, door viewers, smoke alarms, fire sprinkler systems, panic alarms, and emergency phones.

In loco parentis

In 1968 the long-standing tradition of *in loco parentis* was redefined with the passage of the Family Educational Rights and Privacy Act (FERPA, also known as the Buckley Amendment). FERPA was designed to ensure students access to their educational records and to prohibit access or disclosure of those records to third parties without the students' consent. Housing records, including financial and conduct records, became protected in this process, creating a legal barrier between college administrators and parents by severely limiting the communication that could legally occur among them. FERPA affirmed college students as legal adults and afforded the protection from access to educational records of students by others, including parents. Many parents felt that this legislation and the subsequent silence from college and university administrators negatively impacted their abilities to assist in the successful transition of their student into adulthood.

In 1998 FERPA was amended, allowing public college administrators to notify parents if a student was involved in an incident related to illegal drugs or alcohol. Some colleges and universities quickly adopted policies governing parental notification, while others have yet to do so. Proponents of parental notification argue that parents often have a significant financial investment in a student's college education and, therefore, are entitled to information regarding student conduct (Miller, 2003). Whether an institution elects to take advantage of this amendment, there is no question that some parents will insist that administrators provide information as is allowed by this change in law.

As the practice of parental notification for drug and alcohol violations has become more commonplace, so, too, has the practice of communicating with parents on a wide variety of issues. Savvy parents have discovered that proof of dependence as defined by the Internal Revenue Service can provide access to yet more information regarding their student. Some colleges have begun providing information release forms for students and their parents during orientation to better facilitate communication (Savage, 2003). Some housing professionals indicate that they have more contact with parents than with students during some weeks (McCluskey-Titus, 2002).

"Experienced observers on American campuses have begun to notice a new group of mothers and fathers emerging over the past two years. Informally they're called 'helicopter parents' because of the way they hover over their offspring well beyond the standard moment to say goodbye" (Martin & Samels, 2004). These parents are demanding to be involved in the lives of their children, and many colleges are now responding.

With some of the legal impediments to communication with parents removed, colleges are faced with the more philosophical question: Are parents problems or partners?

Parent services

It is widely held that a supportive student-parent relationship is positively linked to overall college adjustment, persistence, and academic achievement (Austin, 2003; Howe & Strauss, 2000; Pascarella & Terenzini, 2005; Savage, 2003; Tinto, 1987). Parents of Millennials have stepped forward as higher education's newest and perhaps most vocal constituency. Housing administrators will either embrace parents as partners in this joint enterprise or battle with them until their students depart on-campus student housing. Many housing administrators have reported significant increases in recent years in the amount of parent-initiated contact with their offices (Forbes, 2001).

Colleges throughout the country are responding to parents with a variety of parent services. Many campus orientation programs, once for freshmen only, now boast specialized tracks and activities for parents and family members (Kollet & Payne, 2004). These programs are designed to assist family members in better understanding the college experience and to facilitate their involvement. These orientation programs make available to parents books such as *Letting Go: A Parents' Guide to Understanding the College Years* (Coburn & Treeger, 1997), or *You're on Your Own* (Savage, 2003).

While those working within higher education find the functional distribution of services intuitive, parents are often confused and frustrated by the divisions of services and information. Some campuses have established a parents association or an office of parent services to better serve the families of students. These organizations become an important conduit for channeling communication in an efficient and proactive manner. Besides providing an important first point of contact, these groups often distribute newsletters, maintain Web sites, and sponsor family weekend activities to facilitate a sense of connection to the student's collegiate experience.

Technological Expectations and the Digital Divide

"This is the first time in the history of the human race that a generation of kids has overtaken their parents in the use of new technology" (Eio in Howe & Strauss, 2003, p. 85). Described by Taylor (2005) as "a generation wired since birth" (p. 7), more than a few college administrators will admit to turning to their student workers when challenged by one or more computer applications. This generation expects personal privacy and unlimited access, academic and administrative currency, and a high degree of literacy by faculty and staff in all things technological. To keep pace with current college students, Dare (2005) suggests "Ten Technologies to Watch and Learn:"

1. Mozilla Firefox, a new, open-source Web browser increasingly favored by students for its increased security and friendly features over Microsoft's Internet Explorer.
2. Blogs, short for Web log, can range from a personal diary to a series of writings by a group. Good source for insight into student culture for administrators.
3. RSS, or "Really Simple Syndication," is a simplified Web page with just the highlights.
4. The Facebook, an online directory where participants can post photos, keep blogs, and make social connection with others who have an "edu" address. Complicates the lives of campus conduct and judicial officers on a regular basis.
5. Podcasting and Vodcasting, the ability to subscribe to a series of audiofiles and download them to a digital audioplayer (iPod). Vodcasting or "video on demand" is similar to podcasting, but the content is video instead of audio and is more likely played on a laptop than a PMA (Personal Media Assistant) (Meng, 2005).
6. Flash Drives, aka USB drives, thumb drives, and stick drives, are small devices that provide digital storage space.
7. Multipurpose Mobile Devices combine cell phone, PDA and mp3 functions in one instrument.
8. Wi-Fi (wireless connections to the Internet) and Bluetooth (wireless connections between devices such as headsets and mobile phones).
9. Voice Over-Internet Protocol (VoIP) or telephone conversations over the Internet. Fees from VoIP service providers such as Vonage can be lower than those charged by cell phone companies. This technology will soon be replaced by telephones with an Internet port.
10. Instant Messaging, real-time communication via the computer.

As technological proficiency becomes essential to academic pursuits and integral to interpersonal exchange, pre-collegiate experiences and acquired skills become a quasi corequisite for college. "While gender differences in computer usage have dissipated over time, differences based on race have persisted *[in addition to]* disparities in technological preparedness", serving to widen the gap known as "the digital divide" (Sax 2005, p. 1),

College Impact

As this book is designed to elicit strategies for the future of the housing profession, a link between a student's place of residence and his or her college experience seems in order. While the effects are primarily indirect, rather than direct,

> The post-1990 research . . . supports our earlier conclusion that students living on campus are more likely to persist to degree completion than are other similar students living elsewhere. Place of residence has a clear bearing on the extent to which students participate in extracurricular activities, engage in more frequent interactions with peers and faculty members, and report positive perceptions of the campus social climate, satisfaction with their college experience, and great personal growth and development. Abundant evidence in both of our reviews indicates that such involvements positively influence persistence. (Pascarella & Terenzini, 2005 p. 604)

Challenges to the profession

Creating residential communities that add value to the overall educational experiences of current and future students is a central question in the design, construction, renovation, and program review of campus housing facilities. Outside pressures such as enhancement of the overall campus environment, financial return to the institution, and purposeful partnerships with academic and student affairs colleagues to improve student recruitment and retention further complicate decisional processes. When reflecting on the characteristics, behaviors, and expectations of current and anticipated students, many challenges to the profession become evident.

Engaging students with their own learning experiences

As the amount of academic effort expressed by the average student (National Survey, 2005) and the retreat from their lives in the classroom (Seaman, 2005) come into focus, the central task of engaging and investing students in their own academic experience seems paramount. New students feel intimidated by their professors (Keup & Stolzenberg, 2005) and don't see real life connections between what they are studying and who they want to be (Taylor, 2005). The nature and form of information readily available on the Internet have muddied student understanding of academic integrity and original work (Seaman, 2005; Nathan, 2005), and previously experienced lack of rigor has created student expectations of maximum achievement for minimum effort. Student self-reports that "65% of learning occurs outside of classes and class-related activities" (Nathan, 2005, p. 101) reassert the significance of the co-curriculum. "Complementary (not just coincidental) learning opportunities inside and outside the classroom [*must*] augment the academic program" (National Survey, 2005, p. 48) in powerful and relevant ways. Campus housing leaders must address how residential facilities, programs, and staffing structures can advance student engagement with the curriculum and lend additional support for academic success. In an increasingly competitive marketplace for residential students, the failure to realize and demonstrate the academic advantages of on-campus housing may relegate campus residential communities to a perceived single advantage of being proximate to class.

Student expectations for their physical and associational environments

Today's students desire more personal privacy, resisting assignments to halls with group bathrooms, and are more averse to having a roommate (Howe & Strauss, 2003). They are critical of the facilities and services they access most often – including student housing (Keup & Stolzenberg, 2003) – and they would like to eat whatever they want, whenever they want or "24/7" (Howe & Strauss, 2003). The retreat from designed "social space" (Nathan, 2005) adds to the challenge for a facility that holds and fosters community, particularly when students perpetuate their own friendship groups through electronic vehicles such as text and instant messaging. New residence hall designs will undoubtedly balance student demands for amenities and privacy with vested institutional interest in creating affordable communities, where personal and academic encounters and enrichment are possible. The inclusion of wireless technology in public areas is one way that community space can double as alternative study space for residential students.

Student expectations, community norms, and institutional enforcement of policy have been challenged by moderating student attitudes toward marijuana (Sax et al., 2005) and elevating drug use by students. The conventional orientation of today's college students may give rise to "sentiments that drug users aren't popular" (Howe & Strauss, 2003, p. 80) and in turn, call for residence life officials to establish clear expectations, communicate them early and often (Taylor, 2005), and enforce policy consistently. Another outgrowth of today's college students' conventional orientation is an interest in the return of college spirit and large-scale events. While their associational groups may now be smaller, their affiliation interests certainly surpass their circle of friends. Creating opportunities for developing and enlarging students' localized peer group has been a long-standing expectation of residential living. The key may be to transform traditional outreach efforts so that they are relevant for students today.

The Role of Campus Housing in Supporting Diversity and Educational Access

A potential limitation to the conventional (see Table 2) attributes of this cohort of college students is the propensity to be more conformist and less committed to free speech or creative thought (Howe & Strauss, 2003). If appreciation for multiple perspectives is somewhat limited, how does this play into understanding of the importance of a diverse student body? Nathan (2005) asserts, "What makes diversity a 'success' . . .is not only that the university population reflects the diversity of the general population but also that students become more involved in the lives and issues of that diverse population" (p. 58). As the cost of education continues to increase relative to the median family income, more viewpoints will be lost from "the campus conversation." The role of campus housing in creating and sustaining inclusive and celebrative environments cannot be overstated. Residential proximity affords excellent opportunities for cross-cultural encounters, but if shared experiences do not become an extension of those encounters, collegiate friendships typically follow the path of "ego-centered friendships" (Nathan, 2005) built on common backgrounds and interests. Keeping on-campus rent rates in line with campus financial aid packaging is critical to student access and participation.

Responding to campus mental health issues

With the manifestation of student mental health issues as a target of public and parental concern and the concomitant increase in demand on campus resources, an apt institutional response must be comprehensive in nature and broadly communicated to members of the college community. Viewing "emotional development as part of the intellectual, developmental, and spiritual growth that is integral to the college experience" (Kadison & DiGeronimo, 2004, p. 3) provides a holistic frame for constructing campus programs, protocols, and services. The following suggestions for crafting institutional plans are presented as an illustrative framework rather than a comprehensive listing of critical elements.

Education. Broadly educating all members of the college community (including parents) about the normative stressors associated with college life, mental health issues common among college students, and campus and community resources empowers all to access and make appropriate referrals. Aspects of a campus mental health education strategy might include:

- Regular campus communication vehicles to provide accurate information about the signs and symptoms of depression, suicidal ideology, and campus resources to all campus employees.

- The student counseling center in the summer orientation program (Kadison & DiGeronimo, 2004, p. 170), offering a session for parents on available counseling services, prescription dispensing, oversight, and bridging care between home and collegiate providers.
- Broad student education on typical mental health challenges for students (anxiety, depression, eating or substance abuse) to promote prevention. (Kadison & DiGeronimo. p. 167)

Intervention. When students convey via direct communication or behavior that they may have a mental health issue, informed and appropriate staff response is essential. A campus intervention plan should include

- Training and response guidelines for full-time and paraprofessional staff, including role limitations and emergency protocols and services.
- Cross-functional (counseling center, housing, student life) team approach for students with special needs (Howe & Strauss, 2003) or critical issues that threaten successful continuation as a student.
- Identified resources to deal with extremely distressed students, including evaluation and assessment needs. (Kadison & DiGeronimo, 2004 p. 167)

Postvention. The reintegration of a student into campus following a psychological emergency calls for mindful coordination of resources and student accountability measures to ensure that the student can access requisite resources associated with continuation as a student. Designated follow-up care (Kadison & DiGeronimo, p. 175), especially when psychotropic drugs are prescribed, bridging with off-campus providers and resources, and articulated continuation of care plans (Kadison & DiGeronimo, p. 176) should be baseline elements following a serious incident.

Today's Web-savvy students access the Internet with frequency and ease when looking for information of personal and educational relevance. Updating campus Web sites with links to popular sites for information on mental health (Kadison & DiGeronimo, p. 180), anonymous screening for selected mental health issues (Kadison & DiGeronimo, p. 178), and resources for students referred as part of the campus judicial process boost access to accommodate a student's schedule. Whether there is an increase in the incidence of campus mental health issues or a proliferation in the use of campus mental health resources, colleges and universities face rising public sentiments of our "duty to care" (and inform families) for all students, especially those who are distressed.

Parents as partners

Parents are becoming increasingly involved in the day-to-day lives of students living on college campuses. Parents often display a customer-like insistence that their needs be met with promptness and efficiency. Housing administrators must better understand the needs of parents and develop effective systems for meeting them. The following are several key focal areas that warrant further consideration and attention:

- A return to *in loco parentis* expectations now seems apparent. While FERPA may look to limit some forms of communication, the successful housing administrator will need to create systems and negotiate boundaries that respect the rights of students while meeting the needs of involved parents.
- Student safety and security is of increasing importance to both students and parents. Facility upgrades that enhance safety will be an important recruitment and retention tool for the future. Housing administrators will be required to prioritize which measures are of the highest value due to the expense and varied demand on budgets. Security features such as video surveillance, card access entry, door alarms, security screens, and security staff will enhance the confidence of students and staff in the residential environment.
- The misbehavior of other students will require swift and consistent consequences and adjudication. Parents and students will become less tolerant of the inappropriate behavior of others. The background screening of both employees and residents will become imperative.
- A return to an option of single-gender residence hall floors or buildings may increase in demand.
- Substance-free environments may be an important quality for some parents and students.

Conclusion

The role of housing administrators is becoming more challenging. They must be able to leverage their collective resources in new and collaborative ways. They also must be willing and able to market their distinctiveness in a marketplace of unsurpassed competition and choice. Students, parents, and their corresponding expectations have never been more diverse. The successful administrator will embrace this multiplicity of needs and demands with enthusiasm and creativity.

The future of higher education has boundless possibilities.

References

Astin, A. (1993). *What matters in college: Four critical years revisited.* San Francisco: Jossey-Bass.

Austin, D. (2003). The role of family influence on student success. In J. Ward-Roof & C. Hatch (Eds.), *Designing successful transitions: A guide for orienting students to college.* Columbia, SC: The National Resource Center for the First-year Experience and Students in Transition.

Beloit College 2005 mindset list. (2005). Retrieved October 28, 2005, from www.beloit.edu/~pubaff/mindset/

Chester, E. (2005). *Generation why.* Retrieved October 28, 2005, from http://www.generationwhy.com

Coburn, K., & Treeger, M. L. (1997). *Letting go.* New York: Harper Collins Publishers.

Coomes, M.D. (2005). A millennial generation primer. *Talking Stick, 23*(1), 34.

Coomes, M. D., & DeBard, R. (2004). *Serving the millennial generation: New directions for student services.* San Francisco: Jossey-Bass.

Dare, L. (2005, Summer). Ten technologies to watch and learn. *Student Affairs Online, 6*(4). Retrieved November 22, 2005, from http://studentaffairs.com/ejournal/Fall_2005/Ten Technologies.htm

Enrollment highlights of U.S. colleges and universities. (2005, August 26). *The Chronicle of Higher Education, 52*(1), 2, 10, 12, 100.

Forbes, K.J. (2001, September/October). Students and their parents: Where do campuses fit in? *About Campus,* 11-17.

Harper, S. R., Harris III, F., & Mmeje, K. (2005). A theoretical model to explain the overrepresentation of college men among campus judicial offenders: Implications for campus administrators. *NASPA Journal, 42(4),* 565-588.

Howe, N., & Strauss, W. (2000). *Millennials rising,* New York: Vintage

Howe, N., & Strauss, W. (2003). *Millennials go to college.* Washington, DC: American Association of Collegiate Registrars and Admissions Officers, Life-Course Associates.

Kadison, R., & DiGeronimo, T. F. (2004). *College of the overwhelmed: The campus mental health crisis and what to do about it.* San Francisco: Jossey-Bass.

Keup, J. R., & Stolzenberg, E.B. (2004). *The 2003 your first college year (YFCY) survey: Exploring the academic and personal experiences of college students.* Los Angeles: Higher Education Research Institute. Retrieved November 18, 2005, from http://www.gseis.uc.a.edu/heri/ytcy_findings.html

Kollet, G., & Payne, C. (2004, October). *Best practices: Parent orientation programs, family orientation programs, and parents' associations.* National Orientation Directors Association Annual Meeting, Chicago, IL.

Levine, A., & Cureton, J. (1998). *When hope and fear collide.* San Francisco: Jossey-Bass.

Martin, J., & Samels, J. E. (2004, September 14). Why today's parents require better college orientations. *Christian Science Monitor.*

McCluskey-Titus, P. (2002). Book review of *Don't tell me what to do, just send money: The essential parenting guide to the college years. The Journal of College and University Student Housing, 30*(2), 41–43.

Meng, P. (2005). *Podcasting & vodcasting: A white paper–definitions, discussions & implications.* University of Missouri IAT Services. Retrieved November 21, 2005, from http://iatservices.missouri.edu

Miller, A. (2003). A review of parental notification concerning college students' alcohol/ drug violations. In S. Horwood, D.E. Robertson, & C. Hulick (Eds.), *Integrating student learning in higher education: Refining the learning community.* Oxford, England: Oxford International Roundtable.

National Survey of Student Engagement (2005). *Annual report.* Bloomington, IN: Center for Postsecondary Research, Indiana University. Retrieved November 18, 2005, from http://nsse.iub.edu/pdf/NSSE2005_annual_report.pdf

Nathan, R. (2005). *My freshman year: What a professor learned by becoming a student.* Ithaca, NY: Cornell University Press.

Pascarella, E.T., & Terenzini, P.T. (2005). *How college affects students.* San Francisco: Jossey-Bass.

Sacks, P. (1996). *Generation X goes to college: An eye-opening account of teaching in postmodern America.* Chicago: Open Court.

Savage, M. (2003). *You're on your own.* New York: Simon & Schuster.

Sax, L. J., & Harper, C. E. (2005, May). *Origins of the gender gap: Pre-college and college influences on the differences between men and women.* Annual meeting of the Association for Institutional Research. Los Angeles, CA. Retrieved October 15, 2005, from http://www.gseis.ucla.edu/heri/research.html

Sax, L. J., Hurtado, S., Lindholm, J. A., Astin, A. W., Korn, W.S., & Mahoney, K.M. (2005). *The American freshman: National norms for fall 2004.* Los Angeles: Higher Education Research Institute. Retrieved October 15, 2005, from http://www.gseis.ucla.edu/heri/PDFs/04_Norms_Flyer.pdf

Seaman, B. (2005). *Binge: Campus life in an age of disconnection and excess.* Hoboken, NJ: John Wiley & Sons.

Taylor, M. (2005). Generation NeXt: Today's postmodern student – meeting, teaching and serving. In Higher Learning Commission of the North Central Association, *2005 collection of papers.* North Central Association.

Tinto, V. (1987). *Leaving college: Rethinking the causes and cures of student attrition.* Chicago: The University of Chicago Press.

Diversity and Multiculturalism on College Campuses

Mary F. Howard-Hamilton, Ed.D. and Susan D. Johnson

The racial ethnic student composition on college campuses is changing rapidly (Altbach, Berdahl, & Gumport, 1999; Justiz, Wilson, & Bjork, 1994; Wijeyesinghe & Jackson, 2001), and preeminent scholars in the field have predicted these changes for 20 years (Pascarella & Terenzini, 2005). The new demographics have helped motivate the infusion of diversity courses in the academic curriculum, programming that exposes all students to the multicultural landscape and programs that train faculty, staff, and students how to provide a safe space in the institution for everyone on campus. However, diversity issues continue to create challenges for housing operations. Developing creative approaches that provide culturally unique residential experiences is imperative because the preparation phase is over and the implementation process is long overdue.

Administrators and student staff in housing units should be role models and leaders in creating spaces that are inclusive and in encouraging diversity initiatives. Because residence assistants (RAs) are student leaders, they also should be comfortable with the demographic shifts and diversity initiatives on campus. Moreover, administrators and staff should be multiculturally competent to support and challenge student leaders in residence life as well as students they encounter on campus because "respecting and appreciating the variations and nuances within and among cultural groups is an ongoing educational process, and inevitably one cannot know everything about all diverse groups" (Rafuls, Howard-Hamilton, & Jennie, 1999, p. 113). Thus, becoming a multiculturally competent leader involves constant education and reeducation that requires a unique mix of awareness, knowledge, and skills to create a sensitive and affirming campus environment (Pope & Reynolds, 1997; Watt, Howard-Hamilton, & Fairchild, 2003).

Multicultural Competence

Often the terms *diversity* and *multiculturalism* are used interchangeably. However, no broadly accepted definitions exist for either. Some scholars argue for a more race-based definition so as not to undermine the effects of racism (Helms & Richardson, 1997), while some advocate the inclusion of other aspects of our social identities such as sexual orientation, socioeconomic status, physical abilities, and religious beliefs (Pederson, 1988). Still others prefer a more universal perspective along with the recognition, acceptance, and respect of individual differences (Pope, Reynolds, & Mueller, 2004; Reynolds, 2001). For the purposes of this chapter, a single, all-encompassing definition of diversity or multiculturalism is less important than the individual definition of these terms. In other words, the question is not "what does diversity or multiculturalism mean?" but rather "what does diversity or multiculturalism mean to you?" Ultimately, how one personally defines these areas will dictate how they are later operationalized on college campuses. Before a department or unit defines diversity or multiculturalism, there should be extensive discussion among those who will ultimately design and implement related initiatives. The more broadly defined, the greater the likelihood of inclusive services and programs.

At the same time, professionals should not oversimplify definitions of multiculturalism and diversity. In discussions regarding these terms, professionals must challenge one another and avoid the temptation of groupthink. Defining diversity in terms of race and ethnicity is commonplace. To go a step further and reach out to other potential aspects of diversity requires a deeper commitment on the part of the institution. Rather than targeting easily accessible populations, institutions should be cognizant of students missing from the campus environment and work toward filling existing gaps. Recognition of the missing populations and heightening awareness of the various racial, ethnic, and cultural groups on campus involves becoming a culturally competent leader.

Many practitioners and scholars in student affairs have long sought to outline general skills, or competencies, necessary to be effective student affairs professionals (Council for the Advancement of Standards [CAS], 2001; Creamer, Winston, & Miller, 2001; Komives & Woodard, 2003). However, little consensus exists about the most essential competencies (Pope & Reynolds, 1997). Even less agreed upon is the role of multicultural competency in the training and development of student affairs professionals.

Pope and Reynolds (1997), in an attempt to synthesize various sources, suggest seven core competencies, or general awareness, knowledge, and skills, for student affairs practitioners. These competencies are

- Administrative and management, or the ability to complete common tasks.
- Theory and translation, or extensive knowledge of theories applicable to effective student affairs practice.
- Helping and advising, or counseling, conflict management, and advising skills.
- Ethical and professional standards, or knowledge of professional ethics codes and legal precedents.
- Training and teaching, or the ability to teach in a formal classroom setting and present to a variety of audiences.
- Research and assessment, or the ability to conduct and make meaning of research studies and assessments.
- Multicultural awareness, knowledge, and skills, or the self-awareness of biases and knowledge of various cultural groups.

Of particular interest is the final competency: multicultural awareness, knowledge, and skills. Multiculturally related issues can ill afford to be relegated to the responsibility of unknown "others." If multiculturalism is to be truly valued at institutions of higher education, it must be incorporated and integrated into every aspect of the student affairs profession. Professionals can no longer depend solely on the "multicultural expert" for consulting purposes. Instead, professionals must have "a level of multicultural awareness, knowledge, and skills that allows them to competently work with diverse groups of students and colleagues" (Pope, Reynolds, & Mueller, 2004, p. 9).

Multicultural Competencies for Housing Professionals

Repeatedly having to address the impact of the college environment on students' lives, housing professionals are aware of multicultural issues faced by students. They are constantly called on to meet the needs of an increasingly diverse student body living on campus and as such are challenged to develop programs, services, and facilities to enhance the residential experiences of *all* students. While many formalized structures and practices exist to address diversity and multiculturalism on campuses, it is perhaps the informal efforts—the ones epitomized by the campus housing environment—that can best tackle these areas.

Pope and Reynolds (1997) argued that multicultural competence "is a necessary prerequisite to effective, affirming, and ethical work in student affairs" (p. 270). Professionals need the awareness, knowledge, and skills to adequately address both culturally similar and culturally different issues (Pope, Reynolds, & Mueller, 2004). In looking to future diversity challenges for housing operations, we take the awareness, knowledge, and skills that define general multicultural competence in student affairs and offer more specific suggestions for multicultural competency in housing (see Table 3.1).

Table 3.1: Characteristics of a Multiculturally Competent Housing Professional

Multicultural Awareness	Multicultural Knowledge	Multicultural Skills
Personally committed to establishing and maintaining an open and diverse residential environment.	Knowledge about the ways in which various cultures communicate—both verbally and non-verbally—and their history, customs, and obstacles.	Ability and commitment to create a living/learning environment in which diverse cultures feel free to express themselves without fear of retribution.
An appreciation of and respect for cultural differences and the value of those differences.	Knowledge of different cultures and groups.	Ability and commitment to support the needs of diverse cultures and groups in an affordable residential environment (foods, accessibility, theme floors/halls, celebrations).
An acknowledgement of the racism that continues to impact the ability of diverse cultures to gain access and achieve success.	Knowledge of laws, programs, and offices designed to counter racist practices.	Ability and commitment to the hiring of a diverse professional and paraprofessional housing staff.
A self-awareness of personal biases and values that may impact others.	Knowledge of culturally relevant resources.	Ability and commitment to challenge oneself on long-held beliefs and be open to conversations with others (residents, resident assistants, professional colleagues, supervisors, administrators) regarding those beliefs.
An acknowledgment and acceptance of other world views.	Knowledge of development models (identity, moral, religious) and their effect on oppressed groups.	Ability and commitment to conduct diversity programming (race, religion, sexual orientation) in a safe and respectful living/learning environment and confront issues of intolerance.
An openness to dissonance and valuing the growth it brings.	Knowledge of multicultural theoretical frameworks (Critical Race Theory, White Racial Consciousness, Minority Identity Development).	Ability and commitment to continuously challenge and support housing paraprofessionals and professionals through diversity related professional development and training exercises.

Adapted from Pope and Reynolds (1997) and *ACUHO-I Ethical Principles and Standards for College and University Student Housing Professionals* (2001).

A culturally competent professional and student leader (Howard-Hamilton, Richardson, & Shuford, 1998) is one who appreciates the inclusion of diversity topics into the curricula and programming. Furthermore, culturally competent individuals can walk the walk and talk the talk about diversity comfortably without fear of being ostracized by their own counterparts or being non-responsive when they see injustices taking place. Overall, there is an appreciation of who they are as racial/ethnic individuals as well as those cultures similar or different from their own group. There is continual self-reflection and understanding that being different is okay. Cognitively, there is a desire to learn about issues of oppression and how this impacts society as well as themselves personally. There is an understanding of the complexity of multiple identities and the intersections of race, gender, socioeconomic status, lifestyle, and religion. Accordingly, they can connect with people from multiple perspectives and understand from a moral stance that it is unjust to discriminate based upon immutable characteristics or cultural variables.

The greatest challenge for culturally competent students is to step forward when acts of discrimination are taking place and to communicate displeasure and discomfort with the situation and take a risk to change what has occurred. This means a willingness to become involved in social change that may create a complete shift in who the student associates with on a daily basis. This is when educators and administrators should model the way for these students. Colleges and universities struggle to create campus environments that are welcoming and inviting to *all* students. Historically, this responsibility has fallen to student affairs professionals who are generally trained to address student needs outside the classroom. While they play a critical role in fostering a multiculturally sensitive environment, student affairs professionals receive relatively little training specific to areas of multiculturalism (McEwen & Roper, 1994; Pope & Reynolds, 1997). Frequently the first respondents to complicated issues revolving around multiculturalism, student affairs professionals remain ill equipped to understand or appreciate the intricacies of multicultural issues. This may be due to a variety of reasons including limited discussion during graduate school preparation or a lack of self-examination regarding cultural assumptions (King & Howard-Hamilton, 2003; Torres, Howard-Hamilton, & Cooper, 2003). Before student affairs professionals can become multiculturally sensitive and create a community where diversity and multiculturalism are valued, they must first explore and acknowledge their own beliefs and biases. The understanding of appropriate theoretical frameworks allows for the exploration of individual biases so these issues will not be projected upon the student or groups the person is targeting. Theories allow one to engage in multiple perspective-taking and reflection time so there are numerous methods to approach a situation and respect cultural uniqueness.

Multiculturally Inclusive Theoretical Frameworks

Long-established student development theories have been the guiding paradigms for more than 40 years (Howard-Hamilton, 1997). "Institutions have embraced and adopted theories developed by Chickering, Perry, Kohlberg, Holland, Super, Loevinger, and Sanford, to name a few" (Howard-Hamilton, p. 18).

Within the past two decades, new theories or models have been created, researched, and published that have included the voices of women (Baxter Magolda, 1992; King & Kitchener, 1994), people of color (Wijeyesinghe & Jackson, 2001), and other groups that have been marginalized or oppressed (Torres, 1999; Torres & Phelps, 1997; Hardiman & Jackson, 1997). Valuing the cultural differences students bring to college campuses is important for students' personal growth and development. One lens or perspective along with the belief in the traditional melting pot philosophy will only lead to multicultural students feeling less secure about immersing themselves in the university environment. A framework that helps administrators understand the complex behavioral response students have when being challenged to understand or immerse themselves in diversity discussions or cultural immersion activities is the Diversity Awareness and Multicultural Competence model created by Howard-Hamilton and Hinton (2004). This is a cyclical model, because students will recycle or rotate through the varying themes continuously when new information or stimuli are introduced that may create some form of healthy dissonance (see Figure 3.1). The model is based on students' exposure to an immense and intense amount of material related to racial, ethnic, and multicultural (sexual orientation, religion, gender) issues. Their reactions to these stimuli result in a series of behavioral shifts that occur over a span of time after each program, reading, or activity has been introduced and the level of that activity is intensified.

The first theme is anticipatory anxiousness/anxiety in which students exhibit a sense of positive anxiousness or normal anxiety about the course and the things they would be learning. They open their minds and want to delve into the topics planned for them and want to learn more about themselves as well as other multicultural groups. The overall feelings at the beginning of the experience may be excitement, hopefulness, joy, and openness. At the opposite end of the continuum, other feelings of anxiety, anger, frustration, fear, guilt, and shame may be exhibited if the student is unsure about what is about to take place and has never been exposed to diverse groups. When individuals must move from the known to the unknown, they experience varying forms of anxiety (Corey, 2001). If students take risks and use the freedom they have to listen to the subtle message of anxiety, the direction of their lives may change.

Students who begin to open their minds and yield to anxiety become curious with the acquisition of new knowledge about multiculturalism and diversity. At first they are shocked and appalled when they discover that there is so much more to learn about the history of diverse groups and that their current level of education is woefully inadequate. There is a desire and readiness to read and learn more about the history of culturally diverse people. Once they are exposed to programs, lectures, debates, or readings that are antithetical to what was learned throughout high school or from their parents, church, and friends, a sense of intellectual disequilibrium occurs, and the unearned privileges become uncov-

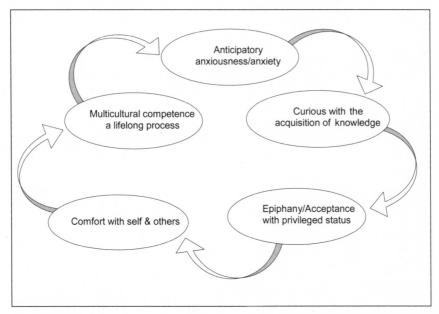

Figure 3.1: Diversity Awareness and Multicultural Competence Model (Howard-Hamilton & Hinton, 2004)

ered. Thus, the next theme, epiphany and acceptance with their privileged status, finds the students recognizing how pervasive privilege is in our society and how many of them have covertly or overtly used these benefits without questioning how or why this power was acquired.

Following the epiphany is the theme of comfort with self and others. It is important for individuals to embrace their racial, ethnic, or cultural heritage so that there is personal peace and empathy for those who also have a cultural connection with meaningful stories. These multicultural stories will be shared, and the learning process continues for everyone. It becomes a lifelong endeavor as noted in the final theme. There is a sense of social consciousness and personal passion to continue the fight against oppression. The students need to maintain a level of normal anxiety, be willing to connect with others not like themselves, and increase their knowledge base so they become multiculturally competent and enhance their level of racial identity development. Students are not the only individuals who need to learn about their privileged status, cultural oppression, and racial identity. Administrators, faculty, and staff should be aware of their own multicultural status and how systemic racism can impede the movement toward inclusiveness. Theories that help individuals understand these personal and institutional complexities are Critical Race Theory and White Racial Identity Development.

Critical Race Theory

Critical Race Theory (CRT) is a theoretical framework generated by scholars of color who study law and legal policies and who are concerned about racial subjugation in society (Delgado & Stefancic, 2001; Smith, Altbach, & Lomotey, 2002; Villalpando & Bernal, 2002). The researchers found that those in power designed laws and policies that were supposed to be race-neutral but still perpetuated racial/ethnic oppression. "This framework emphasizes the importance of viewing policies and policy making in the proper historical and cultural context to deconstruct their racialized content" (Villalpando & Bernal, 2002, pp. 244-245). Ideas such as colorblindness and meritocracy systematically disadvantage people of color and further advantage Whites, as purported by Critical Race theorists. Specifically, Critical Race Theory is based on the following defining elements (Villalpando & Bernal, 2002, p. 245):

- Recognizes that racism is endemic to American life.
- Expresses skepticism toward dominant claims of neutrality, objectivity, colorblindness, and meritocracy.
- Challenges ahistoricism and insists on a contextual/historical analysis of institutional policies.
- Insists on recognizing the experiential knowledge of people of color and their communities of origin in analyzing society.
- Is interdisciplinary and crosses epistemological and methodological boundaries.
- Works toward the end of eliminating racial oppression as part of the broader goal of ending all forms of oppression.

The CRT interdisciplinary connection with education differs slightly "because it attempts to foreground race and racism in the research as well as challenge the traditional paradigms, methods, texts, and separate discourse on race, gender, and class by showing how these social constructs intersect to impact on communities of color" (Solorzano, Ceja, & Yosso, 2000, p. 63). Moreover, there is a focus on a liberating and transformative experience for persons of color by exploring multiple cultural and personal contexts that make up their identity such as race, gender, class, and socioeconomic status. The origins of racial oppression are found in ethnic studies, women's studies, law, psychology, sociology, and history. Discourse then is established so that the common themes and threads are shared.

Methods used to awaken the consciousness of disadvantaged groups are the exposure to microaggressions, creation of counterstories, and development of counterspaces. Conscious, unconscious, verbal, nonverbal, and visual forms of insults directed toward people of color are called microaggressions (Delgado & Stefancic, 2001; Solorzano, Ceja, & Yosso, 2000). These diatribes are pervasive, often covert, innocuous, and nebulous, thus difficult to investigate. This causes tremendous angst among those who experience this racist psychological battering.

Critical Race Theory uses counterstories in the form of discussion, archives, and personal testimonies because it acknowledges that some members of marginalized groups, by virtue of their marginal status, tell untold or different stories based on experiences that challenge the discourse and beliefs of the dominant group (Delgado & Stefancic, 2001; Villalpando & Bernal, 2002). Counterstory-telling is used to cast doubt on existing ideas or myths held by majority group members. A safe place and space, known as counterspaces, should be provided when marginalized groups share their counterstories.

Students of color establish academic and social counterspaces on campus by finding people who look like themselves, and they establish a space that is comfortable and hospitable (Solorzano, Ceja, & Yosso, 2000). These counterspaces may be in a physical structure such as a cultural center or simply the presence of participants in an organization that espouses Africentric values such as Black fraternities or sororities or study groups. The primary emphasis of the counterspace is to find a shelter from the daily torrent of microaggressions and to be in a place that is validating and supportive.

> When the ideology of racism is examined and racist injuries are names, victims of racism can find their voice. Further, those injured by racism discover that they are not alone in their marginality. They become empowered participants, hearing their own stories of others, listening to how the arguments are framed, and learning to make the arguments themselves (Solorzano, Ceja, & Yosso, 2000, p. 64)

White Racial Identity Development

If housing administrators and student leaders are to become open minded about issues related to diversity, the first step is to be comfortable with the idea that everyone is a racial being. The White Racial Identity Development model (Helms, 2000) provides a detailed emotional and cognitive snapshot of how race and racism is viewed, externally and internally, by White people. This is difficult to accept for a large number of White people because they rarely think of themselves in terms of a color or race, but as a human or an American. Thus, understanding the racial identity development of White people is critical to prepare training materials for resident assistants that are sequenced in a manner that is cognitively challenging at a level not too far advanced from their current mode of thinking. In developmental terminology this is considered plus one development, or introducing topics that are one step or stage above the current level of cognitive and psychosocial development.

Helms and Cook (1999) provided an overview of White racial identity and noted there were seven statuses to the model as follows: contact, disintegration, reintegration, pseudo-independence, immersion, emersion, and autonomy. Additionally, these statuses were categorized into two phases: Phase 1, abandonment of racism, consisted of the contact, disintegration, and reintegration statuses; and Phase 2, defining a nonracist White identity, was made up of pseudo-independence, immersion, emersion, and autonomy.

Each status represents different behaviors and levels of discomfort or comfort when engaging in diversity issues. In the contact status, Whites become aware of who they are as a racial being, and they are shocked and surprised to learn about unearned group privileges. During reintegration, there is an "idealization of one's own socio-racial group" (Helms & Cook, 1999, p. 92). Disintegration involves the impact of a racial moral dilemma and how one should react to the person of color as well as to White people with regard to a response. "The Pseudo-Independence status is characterized by an intellectualized commitment to one's racial group in which one identifies with the 'good' nonracist Whites and rejects the 'bad' racists" (Helms & Cook, 1999, p. 92). Once the "good" and the "bad" people have been identified, there is an immersion process that involves a search for honest and accurate information about race and racism, including a "nonracist definition of Whiteness" (Helms & Cook, 1999, p. 92). Once the definition has been cognitively and emotionally processed, the emersion status finds the person working with a community of reeducated White people seeking new information about diversity. In the last status, autonomy, there is a connection to one's racial community, understanding of the complexity of diversity and multiculturalism, as well as an ability to reject or challenge socialized stereotypes and renounce the privileges of racism. If information is introduced that is beyond the person's current psychosocial and cognitive level of development, he or she may close his or her mind to the material and retreat into the original comfortable or privileged position.

Other theories of racial identity development that should be reviewed by housing administrators are the Minority Identity Development model (Rafuls, Howard-Hamilton, & Jennie, 1999; Sue & Sue, 1990); White Racial Identity Development and Cross Cultural model (Sabnani, Ponterotto, & Borodovsky, 1991); and White Identity Development theory (Hardiman, 2001). A thorough review of racial identity theories for multiracial groups, Asians, and Latina(o)s can be found in Wijeyesinghe and Jackson's (2001) text addressing new viewpoints on racial identity development.

Theory to Practice

Housing administrators and campus leaders should maintain a concerted effort to provide appropriate training, supplemental materials, and programming that are relevant to diverse college students. Specifically, in training sessions and other programming efforts, facilitators should teach from an inclusive frame of reference, encouraging dialogue and assigning reflective journals or opportunities periodically during the session to have participants write down an "ah-ha" or enlightening moment during the session. The dialogue and writings could be used to create counterstories when someone is trying to grapple with a racist or sexist incident and it has emotionally impacted her or him. This is the chance to provide the empowering and inclusive circle needed in residence halls for all students. Also it shows students that there is someone available who will listen and challenge any form of oppression that occurs on campus. The first author is reminded of an incident that occurred on campus when her cousin, an African American male college freshman, called one evening and was very distraught and confused because a group of young men on his residence hall floor began referring to Iraqi soldiers as "sand niggers" and that there was complete disregard to his presence in the group. Moreover, he wondered what they said about him behind closed doors. I encouraged him to talk to the resident assistant on the floor about this microaggression, but he was extremely hesitant because there was no personal connection between the two of them. Also, he never sensed that the RA was multiculturally competent. This incident is one clear example of how important it is for RAs, staff, and other housing personnel to make environments inclusive. (Bulletin boards, pamphlets, and brochures that encourage diversity by picturing diverse faces, as well as noting the wide range of diversity programming available, are some ways to promote a diverse environment.) Conversations about race and cross-cultural communication should be part of orientation presentations given at the beginning of each term to incoming students in residence facilities. Occasional evaluations and assessments to surveyresidents on the housing cultural climate will provide insight and ideas for cultural programming and initiatives.

A program at Indiana University that was tremendously successful in opening the dialogue between African American and White women was the "Waiting to Exhale" retreat. The women shared personal stories and discussed similarities and differences about their race, gender, and status in society. The program was an overnight activity held at a sorority house on campus with more than 60 women taking part. The retreat facilitator was a member of a Black sorority on campus, and she enlisted the support of other organizations and administrators to lead get-acquainted activities, group discussions about male/female relationships as well as coping/survival strategies on campus, and goal setting to bridge the gap between White women and women of color on campus. Clearly counterstories were developed, a common space was discovered and shared, and the level of White racial identity development was heightened when all voices were heard. Specifically, all of the women saw a new way of becoming united in their struggle against oppression when solidarity was sought.

Racial microaggressions that occur within academic, residential, and social spaces have been studied by Solorzano, Ceja, and Yosso (2000), who found there is a direct impact on the academic and social life of students that in turn leads to the formation of academic and social common/counterspaces. "These counterspaces serve as sites where deficit notions of people of color can be challenged and where a positive collegiate racial climate can be established and maintained" (Solorzano, Ceja, & Yosso, 2000, p. 70). Thus, the university community should be prepared to support diverse students when they seek a safe haven within predominantly Black student associations, Black sororities, Black female or male support groups (spiritual and academic), and self-made residence hall communities. The researchers also found that African American students create academic and social counterspaces defined by race or gender in response to their marginality on campus. Specifically, "in separating themselves from racially or gender-uncomfortable situations, this group of African American college students appeared to be utilizing their counterspaces on their own terms" (Solorzano, Ceja, & Yosso, 2000, p. 71). Therefore, survival for Black students is contingent on their ability to find a place to describe their experiences among persons like themselves. It is important that faculty and administrators are comfortable with all students of color establishing these spaces and understanding that others from marginalized groups share their sentiments, or else a vicious oppressive cycle will persist, with the dominant group maintaining the status quo on campus and all others remaining outliers within their own academic community.

Housing programs often struggle with whether to intentionally designate themed areas. To do so requires both a philosophical and financial commitment from professionals and the institution. At the philosophical level, housing personnel must be intentional about enhancing learning outside the classroom and must agree that themed areas will ultimately benefit student development. The goals of themed areas should also be in line with the educational mission of the institution. Financially, housing programs must appropriate adequate funds to support the programming and service efforts associated with theme housing as well as the characteristics of a multicultural living environment as shown in Table 3.2. Without the financial ability to sustain theme living areas, the less likely housing programs will be able to maintain a living/learning community that educates and engages its students.

One institution that has invested in the creation of several unique learning environments is The Ohio State University Housing Office. The programs offered not only include cultural initiatives but honors themes, a life style community, and specific academic categories.

The communities established on The Ohio State University campus have existed for several years and are highly successful in creating an environment and atmosphere of inclusiveness as well as celebration for diversity and differences among the students on that campus.

The Afrikan American Living-Learning Program: Those taking part in this program will experience the music, histories, and foods of African and African American communities. Students also have the opportunity to participate in travel that highlights multicultural experiences in the United States. Academic support groups for both men and women further help to provide a balanced experience for students—both academically and socially.

Table 3.3: Characteristics of a Multicultural Living Learning Environment (MLLE)

MLLE Components	Multicultural Awareness	Multicultural Knowledge	Multicultural Skills
Programming	Directly relates and pertains to an array of multicultural theories and frameworks.	Evokes the desire to learn more of various cultures and different others.	Ability and commitment to challenge existing belief systems about diverse cultures and groups.
Students	An openness to learn from and teach different others.	Willing to gain knowledge through interaction both inside and outside an MLLE.	Ability and commitment to actively and consistently take part in multicultural activities specifically designed to enhance living learning environments.
Professional and Para Professional Staffing	Personally committed to the education and development of MLLE residents.	Extensive knowledge of the history and customs of various cultures.	Ability and commitment to confront instances and issues of intolerance.
Resident Contracts	Addresses the definition of diversity and multiculturalism.	Clearly outlines expectations of residents and available learning opportunities.	Ability and commitment to ensure students of the benefits and rewards of living in a diverse learning environment.
Facility	An acknowledgement of resident needs as they relate to the layout of, amenities, and academic resources in the floor and/or building designated as an MLLE.	Knowledge of residential facility trends that directly impact the mission of an MLLE.	Ability and commitment to alter and enhance the facility to preserve the purpose of the MLLE.

MUNDO (Multicultural Understanding Through Nontraditional Discovery Opportunities): Cross-cultural awareness is the key to this themed housing. A sense of global interconnection is woven into the nontraditional living/learning experience. Residents take part in an annual alternative spring break activity and have the opportunity to study abroad. The College of Arts and Sciences and the College of Education work closely together to develop skills that address social justice and leadership issues.

Spanish Language and Culture Community: In this community, students have conversation tables with faculty, students, and staff to enhance language and cultural awareness skills. Recognizing that acquisition of a second language is both personally and professionally beneficial, linguistic and cultural proficiency are emphasized in this environment. Volunteer work with local Latino communities is also part of the experience.

New learning communities for first-year students also have been introduced at the University of Iowa in Iowa City ("Learning communities," 2005). The Multicultural Studies and Leadership program is designed for students interested in learning about American cultural groups and in developing leadership skills. Additionally noteworthy theme housing programs are available at Stanford University, Macalester College, and the University of California-Santa Barbara.

Challenge to the Housing Profession

The living-learning community is enhanced when all individuals are respected and their voices are heard in the creation of that environment. The creation includes having students actively engaged in programming efforts and staff cognizant of activities that do not challenge, support, or have relevance to all persons within the unit. If multicultural students are to feel welcome on college campuses, the first impression (residence halls and staff) will be the lasting impression (successful matriculation and graduation) for many diverse students. Additionally, if the living environment is supportive, diverse students may become interested in becoming RAs and engaging in other leadership opportunities within the residence hall organization. In a sense, universities can "grow their own" leaders by having both multiculturally competent students of color and majority group students who are comfortable supporting diversity initiatives. Failure to provide multicultural programming and a living environment that embraces diversity could negatively affect the recruitment of students and potential future culturally competent administrators and campus leaders. Students could become complacent and ignorant of the changing population that is reflected in the "real world" or their future work environments. They will be incapable of communicating effectively or tackling difficult issues if they lack exposure to and a sound educational experience with racially and ethnically diverse people.

Maintaining and creating supportive environments for diverse students is a lifetime educational responsibility for faculty, administrators, and students who are part of the housing arena. The responsibility of enlightening majority group members about race, ethnicity, and social justice should not rest on the shoulders of people of color and other marginalized groups. It must be the day-to-day mantra of those who have the power to change the environment: housing administrators and institutional leaders. Administrators need continuous professional development opportunities specifically dealing with multicultural issues. Demographic shifts and changes in the campus population make attending to the needs of students of color more paramount.

It is the hope of these writers that administrators will not remain stuck in the first phases of contact, disintegration, and reintegration, but will challenge themselves to move into a nonracist White identity. Campus leaders should first recognize and reconstruct their own cultural White identity (Ortiz & Rhoads, 2000) by examining family background, exposure to other cultures, information about other cultures, and how they develop biases. At this point they should find a way to reexamine their privileges and change their preconceived notions about race and Whiteness. The voice of inclusiveness must start somewhere, and the ideal place would be in living-learning communities, specifically in residence halls. The champions for these changes should be residence life students and full-time professional staff. If these initiatives are not begun immediately and if when students arrive on campus and do not see individuals fighting for equality or people who are multiculturally competent, this sends a message to the institution that diversity and inclusiveness are not important. The campus remains stagnant and the status quo prevails.

References

ACUHO-I ethical principles and standards for college and university student housing professionals (2001). http://www.acuho.ohio-state.edu/resource%20center/ethical.html

Altbach, P.G., Berdahl, R.O., & Gumport, P.J. (1999). *American higher education in the twenty-first century: Social, political, and economic challenges.* Baltimore: Johns Hopkins University Press.

Baxter Magolda, M.B. (1992). *Knowing and reasoning in college: Gender related patterns in students' intellectual development.* San Francisco: Jossey-Bass.

Corey, G. (2001). *Theory and practice of counseling and psychology.* Belmont, CA: Brooks Cole.

Council for the Advancement of Standards for Student Services/Development Programs (CAS). (2001). *Council for the Advancement of Standards: Standards and guidelines for student services/development programs.* Washington, DC: Author.

Creamer, D. G., Winston, R. B., & Miller, T. K. (2001). The professional student affairs administrator: Roles and functions. In R.B. Winston, D.G. Creamer, & T.K. Miller (Eds.), *The professional student affairs administrator: Educator, leader, and manager* (pp. 3-38). New York: Brunner-Routledge.

Delgado, R., & Stefancic, J. (2001). *Critical Race Theory: An introduction.* New York: New York University Press.

Hardiman, R. (2001). Reflections on White identity development theory. In C.L. Wijeyesinghe & B.W. Jackson III (Eds.), *New perspectives on racial identity development: A theoretical and practical anthology* (pp. 108-128). New York: New York University Press.

Hardiman, R., & Jackson, B.W. (1997). Conceptual foundation for social justice courses. In M. Adams, L.A. Bell, & P. Griffin (Eds.), *Teaching for diversity and social justice: A sourcebook* (pp. 16-29). New York: Routledge.

Helms, J.E. (2000). *A race is a nice thing to have: A guide to being a White person or understanding the White person in your life.* Topeka, KS: Content Communication.

Helms, J.E., & Cook, D.A. (1999). *Using race and culture in counseling and psychotherapy: Theory and process.* Needham Heights, MA: Allyn & Bacon.

Helms, J. E., & Richardson, T. Q. (1997). How multiculturalism obscures race and culture as differential aspects of counseling competency. In D.B. Pope-Davis & H.L.K. Coleman (Eds.), *Multicultural counseling competencies: Assessment, education and training, and supervision* (pp. 60-82). Thousand Oaks, CA: Sage.

Howard-Hamilton, M.F. (1997). Theory to practice: Applying developmental theories relevant to African American men. In M. Cuyjet (Ed.), *Helping African American men succeed in college* (pp. 17-30). San Francisco: Jossey-Bass.

Howard-Hamilton, M.F., & Hinton, K.G. (2004). Using the entertainment media to inform student affairs teaching and practice about multiculturalism. In D.S. Forney & T.W. Cawthon (Eds.), *Using entertainment media in student affairs teaching and practice* (pp. 25-36). San Francisco: Jossey-Bass.

Howard-Hamilton, M.F., Richardson, S., & Shuford, B. (1998). Promoting multicultural education: A holistic approach. *College Student Affairs Journal, 18,* 5-17.

Justiz, M.J., Wilson, R., & Bjork, L.G. (1994). *Minorities in higher education.* Phoenix, AZ: American Council on Education and The Oryx Press.

King, P.M., & Howard-Hamilton, M.F. (2003). An assessment of multicultural competence. *NASPA Journal, 40*(2), 119-133.

King, P.M., & Kitchener, K.S. (1994). *Developing reflective judgment.* San Francisco: Jossey-Bass.

Komives, S. R., & Woodard, D. B. (Eds.). (2003). *Student services: A handbook for the profession* (4th ed.). San Francisco: Jossey-Bass.

Learning communities at Iowa. (2005, Winter). *Iowa Update, 8.*

McEwen, M. K., & Roper, L. D. (1994). Incorporating multiculturalism into student affairs preparation programs: Suggestions from the literature. *Journal of College Student Development, 35,* 46-53.

Ortiz, A.M., & Rhoads, R.A. (2000). Deconstructing Whiteness as part of a multicultural educational framework: From theory to practice. *Journal of College Student Development, 41*(1), 81-93.

Pascarella, E.T., & Terenzini, P.T. (2005). *How collage affects students: A third decade of research* (Vol. 2). San Francisco: Jossey-Bass.

Pedersen, P. (1988). *A handbook for developing multicultural awareness.* Alexandria, VA: American Association for Counseling and Development.

Pope, R.L., & Reynolds, A.L. (1997). Student affairs core competencies: Integrating multicultural awareness, knowledge, and skills. *Journal of College Student Development, 38,* 266-277.

Pope, R.L., Reynolds, A.L., & Mueller, J.A. (2004). *Multicultural competence in student affairs*. San Francisco: Jossey-Bass.

Rafuls, S.E., Howard-Hamilton, M.F., & Jennie, J. (1999). Multicultural models and campus ecology theory: Applications to diversity in apartment communities. In D. Casey-Powell (Ed.), *College and university apartment housing* (pp. 93-118). Columbus, OH: The Association of College and University Housing Officers-International.

Reynolds, A.L. (2001). Embracing multiculturalism: A journey of self-discovery. In J.G. Ponterotto, J.M. Casas, L. Suzuki, & C. Alexander (Eds.), *Handbook of multicultural counseling* (2nd ed., pp. 103-112). Thousand Oaks, CA: Sage.

Sabnani, H.B., Ponterotto, J.G., & Borodovsky, L.G. (1991). White racial identity development: The Olentangy Project. In D.G. Creamer (Ed.), *College student development: Theory and practice for the 1990's* (pp. 155-180). Washington, DC: American College Personnel Association.

Sheridan, D., & Anderson, B. (2001). The multicultural competence of resident assistants in Christian colleges and universities, *Growth: The Journal of the Association for Christians in Student Development 1,(1)*.

Smith, W.A., Altbach, P.G., & Lomotey, K. (2002). *The racial crisis in American higher education: Continuing challenges for the twenty first century*. New York: State University of New York Press.

Solorzano, D., Ceja, M., & Yosso, T. (2000). Critical Race Theory, racial microaggressions, and campus racial climate: The experiences of African American college students. *The Journal of Negro Education, 69(1/2)*, 60-73.

Sue, D.W., & Sue, D. (1990). *Counseling the culturally different: Theory and practice* (2nd ed.). New York: Wiley.

The Ohio State University, University Housing. Retrieved October 12, 2005, from the Afrikan American Living- Learning Program http://housing.osu.edu/llps.asp?section=current&id=1&type=18

The Ohio State University, University Housing. Retrieved October 12, 2005, from Allies for Diversity http://housing.osu.edu/llps.asp?section=current&id=21&type=18

The Ohio State University, University Housing. Retrieved October 12, 2005, from International House http://housing.osu.edu/llps.asp?section=current&id=9&type=18

The Ohio State University, University Housing. Retrieved October 12, 2005, from MUNDO (Multicultural Understanding through Nontraditional Discovery Opportunities) http://housing.osu.edu/llps.asp?section=current&id=16&type=18

The Ohio State University, University Housing. Retrieved October 12, 2005, from Native American Cultural Community http://housing.osu.edu/llps.asp?section=current&id=23&type=18

The Ohio State University, University Housing. Retrieved October 12, 2005, from Spanish Language and Culture Community http://housing.osu.edu/ llps.asp?section=current&id=24&type=18

Torres, V. (1999). Validation of a bicultural orientation model for Hispanic college students. *Journal of College Student Development, 40*(3), 285-299.

Torres, V., Howard-Hamilton, M.F., & Cooper, D.L. (2003). *Identity development of diverse populations: Implications for teaching and administration in higher education* (Report Vol. 29, No. 6). San Francisco: Jossey-Bass. (ERIC Document Reproduction Service No. ED479151)

Torres, V., & Phelps, R.E. (1997). Hispanic American acculturation and ethnic identity: A bicultural model. *College Student Affairs Journal, 17*(1), 53-68.

Villalpando, O., & Bernal, D.D. (2002). A Critical Race Theory analysis of barriers that impede the success of faculty of color. In W.A. Smith, P.G. Altbach, & K. Lomotey (Eds.), *The racial crisis in American higher education: Continuing challenges for the twenty first century* (pp. 243-269). New York: State University of New York Press.

Watt, S.K., Howard-Hamilton, M.F., & Fairchild, E. (2003). An assessment of multicultural competence among residence advisors. *Journal of College and University Student Housing, 32*, 32-37.

Wijeyesinghe, C.L., & Jackson III, B.W. (2001). *New perspectives on racial identity development: A theoretical and practical anthology.* New York: New York University Press.

Academic Integration and Campus Transformation

William J. Zeller, Ph.D.

Teaching and learning is in the midst of dramatic transformation. Traditional classrooms designed solely for lecture-style pedagogies may well disappear in the not-too-distant future (Dolence & Norris, 1995; Duderstadt, 1997; Lezner & Johnson, 1997; Morrison, 2003; Varn, 1999). Learning and teaching on tomorrow's campuses will move beyond the simple exchange of information to embrace teaching models that will require greater engagement and active learning methodologies. The impact on residential facilities, programs, and staff will be significant.

Instruction and faculty-student interaction outside of the classroom will transcend traditional boundaries of the campus, and teaching will occur more seamlessly throughout the physical campus and in settings away from the physical campus environment. Instruction modules of the future will allow information to be conveyed asynchronously — any time, anywhere and by anyone — thus liberating faculty and students to have richer interactions when face-to-face instruction occurs. Campus residential environments may well become the setting where the most intensive deep learning interactions will occur, as students and faculty are able to fully exploit the potential of living-learning opportunities.

Over the past decade, reform initiatives in teaching and learning have created more collaborative connections between students and faculty, with students being more active in the teaching and learning process. Learning communities have taken hold as a primary venue for achieving new instructional outcomes. As campuses move into the future, the ever-evolving learning community may become the primary form of teaching and learning within the physical campus environment.

In the future, traditional classroom learning will be transformed and will most likely disappear as new and expanded teaching and learning environments appear on our campuses. Campus facilities, and particularly residential facilities, will need to be designed to support student learning and teaching. Residential staff will need to be successful managers of these new learning environments. These new approaches to student housing will demand a full integration of academic and cocurricular experiences, allowing the entire campus environment to serve as a classroom.

Academic Integration Trends

Undergraduate education reform initiatives that began in the 1980s and '90s created a sense of commitment among faculty and student-affairs professionals toward improving student learning experiences. The reform movement includes renewed focus on first-year student success and retention, new learning community models, and pedagogies that emphasize learning rather than teaching.

Research in this time has shown that undergraduate learning is significantly enhanced when outside classroom activities complement formal classroom instruction (Astin, 1993; Boyer, 1987; American College Personnel Associations [ACPA], 1996).

Campus educators who have pursued these initiatives often find that the most effective means for achieving their goals is the development of residentially based learning communities, where innovative curricular and pedagogical practices can be implemented by creating connections between students' experiences inside and outside the classroom. The connections between the classroom and residence hall environments ultimately provide deeper learning experiences by merging cognitive and affective elements into individual and group educational activities.

Since the early 1980s, living-learning programs have proliferated on campuses across the United States. They have been developed through the advocacy of student affairs administrators, academic departments, and individual faculty, and by executive officers, including campus presidents. The source of sponsorship shapes these programs, and although each campus has different models, strong connections between academic- and student-affairs professionals are an essential ingredient. So too is the ability for campuses to develop programs that specifically fit their needs.

The Registry of Living-Learning Programs and Residential Colleges (2005) lists 67 U.S. campuses with living-learning programs. The registry reveals a wide variety of program models. The National Study of Living-Learning Programs (Inkelas, 2005), sponsored by the Association of College and University Housing Officers-International (ACUHO-I), received responses from 23,910 students on 34 campuses, 11,669 of which came from control subjects not in living-learning communities. Survey results show distinct promise for living-learning participants. For instance, the responses revealed that students in the living-learning environment were more likely than students in the control group to have academic discussions, establish mentoring relationships with faculty, and make a smooth transition from high school into college. Living-learning students reported less drinking and more volunteer activities than non-living-learning counterparts and consider themselves to have improved their critical thinking and analysis abilities. Even though both groups were randomly selected, however, there were a few essential differences between the two that suggest there may be some self-selection into living-learning programs that accounts for some results. For instance, living-learning participants reported higher high school grades on average than did the control group. But other characteristics were shared. Responses came from women in both groups, and both also had similar family backgrounds (educational attainment and income).

The Emergence of a High-Tech Culture

On today's campus, the use of technology, particularly residential technologies, is changing the way students learn, study, and socialize.

The campus environment is being significantly transformed through the use of technologies. Students are interacting with expanded peer groups in new and different ways. They are interacting with faculty more frequently than in the past, but through the use of technology.

An example of this is a male engineering student with a 3.7 grade point average who does not attend classes. He receives lecture notes and homework assignments from his instructors' course management sites and joins study groups with his peers. Classes, he says, are boring, and he believes most students would choose not to go to them if they believed they could still be successful (or would not get an automatic failing grade for failing to attend class).

A growing number of today's students, whose cognition was formed in the digital age, are accustomed to using technology to access, organize, and integrate knowledge. Learning and information gathering with faculty, peers, and new knowledge bases is taking place online. These students come to campuses often bewildered at first, later disappointed, and finally disillusioned by passive, traditional learning experiences (Barone, 2003).

Students expect high bandwidth information access and are disappointed if they don't get it. Although in-room connectivity is still important, students also desire wireless zones in their campus and residential environments, allowing them to work any place at any time. Traditional land-line residential telephone services are quickly becoming obsolete and unnecessary.

Students are actually taking responsibility for creating the type of learning environment they expect. This use of technology has created an invisible subculture on our campuses that must be understood and managed effectively by faculty and student affairs professionals.

Alexander Astin's longitudinal study in 1993 identified key campus characteristics that are essential to achieving general education outcomes, including student-student interaction, student-faculty interaction, faculty that is student-centered, a quality study environment, racial and ethnic issues discussions, and socializing with other students

Just a decade ago, these were strictly face-to-face interactions. For many of today's students and faculty, the primary venue for these interactions is campus and residential technologies. Students are often interacting more with each other through e-mail, instant messaging, and blogging technologies than face-to-face interaction. In-depth dialogues among students are now occurring more through blogging technologies than through late-night "bull sessions" in residence-hall rooms and lounges. On many campuses, the main venue for faculty-student interaction has become e-mail, and students may only seek out a personal interaction with a faculty member if electronic communication fails.

Some campuses have developed online chat rooms for students to discuss important issues, such as racial or ethnic relations, which before took place in group programs.

And students are using technologies more for recreation. Students play Web-based virtual games to compete and socialize with a community of peers anywhere. They share music and movies online. Meeting new friends and even initiating dating is not bounded by campus, much less state or national borders.

Ultimately, the seamless use of technologies within the physical campus environment will allow for the seamless integration of curricular and cocurricular experiences. Traditional campus boundaries will be overcome to allow learning to occur throughout the campus. This transformation of the campus will shape residence hall facilities, staff, and programs in exciting new ways.

The Design of Residential Facilities

The integration of academic and residential life over the past 20 years has significantly impacted the design of residential facilities and will continue to do so into the future. Campus attempts to retrofit academic and academic support spaces into existing facilities created an ongoing tension between the student life and programmatic needs of the community and the new academic goals of living learning-programs. As campuses began to initiate major renovations, or build new facilities, living-learning features have been more easily incorporated. The new amenities in residential facilities included classrooms, academic resource centers, computer labs, libraries, group study spaces, tutorial facilities, faculty offices, faculty living quarters, and more. Significant thought went into making spaces flexible, so use could change at any time, even from day time to evening.

A number of campuses have also found that residential facilities specifically designed to support learning outcomes attract new funding sources, including development funds, general funds, or shared funding with academic departments.

New Staffing Roles and Responsibilities

The integration of academic and residential life will also shape the roles of residential life staff. The evolution of staff will occur within the profession and will also be influenced by the individual campus requirements and outcomes. Besides requiring a keen understanding of the academic culture and the ability to form successful partnerships with academic professionals, residence life professionals and paraprofessionals of the future will need to know how to connect cognitive and affective learning experiences, particularly in the residential setting.

The need for residential staff to become *learning specialists* will shape new identities for residential life and student affairs professionals of the future (Zeller, 1999; Zeller & Hummel, 1999). The Student Learning Imperative, which arose from the Student Learning Project of the American College Personnel Association (ACPA, 1996), called for a new type of professional expertise in applying learning theory, which traditionally had not been a part of student affairs training. In 1996, ACPA already was saying that the need for this expertise would grow exponentially as learning-centered initiatives proliferated. Professional residential life staff will have résumés that exhibit an ability to work with faculty. Some campuses already also are connecting the academic backgrounds of residential staff to the focus of a living-learning program. For instance, in a science living-learning program, a hall director may have a master's in student affairs but a bachelor's in biology. Residential life professionals will comprise learning specialist and student affairs experts.

Student paraprofessionals will be trained to support teaching and learning, making their experiences more applicable to future career goals. They too may have academic concentrations that complement the living-learning theme.

A Glimpse Into the Future

Taking all these things into consideration, one could conclude that the future of the student housing profession will be predicated on two primary assumptions. First, technology and the virtual education enterprise will make accredited degree-granting higher education available anywhere, anytime, and to anyone. As the sophistication of virtual learning increases, these offerings will become the first choice of many students in the future. Second, the traditional campus experience will continue to exist and will be chosen by many students who want or need a richer learning experience than they can get electronically.

The part of the campus that most likely will become extinct is the traditional classroom. Students will, however, choose a campus-based education over an electronic-only experience in order to participate in deeper learning experiences and intensive learning interactions. Faculty will move from being the "sage on the stage" to being the "guide on the side," with coaching as the teaching paradigm of the future. On-campus pedagogical practices will need to integrate both cognitive and affective components in order to better achieve the deep learning experiences campuses will be expected to provide their students.

As students have already begun to prefer technology for interacting with faculty, peers, the library, and other campus resources, it isn't too difficult to extrapolate this phenomenon out for 12 years when today's first graders reach college age. As their skills and the technology they are using become more sophisticated, virtual and distance education will take hold for the majority of students across the United States.

One could predict that most traditional higher education institutions will respond to this trend and stay viable in the higher education market place. With the change in traditional classrooms, campuses will establish environments for learning interactions, where faculty "coaches" work with students in intensive learning experiences that cannot be duplicated virtually and will integrate cognitive and affective domains.

One of the best locations on campus for providing the deep learning environments of the future may well be the residential facility, specifically designed to integrate academic and cocurricular experiences of students. The undergraduate degree of the future may be one that has a residency requirement, where students would accumulate some academic credit through virtual education venues and would be expected to be on campus at times for supplemental learning experiences. Students may come to the campus for short periods and return home or may be on campus for one or two years during a four-year degree. In addition, more nontraditional students will be using campuses for career development and retooling.

The residential environment designed to provide intensive interaction between faculty and students and among student peer groups may be the primary campus learning environment of the future. These facilities will need to provide spaces for experiential learning, research, and new forms of teaching and learning that might evolve. The experiences provided in this environment will be the reason students choose to come to campus in the future.

These benefits will be achieved only through strong collaborations between campus constituents, particularly between academic faculty and student affairs professionals. Linkages between the curriculum and cocurriculum will be more intentionally designed. Student affairs professionals will provide more formalized co-curricular offerings in support of the formal curriculum, developing faculty-sanctioned undergraduate research opportunities, service learning, experiential learning, tutorial services, and study groups.

In order to serve in this new capacity, student affairs professionals will become grounded in student learning and cognitive psychology theories and practice. Meanwhile, student-housing professionals will become experts in designing campus environments that support student learning. Faculty and student affairs collaborations will be essential to create this type of environment, and all components of the future residential campus will complement student learning: residence halls, dining centers, study spaces, formal and informal social spaces, libraries, and outdoor public spaces. Student housing professionals will have to design facilities flexible enough to adapt to the coming changes and still be usable over their 20-to-50 year life spans so that they provide quality living-learning environments for years to come.

References

American College Personnel Association [ACPA]. (1996). *The student learning imperative.* Retrieved Septenber 15, 2005, from http://www.acpa.nche.edu/sli/sli.hm

Astin. A.W. (1993). *What matters in college?* San Francisco: Jossey-Bass.

Barone, C. A. (2003, September/October). The changing landscape and the new academy, *EDUCAUSE, 38*(5), 41-47.

Boyer, E.L. (1987). *College: The undergraduate experience in America, the Carnegie Foundation for the Advancement of Teaching.* New York: Harper & Row.

Dolence, M.G., & Norris, D.M. (1995). *Transforming higher education: A vision for learning in the 21st century.* Ann Arbor, MI: Society for College and University Planning.

Duderstadt, J.J. (1997, March 7). *The future of the university in an era of change.* Atlanta, GA: The Association of the Collegiate Schools of Planning, Georgia Institute of Technology College of Architecture.

Inkelas, K. (n.d.). *The national study of living-learning programs.* Retrieved September 23, 2005, from http://www.livelearnstudy.net/pages/12/index.htm

Lezner, R., & Johnson, S.S. (1997, March 10). Seeing things as they really are. *Forbes, 159*(5), 122-128.

Morrison, J. (2003). U.S. higher education in transition. *On the Horizons, 11*(1), 6-10. Retrieved September 15, 2005, from http://horizon.unc.edu/courses/partners/intransition.asp

The residential learning communities international registry. (2005). Retrieved October 13, 2005, from http://www.bgsu.edu/colleges/as/clc/rlcch/submissions/

Varn, R. (1999). *Higher education – From industrial age to information age education.* Retrieved September 15, 2005, from http://www.centerdigitaled.com/converge/index.php?pg=magstory

Zeller, W. J. (1999, September/October). The learning specialist. *About Campus*
    4(4), 31–32.
Zeller, W. J., & Hummel, M. L (1999). Academically sponsored residential learn-
    ing programs. *Educational Programming and Student Learning in College*
    and University Residence Halls, 5, 81-96.

Part II

The Management and Administration of Housing Operations

Residence life departments are complex entities, comprised of a variety of interrelated programs or functions that can sometimes feel disparate. This complexity requires housing administrators to develop an understanding of the many nuances inherent within housing programs in order to meet the needs of the various audiences those departments serve.

Part II of this book explores the three portions that serve as the foundation to most every aspect of the administrative duties of residence life work: the people that run the operations, the technology that helps them do it, and the facilities they must support. Plus, in this section, the authors explore the reasons why colleges and universities may enter into relationships with private developers.

Human Resources in Residence Life

Holley Belch, Ph.D. and Gary Kimble

> *The lifeblood of a higher education institution is the individuals who populate it. Without students, faculty, and staff, no college or university can exist. Human capital is higher education's principal resource, development of which is its raison d'être. (Winston & Creamer, 1997, p. 1)*

At the very core of residential programs on college campuses are staff members, who at their best are committed, competent, and dedicated, thereby representing the human capital that Winston and Creamer have so aptly identified as central to institutions of higher education. On several campuses, staff members are a blend of paraprofessional (students), professional (both new and seasoned), and allied or support persons. Each group has an important role in the overall day-to-day operation of residential facilities, including growth and development of college students who reside in the residence halls. Among those are the entry-level residential life human resources: student staff, who are often called resident assistants — or RAs — and the entry-level live-in professional staff, commonly designated as residence directors or hall directors.

Historic Context of Residential Staff

Residential facilities, originally rooted in the English model of higher education, were considered the educational center of an institution. The original intent and design of these facilities was to bring students and faculty together (Brubacher & Rudy, 1968; Frederiksen, 1993). Dormitories, as they were called, served an essential purpose in the early history of higher education.

Although modeled after the English system of higher education, the American system lacked the personnel that their English counterparts viewed as vital. In the English system, staff members were responsible for student supervision and discipline while faculty focused on instruction. The American colonial colleges had no residential staffing, leaving faculty to focus their attention on supervision and disciplinary issues related to students (Rudolph, 1962). It was simply a matter of time, however, before administrative positions would emerge to address needs of students, particularly those living in residential facilities on campus (Brubacher & Rudy, 1968; Frederiksen, 1993), so that faculty members could concentrate on their increasing academic demands.

By the 20th century, educational leaders acknowledged the need for professionals devoted to student needs outside of the classroom. Dean of Men positions emerged on many campuses. During this time the courts gave higher education the authority to carry out the job. The courts ruled in *Gott v Berea College* (1913) that college authorities were to act *in loco parentis,* meaning in lieu of parents. The court stated that, "College authorities stand in loco parentis concerning the physical and moral welfare and mental training of the pupils, and we are unable to see why, to that end, they may not make any rule or regulation for the government or betterment of their pupils that a parent could for the same purpose" (as cited in Young & Gehring, 1977, p. 2).

Subsequent changes to higher education in the 20th century all played a significant role in the need for and construction of residential facilities on college campuses (Schroeder & Mable, 1994). These changes included admitting women and ethnic minorities, rapid emergence of public higher education institutions, and federal support for veterans to attend college. Although it is not well documented throughout history, some campuses used older students as staff members to supplement the limited number of adult staffers in the residence halls (Winston & Fitch, 1993).

The middle of the 20th century brought further recognition that the changes in faculty roles, student needs, and the diversity of students enrolling in higher education necessitated more staff on campus to deal with the non-classroom life of students. Although the student affairs profession was emerging, the housemother model in campus residence halls was common, remaining almost literal to the *in loco parentis* notion (Frederiksen, 1993; Schroeder & Mable, 1994). Housemothers lacked preparation or training for their responsibilities (Winston & Fitch, 1993). Among the many changes in higher education that student activism in the 1960s and 1970s precipitated were changes in residential facilities' roles in the education side and the need for residence hall staff to act as more than behavior monitors (Schroeder & Mable, 1994). Over the course of the last 30 to 40 years, the student affairs profession has refined and articulated the role of the co-curriculum in student education and development, placing emphasis on providing learning environments that tie into the academic mission of the institution.

As a result, housing departments developed more specialized and professional job functions, created residence-hall-based programming focused on education outside the classroom, championed collaboration with faculty to develop meaningful living-learning environments, and pioneered the construction of innovative facilities that no longer were double-loaded corridors, but were instead clustered living arrangements for students (Frederiksen, 1993; Saunders, 1993; Schroeder & Mable, 1994). Once student affairs staff members had more specialized training, paraprofessional staff reemerged as an acceptable, important, and necessary adjunct (Winston & Fitch, 1993).

Essential Human Resources in Residence Halls

At the core of any established student affairs organization at a residential college is a strong residence hall program. Life outside the classroom is amplified here. It provides more opportunities to influence student growth and development in the first year or two of college than almost any other program in student affairs. Although educational opportunities are offered through a variety of student affairs programs and departments, none are as pervasive in scope or have the potential to influence as many students as residence hall [educational opportunities] do. (Blimling, 1993, p. 1)

Many in the student affairs profession share the sentiments Blimling expresses, recognizing the potential for learning and growth within a residential setting. The experience, however, extends beyond the proximity of simply living in a residence hall. Critical to the experience is having staff members who are responsible for facilitating learning and growth opportunities, assisting students in developing community, and administering standard -maintenance functions associated with a residential facility. Staff clusters comprise undergraduate students, graduate students, and professionals. A variety of titles exist to identify personnel. For purposes of this discussion, undergraduate student staff members are referred to as resident assistants (RAs) and professional staff are identified as entry-level live-in professionals (e.g., residence and hall directors). Although specific responsibilities of staff vary across campuses, their importance to the educational experience of students is universal.

Resident Assistants

RAs are peer helpers who live on each floor in the residence halls and are charged with developing community among residents; assisting new students with their transition through individual interactions; and developing orientation programs, hall socials, and educational initiatives. RAs play a major role in program- and policy implementation through which goals of a residence life program can be achieved. The primary goal is the development of an environment conducive to the academic and personal growth of students living in the residence halls. Additionally, as peer counselors, RAs provide support for individual students with personal concerns, offer roommate mediation assistance, and share referral information with students. RAs are crucial because they maintain the closest and most enduring contact with resident students.

The RA position is one of the most comprehensive student positions within higher education. Since its inception, the role has changed little, remaining as valuable today as it was when introduced. The overriding principle continues to be helping students in campus residences integrate into the college experience, academically and personally, and to provide a role model. In 1981, Blimling and Miltenberger introduced *The Resident Assistant: Working with College Students in Residence*. It identified four principal roles for the RA: teacher, role model, counselor, and student. It is reasonable to conclude that these four roles remain today as key to the success of the position as they were in 1981.

As much as ever before, RAs have the power to influence student residents in a positive way. Take, for instance, their role in community building. Through interaction and example, RAs develop and exercise social skills, communication skills, conflict resolution, collaboration, and friendship. An RA is able to provide comfort and advice. As peers, RAs theoretically have an excellent opportunity to develop a positive rapport with students, whether explaining the rationale for policies or confronting a policy violation. In many ways RAs serve as a "peer mirror," reflecting for the resident what he/she is capable of achieving within the university setting, assuming that RAs demonstrate academic discipline, attend class, have positive study habits, and maintain good grades.

Through planning and implementing programs, RAs support the development of students and promote an institution's educational mission. By participating in fun and meaningful programs, residents gain experiences that support their personal growth. In addition, RAs serve as an advocate for students and student issues because they have the attention of campus administrators.

There are significant differences today in the experience of the RA, compared with previous generations of RAs. The differences often appear as great as was the difference between what was reported by public school administrators about the general problems encountered between 1963 and 1988. In 1963, school administrators reported the top five school problems as failure to secure a hall pass, getting out of line during a drill, inappropriate dress, holding hands, and chewing gum (Komives, 1993). In 1988, the same school administrators reported the top five problems as gangs and gang culture, destruction of school property, physical assault and harassment, cheating, and substance abuse (Komives).

Campus violence

Campuses of the new millennium have experienced shootings, murder-suicides, homicides, hate crimes, suicides, assaults, hazing, and arson. Although the rate of crime on campus has decreased (Baum & Klaus, 2005), today's RA and campus staff must be prepared to deal with crime and its consequences. According to the report on the violent victimization of college students report (Baum & Klaus, 2005), between 1995 and 2002, college students from age 18 through 24 were victims of approximately 479,000 crimes of violence annually, including rape or sexual assault, robbery, assault, and aggravated assault. In some cases, college students faced rates of crime higher than the general population of non-students.

The nature of college-student victimization is overwhelming. According to Baum & Klaus (2005), approximately 15% to 20% of female college students have experienced forced intercourse (rape), and approximately 5% to 15% of college men have acknowledged that they forced intercourse on another person. In a collection of crime statistics reported by Baum and Klaus, it was noted that simple assaults account for about two-thirds of college student violent crimes, and alcohol and drugs are implicated in approximately 55% to 74% of sexual assaults on campuses. Male college students were twice as likely to be victims of overall violence, and in 41% of violent crimes against college students, the offender was perceived to be under the influence of drugs and/or alcohol. One surprising statistic stated that 7% of all college students were in a physical fight.

Crime statistics are occasionally flawed due to a significant underreporting among victims. Between 1995 and 2002, for instance, students reported to police only 35% of acts of violence they experienced (Baum & Klaus, 2005). Most significant is that living quarters crimes (i.e., burglary, larceny, vandalism, threats, and harassment) constituted as much as 30% of all crimes experienced during that period and often involved residence life personnel directly (Baum & Klaus). RAs may be harassed and intimidated by violence prone students in or outside the classroom, impinging on academic freedom, policy enforcement, and their own safety and welfare. Student staff members who are victimized can feel overwhelmed and need a great deal of support. If they do not sense that this support is there, they will be less likely to report and seek help.

Mental health issues

The RA of today will cope with many issues. None, though, may be more demanding or more challenging to address than those involving mental health issues. According to Zabel, writing for the ERIC Clearinghouse on Handicapped and Gifted Children in 1988, at some point in their lives, most individuals exhibit behavior that others consider excessive or inappropriate for the circumstances. Unlike some other disabilities, though, emotional and behavioral disorders are not necessarily lifelong conditions. Recently, the term *behavioral disorder* has gained favor in describing patterns that depart significantly from the expectations of others. Whether the student is unable to build or maintain satisfactory interpersonal relationships or displays inappropriate types of behaviors or feelings under normal circumstances, it is often RAs who are faced first with handling such students. It might be aggression, irritability, withdrawal, anxiety, or depression. There has been a significant increase in the number of college students experiencing psychological problems, in the severity of the problems (e.g., learning disabilities, eating disorders, substance abuse, self-injury), and in those seeking counseling services (Gallagher, Sysko, & Zhang, 2001; Kitzrow, 2003; Levine & Cureton, 1998; Pledge, Lapan, Heppner, & Roehlke, 1998). In fact, the level of severity goes well beyond the more traditional transition issues that were common among college students 40 years ago (Pledge et al., 1998). There is scant data to confirm the exact number of students with psychological issues attending college (Sharpe, Bruininks, Blacklock, Benson, & Johnson, 2004). However, campus counseling center directors reported that 40% of their clients have severe psychological problems (Gallagher, 2002).

Students with psychological issues often demand more time and energy from counseling center staff (for those that seek counseling services) and others in the students' realm, such as roommates, classmates, faculty, and staff (Kitzrow, 2003). In residence halls, RAs often are on front-line staff, handling the impact of affected students' behaviors and any repercussions among other fellow residents. RAs often are initial responders during a presenting crisis.

Training

With issues of mental health, violence, learning disorders, relationship problems, and social and sexual diseases, student affairs practitioners must focus more attention on training and support systems to recruit, retain, and continually train RAs who can capably handle these complex problems.

Effective training for RAs should be as experiential as possible, providing role-playing activities for developing and practicing competence with the responsibilities of the position. Role-playing situations also enable supervisors and trainers to offer feedback and assess RA staff skills. In particular, housing professionals have successfully used role-playing in confrontation and discipline training, check-in procedures, the first floor meeting, and counseling. Professional staff members must strive to seek additional ways to implement role-playing in training.

RA training is quite broad based. It must include enhancing RA self-confidence and self-esteem. RAs must understand human development, be effective communicators, understand group dynamics, and appropriately confront peers when necessary. Today's RAs must be effective listeners and have the capacity for empathy, have basic counseling skills, and know campus and hall policies and regulations. Add to these perennial skills such as effective time management and organization.

As more residence life operations return to the residential college concept or collaborate with academic entities, RAs will be front and center. It will be imperative for the RA to develop strong relationships with faculty and the residents. Residence life professionals must take the lead in training RAs to support the living learning centers and in fostering important peer relationships in living-learning circumstances. Substantial evidence exists confirming the positive impact of peer interaction on social integration (Tinto, 1975; 1987; 1993) and cognitive development (Pascarella & Terenzini, 2005). Of special interest will be training to enhance communication skills among roommates and floor residents.

Finally, in addition to facilitating a sense of community, living-learning communities foster student involvement (Jones, 2000), provide more frequent student-faculty interaction (Garrett & Zabriskie, 2004; Inkelas, 1999), and positively influence academic achievement (Winston & Anchors, 1993). Almost any one of these alone would be a desirable outcome for a housing operation. The fact that all are potential outcomes is notable and makes RA training in this area particularly important.

Another area of training that increases in importance as campus demographics shift is multicultural and diversity awareness encompassing race, ethnicity, gender or gender identity, sexual orientation, or ability. Training programs in these areas must extend beyond the surface and challenge student staff members to examine their personal views. Data from the Higher Education Research Institute indicated that in 2001 interracial interaction among college freshmen reached a record high (Sax, Lindholm, Astin, Korn, & Mahoney, 2001). Student staff members have a prime opportunity to discuss stereotypes, discover sources of prejudice, and promote diversity among students. Staff training programs should enhance sensitivity, teach about cultures, enhance an awareness of issues for underrepresented populations, teach staff how to develop a system of allies, demonstrate how to facilitate healthy discussions and positive interactions, and teach how to acknowledge and truly appreciate differences.

Training for RAs in the future will also need to encompass many of the traditional components of a residence life operation, such as policies and procedures. With the reality of violence on local and more global scales, crisis management skills will become imperative. For example, an RA may need to develop more sophisticated skills in defusing a volatile situation between residents in order to stabilize a situation before having time to sort out the details of the encounter. There is no doubt campus housing and residence life staff members have witnessed an increase in inappropriately handled disagreements and arguments. It has not been unusual for males and females to physically fight or for roommate disagreements to escalate into violence. Students also are exhibiting the need for learning to control emotional situations and finding appropriate ways to resolve conflict.

The campus of the next 20 years also will have to pay heed to RAs' needs. On a practical level, they need ready access to campus police and safety personnel and backup professional counselors. Today's and tomorrow's students come to campus with a pharmacy of prescription drugs, and therefore health-center personnel must be available to RAs for training, consultation, and intervention.

Backup must also come in the form of comprehensive yet concise campus policies, clearly articulated to students, parents, and other constituents. In addition, for everyone's safety, campuses will have to adopt zero-tolerance policies for specific behaviors that are violent or threatening in nature.

Tomorrow's RA

If the Millennial generation literature is on target (see chapter 2), RAs will be a different breed than those students from a time as recent as the late 1990s. Furthermore, if colleges and universities are to be successful in designing recruiting programs and management systems based on their values and needs, the institutions must continually seek to create the kinds of environments that will attract, retain, and motivate the members of this generation.

It is important to understand the trends of their early years that had such a profound effect on their generational personality. In her work, *Connecting Generations*, Claire Raines (2002) noted eight key trends of the 1990s and 2000s, which influence these students' attitudes toward work. Raines' research, which generally confirms the work of Howe and Strauss, offers insight into the possible work ethic of today's generation. Her eight trends include the popularity of and spotlight on children; scheduled and structured lives; increased daily interaction with other ethnicities and cultures; devastating events such as the bombing at Oklahoma City, the school shooting in Columbine, Colorado, and the terrorist attacks of September 11; re-emergence of the everyday hero and the extent to which national pride and patriotism are popular; advocacy and involvement of parents interceding on behalf of their children; and global connectedness as a common experience of this generation.

Research on the Millennial generation would also lead one to think that future RAs may have an admirable work ethic, based on predictions that they will be sociable, talented, well-educated, collaborative, open-minded, influential, and achievement oriented. They also will expect a challenging, collaborative, creative, fun, and financially rewarding workplace. They may, for instance, arrive for the first day on their floor with personal goals on paper. Millennials are civic minded and have been taught to think in terms of the greater good. They have a high rate of volunteerism. They will expect campus to contribute to its community. Accustomed to teams where everyone gets the honorable mention, they'll likely make certain no one is left behind. They'll expect a floor community that is fair to all, where diversity is the norm, and they'll use their collective power if they feel someone is treated unfairly. They are so well connected that if their expectations are not met, and they encounter dissatisfaction, they can tell thousands of their peers with one click of the mouse.

RAs of the future will challenge residence life professionals to be role models and exhibit honesty and integrity. They'll want work that is stimulating and provides learning opportunities. In her study Raines (2002) noted a Randstad survey that found that "trying new things" was the most popular item, providing support that Millennials are seeking work which offers new learning experiences.

Millennials say they like being friends with coworkers. Hall directors who provide for the social aspects of work will find those efforts well rewarded. It has been noted that some companies of today are even interviewing and hiring groups of friends. Companies of the future will be challenged to seek new and innovative ways to make the work environment more attractive to today's student. Many Millennials will enter the workforce believing their ideas deserve to be given consideration from supervisors regardless of the length of time of their service to the company (Raines, 2002). Further, this generation is so accustomed to a high degree of participation in a variety of activities that they will expect supervisors to be flexible with their schedules in order to meet their needs (Raines).

The students who take on the responsibility of the RA position will bring to our residence life operations the philosophical elements which we have long espoused, including teamwork, technology, structure, entertainment and excitement, and experiential activities. With mentoring and encouragement, we will undoubtedly be in a position to learn from them.

Recently, Kimble, Timson, and Oltersdorf (2004) confirmed the positive impact of this generation of students on the RA position in a study of 2,361 RAs and student leaders, which assessed their interests and thoughts about potentially entering residence life and student affairs careers. The respondents represented more than 300 institutions, with 31% males and 67% females. The results were rather remarkable for the future of our profession. More than 51% indicated they had given consideration to a career in the field of housing and residence life. When asked what they perceived as the most positive factors associated with the work, 81% reported it was fun and enjoyable work, 78% indicated it offered positive leadership and relationship experiences, and 75% believed the work was interesting and meaningful. Negatives included the nature of the "fishbowl" existence of the profession (64%), salaries (57%), and length of work week (56%). The positives certainly outweigh negatives and reinforce positive characteristics of this generation, including a desire for challenge with learning opportunities, development, and a career path. After all, they appear to have interest in our positions and find the work meaningful. Any negatives reported in the study are of the nature that we, as professionals, have the ability to change in order to make the positions more attractive. Lastly, it is encouraging that the positives they noted are factors inherent in the work of the housing professional.

Entry-Level Live-In Professionals

The value and importance of new professionals in student affairs has been affirmed in the literature (Amey & Reesor, 1998; Barr, 1990; Belch & Mueller, 2003; Coleman & Johnson, 1990; Dalton, 1996; Kinser, 1993; Tederman, 1997).

Historically, entry-level live-in positions have functioned as a key entry point into the profession for years (Belch & Mueller, 2003). As the student affairs profession evolved, and with it the role of residence life and housing on college campuses, staff members in these type of positions have been instrumental in incorporating the learning side of university experience into residence life and are strong perpetuators of a multidimensional residence community.

Although many entry-level professionals have newly acquired master's degrees from preparation programs, a significant number of staff come directly from their undergraduate experience, from the general workforce, or from other types of graduate level programs (Cooper, etal., 2002; Creamer, 1997; Helm, 2004). In an international study of entry-level live-in staff, more than half (58%) of the senior housing officers surveyed indicated that the minimum educational level was a bachelor's degree, while 31% said a master's degree (St. Onge & Nestor, 2005). Minimum degree requirements appear to be tied to institutional philosophy and practice and to market forces in the hiring of entry-level live in professionals.

Roles and responsibilities

The roles and responsibilities will vary, but some general job responsibilities are more universal to a typical entry-level live-in position. These may include: supervision of staff (both student and clerical); advising student groups developing and coordinating student programs and activities; enforcing policy and addressing student behavior; individual counseling; and acting as liaison to food service, custodial, and maintenance staff (Kearney, 1993). More recently, job responsibilities have also included fostering and supporting the educational mission of the institution as part of the residential experience (Devine, 2001; Kearney, 1993).

Because the living-learning connection is becoming and will continue to be important in residence life, entry-level staff will have to be trained differently from their predecessors. A study of roles and perceptions of live-in resident directors found that general management duties often overshadow educational initiatives (Devine, 2001, p. 34). Devine warns that this will cost the residence life program its quality. It is vital that entry-level live-in professionals are provided with a comprehensive understanding of faculty culture, what specifically is recognized as "service" for faculty in the promotion and tenure process, and what responsibilities faculty members have beyond teaching. The culture of faculty is unique, and individual campuses have their own ways of shaping that culture. Without this understanding, entry-level residence life staff members will find it hard to partner effectively with faculty—one of their prime roles.

Live-in professional staff will face the same kinds of challenges already noted for RAs. These issues heighten responsibilities of professional staff both as facility managers and supervisors to RAs. Skills in managing crises, dealing with the students involved, sorting out the details, and debriefing and attending to RAs that were involved or affected are as important as they ever were.

The same goes for multicultural awareness and competence (Mueller & Pope, 2001, p. 133), which must be viewed as integrative and relational rather than as a distinct competency unto itself (Pope, Reynolds, & Mueller, 2004). The key for professional live-in staff now is to apply that skill and competence to the living-learning environment in a manner that truly creates a multicultural campus environment.

Recruitment and retention of staff

An emerging body of research has brought attention and perspective to the challenge of recruiting and retaining entry-level live-in staff (Belch, 2005; Belch & Mueller, 2003; St. Onge & Nestor, 2005). Senior housing officers believe that the challenges of recruiting and retaining these key staffers are something the entire residence life profession must address (St. Onge & Nestor, 2005).

Recruitment, selection, and training of new staff is time consuming and costly (Buck & Watson, 2002). Unwanted or voluntary departures can drain resources and affect morale (Buck & Watson). Therefore, understanding the experience of today's and tomorrow's candidates is as important as establishing the details of the interview and selection processes. In an older study of master's degree graduates, 30% thought they were not treated professionally in the application process (e.g., no acknowledgement of or response to submitting an application) or the interview process (e.g., no communication after the campus visit; verbal promises made during the interview or negotiation yet not received after accepting the job) and that the campus interviews did not provide them with a good idea of the institution (Kinser, 1993). Each year following placement services at national conferences, master's degree students often convey stories of receiving correspondence about jobs they haven't applied for, envelopes addressed to them containing letters addressed to another candidate, or campus visits where they were left alone to navigate the campus environment for interviews. Consequently, the job search process can seem frustrating and lead them to question the professional nature of the field (Belch, Dunkel, & Wilson, 2005).

Senior housing officers reported that allowing pets, offering flexible work schedules, and providing professional development funds are all attractive enticements in the recruitment for entry-level live-in positions (St. Onge & Nestor, 2005). Further, the researchers indicated that salary, availability of professional development funds/opportunities, job responsibilities, and the reputation of the department or institution have a significant impact on recruitment efforts as well. In a study of best practices in the recruitment of entry-level live-in staff, senior housing officers confirmed that current staff and alumni staff played a significant role in the recruitment of new live-in professional staff (Belch, etal.,).

It would appear, however, that larger institutions with large residential programs are at a distinct advantage in the recruitment process. Studies indicate that
larger residential systems with more staff have more available resources and
greater flexibility and can often offset geographic limitations in ways that are not
often possible at smaller institutions (Belch, etal., 2005; St. Onge & Nestor,
2005). The opportunity to interact with a significant number of colleagues in
entry-level live-in positions is an important factor for new professionals in their
decisions about employment (Belch, etal., 2005).

Residence life programs identified as having best practices in the recruitment
of entry-level live-in professionals have clear goals and established timelines,
and they consider recruitment to be a year round activity (Belch, etal., 2005). In
addition, they are characterized by a genuine enthusiasm for the process and
experience: valuing and respecting the personal experience of a candidate, dis-
playing a sincere ethic of care for candidates in each step of the process having
a midlevel professional staff person responsible for conducting and coordinating
the recruitment efforts maintaining consistent and clear communication with all
candidates regardless of where they are in the search process and defining clearly established and highly regarded roles and responsibilities for professional staff
for on-campus interviews (Belch, etal., 2005).

Retaining these professionals over a period of time is of equal importance. In
recent years, voluntary separation of entry-level live-in professionals, particularly in midyear, has been cause for concern by some senior housing officers.
According to an international sample of senior housing officers, the average
length of employment at an institution in an entry-level live-in position is 2 to 4
years (St. Onge & Nestor, 2005). It was found that length-of-stay in a live-in
position positively correlated with institutional size (individuals stay longer at
larger institutions with larger housing programs), organizational structure (institutions with separate housing and residence life systems), and average starting
salaries (St. Onge & Nestor). Other factors that contribute to retention are availability of health benefits, parking (at a cost), professional development funding,
retirement plans, and opportunity for tuition support (St. Onge & Nestor).

There is some evidence to suggest that the disparity between what new professionals believe to be true about an entry-level live-in position and the reality
may differ. In a study of new professionals, participants were surprised at the
number of hours they worked because they didn't perceive their resident director
(when they were graduate students) working as many hours (Pedigo). Further, the
volume of administrative responsibilities (for example, the number of meetings,
amount of committee work, etc.) astonished the respondents (Pedigo, 2002).
Similarly, one quarter of master's degree graduates said the job title did not
reflect the responsibilities they had, and nearly one half (44%) were surprised by
many things related to their jobs (Kinser, 1993).

For professional live-in staff, living accommodations and conditions are an
essential aspect of their satisfaction with the overall experience, their ability to

achieve a level of quality of life that is meaningful, and in some cases their measure of value to the organization. Campus housing operations must invest in maintenance and remodeling (new kitchen cabinets, new carpeting, new lighting fixtures, resurfacing interior doors, and so forth) of live-in staff apartments and develop a plan for such renovations. Simply offering new staff the opportunity to select new furniture, albeit important, is not enough. In many cases, cinder block walls are a constant reminder of institutional living, yet attention to other aspects of the physical environment can serve to mediate the impact. Entry-level live-in staffs understand the financial considerations and limitations of gutting all staff apartments and are often motivated by knowing that a renovation plan exists, especially if they see evidence (Belch, etal., 2005).

Compensation

The concept of compensation is far more complex than simply salary and apartment accommodations. For entry-level live-in positions, the compensation package has historically included salary, health benefits, apartment, and possibly a full or partial meal plan.

Senior housing officers have noted their concern regarding salary levels particularly in relation to the recruitment and hiring of entry-level live-in professionals, yet graduate students did not express the same level of concern regarding salaries in these types of positions (Belch & Mueller, 2003). Predictably, though, entry-level live-in professionals had a more heightened awareness of salary and its potential importance once on the job (Belch, 2005; Belch, etal., 2005). The range of salaries reflects the variance in higher education among institutions and across geography. For example, institutions with some of the highest salary rates for entry-level live-in positions are typically located in high-end economic and real estate markets (California, New York City), while some of the lowest paid live-in positions are at institutions with a religious affiliation or located in very rural areas (Horowitz, 2005). It is no wonder that institutions offering, for example, $20,000 for a 10-month contract with $250 in professional development funds struggle in the recruitment of live-in professionals compared to an institution offering $28,000 to $30,000 and $1,000 in professional development funds for a comparable position. It is important, however, to examine salaries judiciously and to make certain that the actual live-in positions and responsibilities are analogous.

Recent compensation packages have been crafted to define benefits in a much broader sense by including items such as pets (specifically cats and dogs), flexible work schedules, professional development funds and opportunities, parking, a clothes washer and dryer in the apartment, non-campus fitness club memberships, retirement options, tuition support, private entrances to apartments, and coveted sporting event tickets (Belch, 2005; Belch, etal., 2005; St. Onge & Nestor, 2005). In fact, some institutions offer partial meal plans to spouses/children in addition to the staff member in an effort to acknowledge the family that lives in residence and not solely the staff member (Belch, 2005). The availability of a variety of benefits appears to be directly related to the size of the residence life operation/institution (larger institutions are at an advantage) and does correlate positively with length of time in an entry-level live-in position (St. Onge & Nestor, 2005).

For some residence life operations, policies regarding the use of apartments for professional staff have undergone scrutiny and change in recent years. Departmens are popular that have policies allowing live-in professionals the discretion to welcome another person or persons to live in their apartments whether a spouse, child, significant other, partner, friend, or other family member have gained popularity. Ultimately, a number of factors (state law, institutional policy, institutional mores, and support from the leadership) need to be considered in policy development and/or change (Kearney, 1993).

Professional development opportunities, experience to work with and/or shadow other professionals, and financial support are important to entry-level live-in professionals and appear to be essential components in the recruitment and retention process (Belch, etal., 2005). These professionals are eager to learn more in order to accomplish the goals in their current live-in positions and prepare themselves for the next level in their careers. Highly regarded residence life operations offer a variety of opportunities including membership on or chairing important internal committees, appointment to and active membership within institution-wide committees, some release time and/or quarter-time assignment in another functional area of interest, and selection to institutionally sponsored professional development activities (Belch, etal., 2005).

There will always be institutions that can do more, offer more, and provide more. But even more budget-strapped operations can be creative in developing compensation packages for professional live-in staff (McCuskey, 2003). Moreover, operations should consider personalizing compensation in ways that are attractive to candidates and staff. That might mean allowing staff to bundle compensation items from a variety of options and change options as priorities shift. This could also help senior housing officers apportion limited resources in a more effective manner. The degree to which a senior housing officer has influence and/or control over all aspects of compensation will rely not only on her or his political, budgetary, and analytical skills, power, and abilities but also on institution type, size, and culture.

Quality of life

The work-life balance or quality of life, a term often used in conjunction with live-in professional positions, is one that has been identified as a significant concern among graduate students and professional live-in staff (Belch, 2005; Belch & Mueller, 2003). In fact, some graduate students will not pursue live-in professional positions because they do not believe that there is any quality of life personally or professionally as a live-in staff member (Belch, 2005). Senior housing officers also identified quality of life to be an issue for these new professionals (Belch & Mueller, 2003; St. Onge & Nestor, 2005).

The balance between work and life activities seems to be a fundamental struggle endemic to our society. The proverbial personal and professional high-wire act that can befuddle us to no end serves as a source of frustration, becomes an elusive dream, and/or functions as a mantra to keep us ever vigilant in our quest for fulfillment and satisfaction in life. Some would suggest that the culture in student affairs rewards long work hours and does not value balance (Padulo, 2001). However, changes in society have impacted the way in which people value work and personal life and the extent to which they will compromise personal relationships over career (Littlefield, 2003).

The idea of creating and maintaining perspective and balance between work and life activities is a particularly salient one for recent generations. Members of the identifiable Gen X and Gen Y groups are questioning the purpose and meaning of work (Chalofsky, 2003). The idea of meaningful work is more than work for pay; it encompasses all of the work in our lives, how we live, and how we are able to align meaningful elements of our lives (values, purpose, relationships, activities; Chalofsky, 2003). Some cynics have concluded that the current generation is lazy and opposed to work. An emerging body of research reveals that the productivity of employees and their organizational commitment can be positively affected through the employer's understanding and sensitivity to the work-life connection (Bailyn, 1993; Galinsky, Bond, & Swanberg, 1998).

The literature about new professionals in student affairs specifically offers advice on the importance of finding balance between work and life activities (Hamrick & Hemphill, 1998; Tennant & Brungardt, 1998; Toma, Clark, & Jacobs, 1998; Toma & Grady, 2002). The idea of creating and maintaining balance is a joint quest by both employers and the employees, more complex than simply being efficient and developing a better time management plan (Toma & Grady, 2002). Entry-level live-in professionals need to utilize effective strategies to balance the demands in their work lives (high levels of contact with people, limiting what can become unlimited access by students and supervisors, constant conflict resolution, living within a fishbowl, and so forth) with their individual needs or desires for fulfilling personal lives. It is equally important that these strategies are varied and unique to the individual, simply because the work-life balance is defined differently by every individual (Hartley, 2004). For example, leaving campus for a weekend may be a useful strategy for some, while others might welcome better opportunities to get outside the residence hall and connect with the life of the community.

Balance also requires fluidity. "Balance means that nothing is absolutely static and unchanging – routines cannot be rigid and unchangeable. They must be flexible, which means you, as the master/mistress of your routines, must have the flexibility to maintain a balance" (Burton, 2004, p. 12).

Organizations must be sensitive to what balance is for different individuals. For example, a staff member who spends most of her time on work-related endeavors may do so because she is less confident in her personal life. She may require help connecting to non-work groups that will welcome her and make her comfortable. A different staff member may be dissatisfied with his overall work experience because he lacks a sense of accomplishment or confidence on both sides. He may need assistance identifying what he has achieved professionally and personally as well as creating short- and long-term goals in each area. Work environments that are created to support staff in achieving the work-life balance or some meaningful measure of quality of life as they define it (not as the organization defines it) are characterized as organizations with exceptional leadership (Spinks, 2004).

In order to find an appropriate fit for employment, entry-level live-in professional staff should pay close attention to institutional and organizational values. Equally important, leadership in housing and residence life departments must value the importance or relevance of quality of life. At times, however, the will to change policy far outweighs the ability to do because institutional mission, values, or politics pose constraints.

The perception of a lack of quality of life for live-in staff is real both for those that live in and those that do not (Belch, 2005). The dictates of the job mean that certain luxuries cannot come with the territory, such as short work weeks or vacation schedules that differ from the campus calendar. And residence life positions are no longer the dominant option on campus. Graduate assistantships of many sorts have proliferated. In order to avoid live-in positions being second-rate options for employment (McCuskey, 2003), senior housing officers will find it more and more essential to find ways to ensure quality of life for live-in positions.

Socialization

Entry into a new work environment can be stressful, moreso when it is one's first professional position. "The entry of new employees into organizations is a critical human resource process that cannot be underestimated" (Holton & Russell, 1999, p. 1). New professionals in particular may experience cognitive dissonance and a sense of isolation (Amey, 1998; Hunter & Beeler, 1991). Despite claims of importance and relevance, the orientation of new staff to their new institution remains one of the most neglected aspects of managing human resources (Winston & Creamer, 1997).

In fact, Winston and Creamer (1997) revealed that only 61% of staff in new positions had any type of orientation. An effective orientation and socialization process (e.g., support, access to information, knowledge acquisition) is key to satisfaction (Ashforth & Saks, 1996; Morrow & McElroy, 1987; Nelson & Quick, 1991), performance (Ashforth & Saks, 1996; Meyer, Pavnonen, Gellatly, Goffin, & Jackson, 1989), and commitment to the organization (Allen &

Meyer, 1990) and the profession (Ashforth & Saks, 1996; Nelson & Quick, 1991).

Socialization relates to how an individual gains knowledge and skills to become effective in the environment (Weidman, Twale, & Stein, 2001). "Socialization is also subconscious, allowing people to incorporate the organization's culture and identify and bond with their environment or professional" (Weidman et al., 2001, p. 6). Interaction with colleagues provides new professionals with a sense of support and social acceptance and serves to mediate a sense of unmet expectations (Major, Kozlowski, Chao, & Gardner, 1995).

A positive outcome of professional socialization is the evolution of a professional identity (Hunter & Comey, 1991; Weidman et al., 2001), which can lead the employee to having greater commitment to the profession over time. It opens the door for supervisors to mentor these entry-level live-in professionals throughout their careers. This kind of interaction between live-in staff and more seasoned staff also creates an opportunity to expose the variety of employment options that housing and residence life has to offer and help identify where they might be most successful. When an employee begins thinking that they have a career, not just a job, there's more motivation and satisfaction. Retention is enhanced as a result (McCuskey, 2003).

Traditionally, residence life staffs train and orient new staffs, particularly entry-level live-in professionals, to the policies, procedures, and norms of the individual campus. However, because supervisors serve as the strongest source of support for new employees in a new environment (Weidman et al., 2001), to make socialization effective supervisors must go beyond traditional training efforts and bonding experiences typically associated with entry-level live-in professionals. This can be additionally challenging for supervisors on small campuses that hire perhaps only one or two new professionals each year, particularly if the campus is more rural (Pedigo, 2002).

Unionization

Collective bargaining has been a part of higher education for decades. More recently, however, unionization has expanded to a variety of workers in higher education settings (Barrett, Vander Putten, Peterson, & Cameron, 1995; Vander Putten, McLendon, & Peterson, 1997). Much of the literature on unionization in higher education pertains to faculty or graduate teaching assistants (Barba, 1994a; Barba, 1994b; Barrett et al., 1995; Cavell , 2000; Kavanagh, 2000; Lafer, 2003; Lee, etal., 2004; Vander Putten, et al., 1997; Vaughn, 1998), with little if any attention to noninstructional staff (i.e., entry-level professional live-in staff; Vander Putten et al., 1997).

The need for instructional staff to embrace collective bargaining emerged as a result of an economics driven administrative strategy to have graduate students teaching in place of some full-time tenure track faculty. Institutions began shifting the labor force while rationalizing it as an important part of graduate students' training. Institutions of higher education did not foresee that graduate students would turn to unionization to protect rights related to wages, benefits, workload, impartial grievance procedures, and working conditions (Cavell, 2000; Kavanagh, 2000; Lafer, 2003). As this movement for unionization among graduate teaching assistants has moved forward, Lafer warned that it "offers hope of spreading to more campuses and to other parts of the university ranks" (p. 39).

Researchers have noted that as the 1990s took hold, graduate student unions experienced success (Rhoades & Rhoads, 2003). In the 1990s and in the early stages of the 21st century, higher education has experienced a significant increase in unions responding to the corporatization of college and universities across the country (Lafer, 2003). Nonteaching graduate students also have joined the union movement (Lee et al., 2004). Not surprisingly, faculty and undergraduate students have been supportive of graduate students' desires to unionize (Lafer, 2003, p. 37).

Over the course of the last decade or so, collective bargaining and unionization has surfaced in residence life and housing operations on some campuses, from resident directors, area coordinators down to graduate assistants, RAs, and community managers. They have sought support and protection by forming, attempting to establish, or joining other employees' collective bargaining agreements. Although residence life and housing staffers are not specifically addressed in the literature, it is safe to assume that their motivations match others in higher education. Working conditions and workload may be primary concerns that drive efforts to unionize at this level.

Workload and specific work hours are not easily delineated for a live-in staff position. The difficulty with live-in staff is the perception (and sometimes reality) of total access by students and supervisory staff. The challenge is how to structure a work week comprising a specified (and sometimes limited) number of hours worked in an environment where predictability is less certain and fluctuation of hours from week to week may make good sense for the nature of the task. It is not an impossible task to set workload and hours, but it also not necessarily a natural fit to the nature of the job.

Future considerations

Predicting the future of entry-level human resources needed to meet the needs of students in a residential environment is dicey. How do changes in the future affect the type of students we attract to our programs? How do these issues impact who may be interested in working as a live-in professional? What are the nuances that the human element brings to these issues?

Senior housing officers can start by evaluating policies, procedures, and attitudes about the entry-level live-in position. They must set aside, to a certain extent, their experiences as live-in staff so as not to lose sight of how the jobs have evolved and who is or later will be drawn to them. Although it is human nature to do it the same way, success may mean breaking away from conventions in the profession from 10, 15, or 20 years ago.

For instance, with the deepening of the educational component of residence life, it makes less sense for professional, degreed staff members to spend time with facility functions (key lockouts, maintenance requests) that can be accomplished by others, such as support staff or student workers). These functions can cannibalize a considerable wedge of time (Belch, etal., 2005). Consider placing such staff in visible, key areas such as neighborhood and community centers where students can stop by to make requests. Discovering ways to reconfigure duties could provide many benefits, from economizing to optimizing student and staff satisfaction and educational outcomes.

Technology has changed how current graduate students and others identify potential job openings, and that will continue to evolve in the future. Among other things, it becomes more important for higher-level professionals to take a personal, active role in encouraging students to seek residence life careers. Fortunately, the options for those wanting to work in student affairs are greater than they have ever been in our history, and they will continue to expand in the future as new types of services evolve to serve an ever changing student population. Campuses have historically responded to the influx of new student groups (e.g., ethnic minority students, international students, students with disabilities) and to the changing needs of students and thus service providers by creating new programs and service areas. For example, in many areas of student affairs, as well as specifically in housing and residence life, the integration of technology has expanded the qualifications and background of the workforce to extend well beyond those with traditional experiences specific to a functional area. Continued attention on academically focused residential learning environments may necessitate having some staff members who specialize in curriculum development and pedagogy. Ultimately, too, the profession must identify new markets for recruitment while continuing to nurture more traditional avenues for entering the live-in professional staff pipeline. As one example, some hiring agents must be more willing to consider individuals who are skilled and genuinely interested in housing and residence life, regardless of whether or not they have RA experience.

Creating new benefit options, developing collaborations and pooling resources with nearby colleagues and institutions in advertising and recruitment efforts, and assessing the impact of the changes are all necessary components of maintaining a competitive place in the hiring marketplace. Smaller institutions or institutions in more challenging geographic markets may need to form consortium arrangements and adopt a collaborative recruiting philosophy. Formalizing your network of alumni who have worked as live-in professionals at your institution will serve to reconnect colleagues, offer additional mentoring opportunities to staff, and provide a positive network of recruiters for live-in positions.

Staff development has to have a forward-looking makeover. Training must be broad based across the institution instead of sequestered in student affairs or residence life. Supervisors will need to redesign training so it grabs the attention and enthusiasm of current and future professional staff that expect a different type of instructional format and content. Consider having each staff member, in consultation with a supervisor, draft a professional development plan that is linked to resources, personal and professional goals, and outcomes. This will send the message that professional development is a part of, not supplemental to, a person's job. It is important for staffers to understand what is available, how they can participate, and how professional development opportunities relate to their overall goals.

By all accounts, residential life as a program area and the professionals working within it will continue to expand partnerships with the academic community. Residence life staffers need to be well educated in learning theory and pedagogy (learning communities, supplemental instruction, collaborative and cooperative learning, peer education) and to know how to apply them (ACUHO-I Residential Task Force, 1997). Also, a demonstrated ability to work with faculty will be an essential skill for staff as academic partnerships expand and flourish.

Because parents are so involved in students' lives and show signs of remaining so in the future, residence life entry-level staff may need to borrow a model from the disability community and teach students how to advocate for themselves as well as help parents and guardians understand the motives for this educational process. It is incumbent upon staff to learn how to effectively manage the process of developing and working with students while tending to the needs of parents or guardians to be involved and connected.

Conclusion

There is little doubt of the important role RAs and entry-level live-in professional staff play on a residential campus. Both groups engage students in and contribute to the learning environment, provide students with opportunities for growth and development, offer an essential connection to the non-classroom experience, and serve as the foundation of support for residential students on college campuses.

The success and accomplishments of a residence life and housing operation are, in part, inextricably intertwined with the human resources working with students in residence halls. Beyond attending to the standard processes of selecting and training qualified staff, senior housing officers and others must be aware of the values of new generations of students and employees, the issues and concerns of both groups, and the subsequent impact on their interest in working in and entering into this career path. The present and the future necessitate an examination and assessment of traditional roles and responsibilities for these positions and the infusion of creativity, flexibility, and responsiveness in all aspects of human resource development.

References

ACUHO-I Residential College Task Force. (1997). *The residential nexus: A focus on student learning. Setting new directions for making new connections.* Columbus, OH: Association of College and University Housing Officers-International. (ERIC Document Reproduction Service No. ED437883)

Allen, N., & Meyer, J. (1990). Organizational socialization tactics: A longitudinal analysis of links to newcomers' commitment and role orientation. *Academy of Management Journal, 33,* 847-885.

Amey, M. J. (1998). Unwritten rules: Organizational and political realities of the job. In M. J. Amey & L. M. Reesor (Eds.), *Beginning your journey: A guide for new professionals in student affairs* (NASPA Monograph Series No. 21, pp. 5-20). Washington, DC: National Association of Student Personnel Administrators.

Amey, M. J., & Reesor, L. M. (1998). *Beginning your journey: A guide for new professionals in student affairs* (NASPA Monograph Series No. 21). Washington, DC: National Association of Student Personnel Administrators.

Ashforth, B. E., & Saks, A. M. (1996). Socialization tactics: Longitudinal effects on newcomer adjustment. *Academy of Management Journal, 39,* 149-178.

Bailyn, L. (1993). *Breaking the mold: Women, men and time in the new corporate world.* New York: Free Press.

Barba, W. C. (1994a). The graduate student employee union at SUNY. *Journal of Higher Education Management, 10*(1), 39-48.

Barba, W. C. (1994b). The unionization movement. *NACUBO Business Officer, 27*(5), 35-43.

Barr, M. J. (1990). Making the transition to a professional role. In D. Coleman & J. Johnson (Eds.), *The new professional: A resource guide for student affairs professionals and their supervisors* (NASPA Monograph Series, No. 10, pp. 17-29). Washington, DC: National Association of Student Personnel Administrators.

Barrett, M., Vander Putten, J., Peterson, M., & Camerson, K. (1995). *Perceptions of non-instructional staff at the University of Michigan: A content analysis.* (ERIC Document Reproduction Service No. ED387016)

Baum, K., & Klaus, P. (2005). *Violent victimization of college students, 1995-2002* (NCJ Publication No. 206836). Washington, DC: U.S. Department of Justice, Office of Justice Programs, Bureau of Justice Statistics.

Belch, H. A. (2005). *What constitutes "quality of life?": Perspectives from new and emerging professionals in student affairs.* Manuscript in preparation.

Belch, H. A., Dunkel, N., & Wilson, M. E. (2005). [Best practices in the recruitment and retention of entry-level live-in residence life professionals]. Unpublished raw data.

Belch, H. A., & Mueller, J. A. (2003). Candidate pools or puddles? Challenges and trends in hiring resident director candidates. *Journal of College Student Development, 44*(1), 29-46.

Blimling, G. S. (1993). New challenges and goals for residential life programs. In R. B. Winston, Jr., S. Anchors, & Associates (Eds.), *Student housing and residential life* (pp. 1-20). San Francisco: Jossey-Bass.

Blimling, G. S., & Miltenberger, L. (1981). *The resident assistant: Working with college students in residence halls.* Dubuque, IA: Kendall/Hunt Publishing.

Brubacher, J. S., & Rudy, W. (1968). *Higher education in transition: An American history: 1636-1956.* New York: Harper Collins.

Buck, J. M., & Watson, J. L. (2002). Retaining staff employees: The relationship between human resources management strategies and organizational commitment. *Innovative Higher Education, 26*(3), 175-193.

Burton, C. (2004). What does work-life balance mean anyway? *Journal of Quality & Participation, 27*(3), 12-13.

Cavell, L. J. (2000). *Graduate student unionization in higher education.* (ERIC Document Reproduction Service No. ED446647)

Chalofsky, N. (2003). Meaningful work. *Training and Development, 57*(12), 52-58.

Coleman, D. D., & Johnson, J. E. (Eds.). (1990). *The new professional: A resource guide for new student affairs professionals and their supervisors* (NASPA Monograph Series, No. 10). Washington, DC: National Association of Student Personnel Administrators.

Cooper, D., Saunders, S. A., Winston, R. B., Jr., Hirt, J. B., Creamer, D. G., & Janosik, S. M. (2002). *Learning through supervised practice in student affairs.* New York: Brunner-Routledge.

Creamer, D. G. (1997). Quality assurance in college student affairs. In R. B. Winston, Jr., & D. G. Creamer (Eds.), *Improving staffing practices in student affairs* (pp. 353-367). San Francisco: Jossey-Bass.

Dalton, J. C. (1996). Managing human resources. In S. R. Komives & D. B. Woodard, Jr. (Eds.), *Student services: A handbook for the profession* (3rd ed., pp. 494-511). San Francisco: Jossey-Bass.

Devine, J. L. (2001). A case study of the work patterns and job expectations of live-in hall directors as they attempt to accomplish the mission of the Department of Residence Life. *Dissertation Abstracts International, 62*(06), 2004. (UMI No. AAT 3016145)

Frederiksen, C. F. (1993). A brief history of collegiate housing. In R. B. Winston, Jr., S. Anchors, & Associates (Eds.), *Student housing and residential life* (pp. 167-183). San Francisco: Jossey-Bass.

Galinsky, E., Bond, J., & Swanberg, J. (1998). *The 1997 national study of the changing workforce.* New York: Families and Work Institute.

Gallagher, R. (2002). *National survey of counseling center directors.* Alexandria, VA: International Association of Counseling Services.

Gallagher, R., Gill, A., & Sysko, H. (2000). *National survey of counseling center directors.* Alexandria, VA: International Association of Counseling Services.

Gallagher, R., Sysko, H., & Zhang, B. (2001). *National survey of counseling center directors.* Alexandria, VA: International Association of Counseling Services.

Garrett, M. D., & Zabriskie, M. S. (2004). The influence of living-learning program participation on student-faculty interaction. *Journal of College and University Housing, 33*(1), 38-44.

Hamrick, F. A., & Hemphill, B. O. (1998). Pathways to success in student affairs. In M. J. Amey & L. M. Reesor (Eds.), *Beginning your journey: A guide for new professionals in student affairs* (NASPA Monograph Series No. 21, pp. 87-104). Washington, DC: National Association of Student Personnel Administrators.

Hartley, D. E. (2004). The intrinsic equation. *Training and Development, 58*(7), 26-28.

Helm, M. P. (2004). Professional identity, sense-making, and the market effect: Perspectives from new student affairs professionals, *Dissertation Abstracts International,* 65(04) 1274. (UMI No. AAT 3131603)

Holton, E. F., III, & Russell, C. J. (1999). Organizational entry and exit: An exploratory longitudinal examination of early careers. *Human Performance, 12*(3/4), 311-342.

Horowitz, R. (2005). *The 2005 live-in/on report.* Columbus, OH: Association of College and University Housing Officers-International.

Howe, N., & Strauss, W. (2000). *Millennials rising: The next great generation.* New York: Vintage Books.

Hunter, D. E., & Beeler, K. (1991). Peering through the looking glass at preparation needed for student affairs research. In K. Beeler & D. Hunter (Eds.), *Puzzles and pieces of wonderland: The promise and practice of student affairs research* (pp. 106-123). Washington, DC: National Association of Student Personnel Administrators. (ERIC Document Reproduction Service No. ED360598)

Hunter, D. E., & Comey, D. (1991). Common learning in student affairs. *NASPA Journal, 29*(1), 10-16.

Inkelas, K. K. (1999). *A tide on which all boats rise: The effects of living-learning program participation on undergraduate outcomes at the University of Michigan.* Ann Arbor, MI: University Housing, University of Michigan.

Jones, J. B. (2000). *A study of the effects of multiple living-learning programs on residence hall students.* Unpublished doctoral dissertation, Texas Tech University, Lubbock.

Kavanagh, P. (2000). A vision of democratic governance in higher education: The stakes of work in academia. *Social Policy, 30*(4), 24-29.

Kearney, P. A. (1993). Professional staffing. In R. B. Winston, Jr., S. Anchors, & Associates (Eds.), *Student housing and residential life* (pp. 269-291). San Francisco: Jossey-Bass.

Kimble, G., Timson, G., & Oltersdorf, D. (2004, February). *Washed up on the beach*. Paper presented at the annual meeting of the Southeastern Association of Housing Officers, Hilton Head, SC.

Kinser, K. (1993). *New professionals in student affairs: What they didn't teach you in graduate school*. Paper presented at the annual meeting of the National Association of Student Personnel Administrators, Boston, MA. (ERIC Document Reproduction Service No. ED378491)

Kitzrow, M. A. (2003). The mental health needs of today's college students: Challenges and recommendations. *NASPA Journal, 41*(1), 167-181.

Komives, S. (1993, July). *Explore new worlds*. Paper presented at the meeting of the Association of College and University Housing Officers-International, Columbus, OH.

Lafer, G. (2003). Graduate student unions: Organizing in a changed academic economy. *Labor Studies Journal, 28*(2), 25-43.

Lee, J. J., Oseguera, L., Kim, K. A., Fann, A., Davis, T. M., & Rhoads, R. A. (2004). Tangles in the tapestry: Cultural barriers to graduate student unionization. *The Journal of Higher Education, 75*(3), 340-361.

Levine, A., & Cureton, S. (1998). *When hope and fear collide: A portrait of today's college student*. San Francisco: Jossey Bass.

Littlefield, K. L. (2003). Quality of work-life issues: The needs of the dual-career couple. Examining the relationship of organizational commitment and employee perceptions of personnel practices: A study of the northern-lower Michigan dual-earner family. *Dissertation Abstracts International,* (64(09), 3370). (UMI No. AAT 3105576)

Major, D. A., Kozlowski, S. W. J., Chao, G. T., & Gardner, P. D. (1995). A longitudinal investigation of newcomer expectations, early socialization outcomes, and the moderating effects. *Journal of Applied Psychology, 80*, 418-431.

McCuskey, B. M. (2003). *The future of the university housing profession and implications for practitioners: A Delphi study* (Doctoral dissertation, West Virginia University, 2003). Available online at https://etd.wvu.edu/etd/etd-DocumentData.jsp?jsp_etdId=2885

Meyer, J. P., Pavnonem, S. V., Gellatly, I. R., Goffin, R. D., & Jackson, D. N. (1989). Organizational commitment and job performance: It's the nature of the commitment that counts. *Journal of Applied Psychology, 74*(1), 152-156.

Morrow, P. C., & McElroy, J. C. (1987). Work commitment and job satisfaction over three career stages. *Journal of Vocational Behavior, 30*, 330-346.

Mueller, J. A., & Pope, R. L. (2001). The relationship between multicultural competence and white racial consciousness among student affairs practitioners. *Journal of College Student Development, 42*, 133-144.

Nelson, D. L., & Quick, J. C. (1991). Social support and newcomer adjustment in organizations: Attachment theory at work? *Journal of Organizational Behavior, 12*, 543-554.

Padulo, M. K. B. (2001). The balancing act: Work environment issues for women with children in student affairs. *Dissertation Abstracts International, 62*(03), 938. (UMI No. AAT 3007296)

Pascarella, E. T. , & Terenzini, P. T. (2005). *How college affects students: A third decade of research* (Vol. 2). San Francisco: Jossey-Bass.

Pedigo, S. D. (2002). The socialization of new residence life professionals. *Dissertation Abstracts International, 63*(11), 3807. (UMI No. AAT 3071132)

Pledge, D., Lapan, R., Heppner, P., & Roehlke, H. (1998). Stability and severity of presenting problems at a university counseling center: A 6-year analysis. *Professional Psychology Research and Practice, 29*(4), 386-389.

Pope, R. L., Reynolds, A. L., & Mueller, J. A. (2004). *Multicultural competence in student affairs.* San Francisco: Jossey-Bass.

Raban, D. M. (1992). The state of unions in higher education: Is unionization compatible with professionalism? In R. H. Johnson (Ed.), *The impact of collective bargaining on higher education: A twenty year retrospective* (pp. 18-22). New York: The National Center for the Study of Collective Bargaining in Higher Education and the Professions, Baruch College, The City University of New York.

Raines, C. (2002). *Connecting generations: The sourcebook for a new workplace.* Menlo Park, CA: Crisp Publications.

Rhoades, G., & Rhoads, R. A. (2003). The public discourse of U.S. graduate student unions: Social movement identities, ideologies, and strategies. *Review of Higher Education, 26*(2), 163-186.

Rudolph, F. (1962). *The American college and university: A history.* New York: Knopf.

Saunders, S. A. (1993). Allied professional and support staffing. In R. B. Winston, Jr., S. Anchors, & Associates, *Student housing and residential life* (pp. 292-314). San Francisco: Jossey-Bass.

Sax, L. J., Lindholm, J. A., Astin, A. W., Korn, W. S., & Mahoney, K. M. (2001). *The American freshman: National norms for fall 2001.* Los Angeles: Higher Education Research Institute, UCLA Graduate School of Education and Information Studies.

Schroeder, C., & Mable, P. (1994). The role of residence halls in educating students. In C. Schroeder, P. Mable, & Associates (Eds.), *Realizing the educational potential of residence halls* (pp. 3-21). San Francisco: Jossey-Bass.

Sharpe, M. N., Bruininks, B. D., Blacklock, B. A., Benson, B., & Johnson, D. M. (2004). *The emergence of psychiatric disabilities in postsecondary education* (Issue Brief 3[1]). Minneapolis, MN: National Center on Secondary Education and Transition.

Smith, T. B. (1994). Integrating living and learning in residential colleges. In C.

Schroeder, P. Mable, & Associates (Eds.), *Realizing the educational potential of residence halls* (pp. 3-21). San Francisco: Jossey-Bass.

Spinks, N. (2004). Work-life balance: Achievable goal or pipe dream? *Journal for Quality and Participation, 27*(3), 4-11.

St. Onge, S., & Nestor, E. (2005). [An international survey of recruitment and retention of entry-level staff in housing and residence life]. Unpublished raw data.

Tederman, J. S. (1997). *Advice from the dean* (NASPA Monograph Series, No. 18, pp. 99-101). Washington, DC: National Association of Student Personnel Administrators.

Tennant, S., & Brungardt, D. (1998). Voices of experience. In M. J. Amey & L. M. Reesor (Eds.), *Beginning your journey: A guide for new professionals in student affairs* (NASPA Monograph Series No. 21, pp. 105-109). Washington, DC: National Association of Student Personnel Administrators.

Tinto, V. (1975). Dropout from higher education: A theoretical synthesis of recent research. *Review of Educational Research, 45*, 89-125.

Tinto, V. (1987). *Leaving college: Rethinking the causes and cures of student attrition*. Chicago: University of Chicago Press.

Tinto, V. (1993). *Leaving college: Rethinking the causes and cures of student attrition (2nd ed.)*. Chicago: University of Chicago Press.

Toma, J. D., Clark, C., & Jacobs, B. (1998). Reconciling the professional and the personal for the new student affairs professional. In M. J. Amey & L. M. Reesor (Eds.), *Beginning your journey: A guide for new professionals in student affairs* (NASPA Monograph Series No. 21, pp. 67-85). Washington, DC: National Association of Student Personnel Administrators.

Toma, J. D., & Grady, K. A. (2002). Reconciling life and work for the new student affairs professional. In M. J. Amey & L. M. Reesor (Eds.), *Beginning your journey: A guide for new professionals in student affairs* (revised edition, pp. 97-118). Washington, DC: National Association of Student Personnel Administrators.

Vander Putten, J., McLendon, M. K., & Peterson, M. W. (1997). Comparing union and nonunion staff perceptions of the higher education work environment. *Research in Higher Education, 38*(1), 131-149.

Vaughn, W. (1998). Apprentice or employee? *Academe, 84*(6), 43-49.

Weidman, J. C., Twale, D. J., & Stein, E. L. (2001). *Socialization of graduate and professional students in higher education: A perilous passage?* (ASHE-ERIC Higher Education Report Volume 28, No. 3). Washington, DC: George Washington University, Graduate School of Education and Human Development. (ERIC Document Reproduction Service No. ED457710)

Winston, R. B., Jr., & Anchors, S. (1993). *Student housing and residential life: A handbook for professionals committed to student development goals*. San Francisco: Jossey-Bass.

Winston, R. B., Jr., & Creamer, D. G. (1997). *Improving staffing practices in student affairs*. San Francisco: Jossey-Bass.

Winston, R. B., Jr., & Fitch, R. T. (1993). Paraprofessional staffing. In R. B. Winston, Jr., S. Anchors, & Associates (Eds.), *Student housing and residential life* (pp. 315-343). San Francisco: Jossey-Bass.

Young, D. P., & Gehring, D. (1977). *The college student and the courts* (rev. ed.). Asheville, NC: College Administration Publications. (ERIC Document Reproduction Service No. ED187224)

Zabel, R. H. (1988). *Emotional disturbances* (ERIC Digest #454). Reston, VA: ERIC Clearinghouse on Gifted and Handicapped Children. (ERIC Document Reproduction Service No. ED295398)

Technological Change and Residential Operations

Azfar Mian

W hen establishing an information technology system that meets the needs of a collegiate housing program, the challenges are many. Aside from the sheer technological requirements of maintaining a system that has, on some campuses, tens of thousands of end users, administrators must develop a system with pedagogical and recreational features appropriate for a rapidly changing student population. The systems must preserve the essential elements of higher education and the residence hall experience. Finally, this technology must also be able to adapt to changes brought about by residence life issues, facilities, and student activities.

It is even more challenging to predict how far technology will have progressed in the 2010s or especially the 2020s. It's safe to say that many of the devices and systems will be smaller, faster, more powerful, and less expensive. However, specific features and the means by which they will be utilized become a matter of imagination and speculation. What housing professionals can do today, however, is familiarize themselves with the areas in which technology can continue to be utilized to improve the delivery of services and information. They should build at least a basic understanding of the issues that information technology professionals face. While it may not be clear what the future holds, there is no question that technology will play a role in it.

Many colleges and universities, especially the larger, public-supported institutions, maintain an information technology department that serves only the housing department. For those housing operations that do not have a dedicated information technology staff, a worthwhile solution can be to form a strategic partnership with a private service provider or a particular campus information technology area. This allows the housing office to possess the resources necessary to respond to the specific needs of their consumers.

The importance of being able to provide such a service is even more pertinent when considering the students who will be enrolling in colleges throughout the first two decades of this century. Millennial students, as they are known, in many cases have been using computers since kindergarten. The prevalence of technology has made today's students increasingly comfortable at a computer keyboard and has changed the way they interact with each other and the world at large. Communicating via chat rooms, blogs, and e-mail is, in some cases, preferred over in-person interaction. They are more likely than their predecessors to utilize the Internet, rather than traditional libraries, for information and research. Registering for classes and performing other tasks online is preferred, as it offers immediate satisfaction. They expect their instructional materials, such as the class syllabus, to be available online. Information technology is an essential element of their lives.

All of this means that an increasing number of students are arriving on campus with one or more computers of their own. A story in *The Chronicle of Higher Education* (Managan, 2006) quoted a 2005 study by Student Monitor LLC that showed 80% of college students own a computer, and 27% of those surveyed own more than one. This is an increase compared to the 19% who, in 2000, said they owned more than one computer.

When students move into the residence halls with their computers (and perhaps even an Internet-ready gaming system), the question remains where they can plug them in. Students want to use all these items, yet most residence hall rooms offer only a single network port. This means housing operations will need to consider how many machines per port they will allow to be registered. Technologically speaking, it's not a difficult task, but it does require changes in procedural thinking.

In all aspects of their educational experiences these students will expect a higher degree of customer service. Strongly influenced by consumerism, they do not expect, for instance, to wait in lines when they could fill a form out electronically. In fact, students today don't even necessarily expect to come on campus for classes, group meetings, or to visit libraries. Institutions are now making efforts to expand services beyond the campus perimeter. This desire may also exist in the non-traditional, older college students who are returning to the college campus after a stint in the workforce. They may be returning to school for graduate programs, to update their skills, or acquire new talents. Regardless, these non-traditional students are looking for convenient services, easy access to information, and classes when and where they need them. Students, staff, and faculty need to be linked to the world beyond campus for research, teaching, learning, and service. All of these factors draw upon information technology.

The rate at which students are changing, however, pales in comparison with the rate at which the technology transforms. It can be difficult to ascertain what technology a housing operation needs, receive the funding, install the system, and assess its effectiveness before the next big leap occurs. Residence life and housing must strategize carefully when it comes to planning information technology for the next decade and beyond.

Pressing Issues

Considering the large scope of technology issues on a college campus, what concerns should receive the greatest amount of attention? Some answers to that can be found in a 2005 higher education technology study (Green, 2005b) that queried information technology executives and professionals (director level and above) from 501 campuses across the United States. Some of the most pressing issues, as determined by this group, are discussed below.

Network security

Colleges and universities have struggled to find the proper balance between network openness and network security. Universities have raised their minimum security standards and will need to make sure the data remains secure and only accessed by authorized individuals. This safeguard is critical because, as technology develops, so does the tendency for malware – shorthand for "malicious software," which can include viruses, worms, and other harmful programs—to interfere. In this survey, respondents revealed that 50.7% of their institutions experienced hacking or attacks on their campus network operations in the 2004-05 academic year. Also, 41.2% had critical spyware-related infestations, and approximately one-third experienced virus attacks.

Portal technologies

As colleges and universities rely more on online means to distribute information to their populations, the use of portal technologies will continue to grow. Most everyone today recognizes that a Web page or site on the Internet is a valuable means of disseminating information. However, these portal technologies take the static Web page to the next level, allowing the end users (or, to some extent, the portal creator) to customize the portal so that it delivers the specific information that is most useful to them.

These portals are becoming more common commercially in the form of Web sites such as the information site Yahoo.com or several news-oriented sites such as CNN.com or ESPN.com. On sites such as these, the users can purposefully alter the sites so that the information most valuable to them – either because of areas of interest, geography, or any other measure – is arranged to be delivered "up-front." Other sites, such as the online retailer Amazon.com, collect information on past purchases and behaviors and uses that information to push content that it believes will most benefit the uses.

The challenge for university housing operations is to create user-friendly portals to service their clientele in their day-to-day operations. Some of the information that may be of value to students would include bus schedules, parking maps, floor plans of different residence halls, a calendar of events, and a menu of available facilities and their locations. These portals can also accommodate means of communication such as message boards as well as collaborative collections of information such as wikis and blogs.

The basic concept of the wiki is Internet-based cooperation within a virtually endless audience, each member of which can contribute to a central body of knowledge. Meanwhile, a blog is a personal journal made available on a Web site, often being open to comment and contributions from its readers. These tools as part of a portal dedicated to an individual residence hall or a housing department as a whole have the potential to promote community building and knowledge sharing.

Still, the major advantages of portal technologies cannot be reaped until there is one central portal across campus. Through communication and a willingness to work with other departments, housing operations must explore ways to be part of the university's central portal instead of having a separate housing portal.

Wireless networks

Being hardwired into the campus network only from a hub in an office, lab, or residence hall does not fully satisfy students and, in fact, may make them feel restricted. They want technology that allows them access to anything and anyone from anywhere. This is evidenced by the growing prevalence of laptop computers and handheld electronic devices across campus and on the network. To that end, it will become only more important that a wireless network completely covers the college campus.

Fortunately, wireless infrastructure is becoming increasingly affordable. Looking at trends from the first years of the 21st century, access points cost only a few hundred dollars, no longer require expensive power connections, and they feed straight from the network equipment. Looking at pricing patterns, one could predict that, as soon as 2008, a college campus could install a broad-coverage wireless network for less than $500,000, with a three-year life-cycle replacement cost of $140,000 per year. With the continuing drop in hardware costs for wired networks, it is possible over time to absorb network expansion into existing budgets without having to seek new funding sources.

Despite the tremendous advancements, though, wireless serves only as an extension to an existing wired campus network and not as a replacement. Security of data while on the wireless network remains a primary concern of universities. As housing operations add wireless access throughout the residence halls, they will need to add the additional security and make sure their standards are in compliance with the standards of the campus' central information technology department. Also, it is a well recognized fact that a wired infrastructure provides much greater bandwidth than does a wireless infrastructure along with the additional security systems.

Budgeting and infrastructure

Along with finding ways to keep pace with changing information technology, campus housing departments are also working to discover ways to address the need for funding to support the developments. The installation of technology fees is a growing way for campuses to underwrite these costs. It is important to note that housing operations do not receive any of the campus technology fees. Housing operations will have to have their own three-year information technology plan that integrates with the central campus information technology plan.

Green (2005a) highlights that information technology officials, when preparing their budget plans, recognize the need for security and protection. However, the trends are not to be more proactive by integrating security efforts with infrastructure maintenance and enhancement efforts. This movement is also focusing on disaster recovery and emergency response planning, a trend that received increased attention after the terrorist attacks of September 11, 2001, and was revisited after the 2005 Gulf Coast hurricanes. Still, the report states that only approximately half of the surveyed institutions have an actual strategic plan (Green 2005a).

Enterprise resource planning software

Systems that promote enterprise resource planning are attractive for the ways in which they combine information from separate departments (such as human resources, student services, payroll, finance, and more) into one system that updates information in real time. Unfortunately, most of the enterprise resource planning systems that are commercially available do not currently include a housing module as a standard. Still, colleges and universities are purchasing independent housing modules and working to integrate them with the campus' enterprise resource planning software. This may not be a cost-effective solution for smaller housing programs. However, for those institutions that choose to utilize them, these systems can be valuable tools when it comes to processes such as billing for damages, making room assignments, and managing disciplinary records.

File sharing

Institutions of higher education are recognizing the need to support and respond to concerns raised by the music and entertainment industries concerning the unauthorized sharing of files and illegal downloading of songs, television programs, and even full length movies. Regardless of the ethical implications of this practice – which many institutions are addressing through the establishment of "appropriate use policies" and standards – there are also the technological concerns of exposing a campus network to viruses as well as taxing the systems' bandwidth capabilities.

Technology As A Tool

Much of today's technology contains a certain amount of "wow factor," and more than one tech-savvy project has been implemented "just because we can." However, in the business of collegiate housing – which, as an auxiliary department is not eligible for certain development grant dollars – the administrators and information technology managers must justify new projects by pointing to concrete benefits such as reducing expenses or increasing student satisfaction.

One of these areas can be in the recruitment and retention of students, a measuring stick that virtually all collegiate housing operations look to. Some information technology services that housing operations are using to differentiate themselves from private housing competition and to retain students in the residence halls are

- Convert key student services to Web-based systems. Example of these services include housing applications, housing contracts, the updating of preferences, matching roommates, and live chat capability with staff. This Web-enabled format provides students within the ability to conduct transactions at any time of their choosing.
- Connect the campus telephone system with the central data warehouse so that residents are able to retrieve information like room assignments and roommate information themselves via the phone.
- Encourage the use of electronic communication tools. Communities can be strengthened through means including e-mail, chat, digital downloads, and discussion-board capabilities.
- Provide materials online and on-demand. Institutions can quickly and easily share information such as marketing brochures, policies, rules, regulations, phone numbers, and project details through Web sites and other electronic sources. Using the Internet to transmit information reduces the amount spent on publishing hard copies of documents, while also making the information available to customers when they need it, no matter where they are.

Housing operations also utilize technology to reduce administrative costs within specific processes such as housing assignments, roommate matching, call centers, judicials, and live chat capabilities from the department's Web page. The key to increasing funding for other information technology initiatives is to integrate old and new applications in support of redesigned business processes rather than to create all new applications. By bridging the existing and new systems, information can flow across to the desktops of staff members and student residents. To achieve this, housing information technology staff members need to promote consistent user interfaces, define data consistently, and maintain a central data warehouse where all resident data is stored. This gives staff access to data from the central systems that they can blend with their own data to produce queries and reports.

Making Change Affordable

In order to upgrade to the latest technological options and offer the best-of-the-best across campus, work may be completed in phases. It is advisable to put the newest technology where it will do the most good, meaning upgrades can be done as needed and as funding permits.

Because of the differences in needs, information technology professionals should assess where maximum bandwidth is most necessary and focus technology investments in those areas. Does everyone at the university really need 1 Gbps (gigabit per second) of bandwidth today? Or 10 Gbps tomorrow? Or even 100 Gbps as soon as 2015? There may be some departments that do, but there will be plenty of others that do not. The housing professional and the information technology professional must be able to work together to identify the areas of highest priority, serve them as best as possible with the available resources, and establish a tiered approach for the other areas.

Additional technology that reduces bandwidth requirements is also available. For example, one might desire higher transmission speeds for popular desktop video conferencing devices. However, because many of these utilize compression technology, video can be delivered adequately without requiring full bandwidth. Most advanced users and devices can make use of existing bandwidth speeds.

Housing operations might consider freeing funds for new technology purchases and initiatives by first making a modest investment in information technology asset-management software that monitors hardware and software. These tools track purchase dates, what processor the machine uses, who installed what software on them, and how heavily they are being used. One way this saves institutions money is by helping monitor which software products are being used heavily and which aren't. It may be that certain software doesn't need to be renewed as often as it has been, or even at all. This process is still a new concept in higher education campuses and has the potential to grow substantially in the coming decade.

Information Technology Planning and Support

Housing operations must plan, set priorities, and budget for technology updates, enhanced information technology support, and staff training. They should move towards new concepts such as electronic commerce to accept forms and payments online, have a housing portal or have housing information via the campus portal, and facilitate instant messaging and chat among staff and students. The housing portal provides the avenue for staff and students to go to one location, sign on, and retrieve all the information that applies to them. It gives the ability to combine information from multiple systems into one place. As residence halls are renovated or built, technology planning should play a key role because installing the right infrastructure to support the needs of students in the next two decades is critical.

Other strategies for information technology planning and support include

- Evaluate emerging technologies on an ongoing basis and see how housing information technology staff can implement them.
- Implement a program that supports technology hardware being replaced at least every five years.
- Include adequate support costs in the budgets. Also explore the ability to provide support from a distance using remote desktop support software.
- Assess space on an annual basis with a focus on exploring ways to consolidate equipment and closets, if possible, which would potentially make space available for other purposes.
- Develop security standards for departmental systems and servers that mirror the standards for mainframe applications. Mainframe applications in general have traditionally had higher security standards. Making the security standards consistent for all housing systems, servers, and applications will secure all assets well.
- Create Web-based support services that provide information to residents and staff on hardware and software standards, wireless and wired connectivity, e-mail accounts, room assignments, roommates, move in, and campus life before their actual arrival on campus.
- Provide a professional but easy way for hall staff and student leaders to create and manage individual sections of the overall housing Web site.

Coordination With the Rest of Campus

In the interest of making campus information technology secure and efficient, managers are evaluating how to reorganize information technology departments. As systems, networks, and programs evolve, the primary campus information technology office must grow as well to maximize efficiency and minimize expenditure. These departments take their cues from the corporate sector to create consistent standards, equipment, policies, and procedures. Across different campuses the approaches are different, but the result is the same: reorganized information technology departments that are smaller and centralized.

This information technology centralization could become a challenge if services are not provided to a housing operation in a timely manner. On the other hand, information technology centralization on campuses could be an opportunity for housing operations that may not have internal resources to meet their technology needs. Some strategies to consider over the next two decades include

- Know what the latest technologies and trends are (for 2006 that could be blogs and The Facebook.com. Who knows what they could be in the future?) and how they can be applied to your housing operation. Having this knowledge would be beneficial as a housing staff member communicates with central information technology staff.

- Know the costs associated with implementing those technologies so that housing is not over charged.
- Housing information technology staff should study the campus information technology planning structure and participate on their committees. The next step would be to align housing needs with the vision of central IT. Let the campus information technology administrators know what housing needs to achieve over the next five years so housing's needs get incorporated into overall campus initiatives.

Toward new guidelines

As information increasingly is needed to support decision-making, technology professionals must integrate different systems to share data dynamically and make it part of workflow applications. The expectation is that all this information be available electronically through a Web-based portal to help streamline processes, meet student expectations, and hold steady or decrease departmental overhead. Forward-looking housing operations are aiming to perfect their critical business functions. In examining best practices, some guidelines emerge as they relate to technology and infrastructure.

- When considering a new housing management system, select a configurable system rather than a custom software application. Configurable applications require less custom programming integration and maintenance. If the housing department is willing and open to changing some of their existing processes, configurable systems are generally implemented more swiftly. Implementation becomes more complicated and expensive when custom changes need to be made. At that point it would be better for the housing department to have a custom housing management system developed.
- No matter if the housing operation decides to purchase a configurable housing management system or have a custom system developed, ensure that a contact and workflow engine is embedded in that system. The contact engine provides students the ability to receive automatic updates via e-mail and also check their status online as their specific process moves through the various steps involved. The workflow engine is beneficial especially when designated staff members are responsible for different steps in a process. An advantage of the workflow engine is that it keeps the process moving forward by alerting the appropriate staff that it is their turn to take the next step. Once their part of the process is complete, it alerts the next staff member.

- Prioritize the reports and the order of reports that are available for staff through the portal. Without this prioritization, the entire portal project can become overwhelming.
- When developing or buying a system, stress that all data is secure at all times and that it has the flexibility to be updated if some processes require modifications in the future.

Conclusion

There are numerous challenges, strategies, and guidelines that should be part of a college housing department's technology plan. As students demand campus technology and information delivery systems that match their mobile lifestyle, campuses must meet this need or else risk declining student satisfaction or even declining occupancy rates. A successful implementation of these technologies can help better manage administrative costs.

The successful and progressive approach is to embrace technology in order to effectively communicate with all stakeholders and respond to competitive challenges. The application of technology can help a housing department attract and retain residents, provide the delivery mechanism to streamline administrative processes, and help reduce costs. Existing campuses are renovating buildings in an effort to improve connectivity and create access alternatives such as wireless communications or converged systems that support voice, data, and video. Concerns for campus computing security are requiring leading institutions to adopt the same security policies for their servers and end users as those that have been in place for large mainframe systems.

Housing operations are moving towards establishing and hosting complex Web sites that support Web-enabled student services, streaming video, e-commerce, and new protocols that support peer-to-peer messaging and chat features. Institutions that demonstrate such commitment have a need for an information technology staff that brings with it experience, accomplishment, training, and creativity. These staff members must also have the potential to assume a leadership role in exemplifying how technology can support a particular department's vision and mission.

References

Amey, M., & Van Der Linden, K. (2003). The use of technology: Institutional issues. In *The NEA 2003 Almanac of Higher Education (pp. 85-95)*. Washington, DC: National Education Association.

Bamberger, R. H. (2004, April). Learning in a connected world: *Leveraging technology in higher education institutions.* Retrieved September 10, 2005, from *http://whitepapers.zdnet.com/abstract.aspx?promo=50002&docid=92333*

Bradet, K. (2004). *Cornell University unplugged.* Retrieved September 10, 2005, from http://www.campus-technology.com/article.asp?id=9945

Briggs, L. L. (2005). *IT asset management: Watch your assets.* Retrieved July 22, 2005, from http://www.campus-technology.com/print.asp?ID=11043

Bromley, H. (2005). How to tell if you really need the latest technology. *The NEA Higher Education Journal.* 21-27. Retrieved September 10, 2005, from http://www2.nea.org/he/heta98/s98pg21.pdf

Bowers. C. A. (1998, Spring). The paradox of technology: What's gained and lost? *The NEA Higher Education Journal, 49-57.*

Buckalew, L. G. (2005). *Trends in higher education.* Retrieved July 1, 2005, from http://enterprise.usa.siemens.com/company/white/industry/mainColumnParagraphs/0/document/TrendsinHigherEd.pdf

Campus Management Corporation. (2004). *Mapping information technology strategies to answer today's agenda.* Retrieved May 18, 2005, from http://www.campus-technology.com/article.asp?id=10308

Dragoon, A. (2005). *Six simple rules for successful self service.* Retrieved October 17, 2005, from http://www.cio.com/archive/101505/self_serve.html?action=print

Foster, A. L. (2005). Mark essays electronically: A professor uses tablet PC's in a composition course. *The Chronicle of Higher Education, 51*(42), B18.

Freedman, D. H. (2005). *What's next: Service with a smile. Really.* Retrieved October 18, 2005, from http://pf.inc.com/magazine/20051001/columns-dfreedman.html

Gilbert, W. S., & Green, K. C. (2004). *Information technology: A road to the future? To promote academic justice and excellence.* Washington, DC: Office of Higher Education, National Education Association.

Green, K. C. (2002). *Campus computing looks ahead: Tracking the digital puck.* Retrieved May 1, 2005, from http://www.campus-technology.com/article.asp?id-6986

Green, K. C. (2003). *Tracking the digital puck into 2004.* Retrieved May 1, 2005, from http://www.campus-technology.com/article.asp?id=8574

Green, K. C. (2004a). *Tech budgets get some relief: Cautious support for open source applications.* Retrieved October 4, 2005, from http://www.campus-computing.net/Summaries/2004/index.html

Green, K. C. (2004b). *Trust, but verify.* Retrieved October 9, 2005, from http://www.campus-technology.com/article.asp?id=10072

Green, K. C. (2005a). *Growing campus concern about IT security: Slow progress on IT disaster planning. The 2005 national survey on information technology in U.S. higher education.* Retrieved May 1, 2006, from http://www.campuscomputing.net/summaries/2005/index.html

Green, K. C. (2005b). *Planning priorities.* Retrieved October 2, 2005, from http://www.campus-technology.com/article.asp?id=10418

Gritt, P. (2005). *Optimizing agents in an e-service environment.* Retrieved October 15, 2005, from http://www.cio-today.com/news/Optimizing-Agents-and-E-Service/story.xhtml?story_id=101705

Grush, M. (2004a). *A new realm of IT planning.* Retrieved May 18, 2005, from http://www.Campus-Technology.com/print.asp?ID10211

Grush, M. (2004b). *Top 10 countdown.* Retrieved September 18, 2005, from http://www.Campus Technology.com/print.asp?ID11722

Junnarkar, S. (2005). *Digital cameras, in school and on call.* Retrieved August 5, 2005 from *clnet.com* at http://news.com.com.2102-1041_3-5737820.html?tag=stu.utl.print

Managan, K. S. (2005). Make videos: An educational course puts students in director's chairs. *The Chronicle of Higher Education, 51*(42), B6.

Managan, K.S. (2006). For many students, one computer is not enough. *The Chronicle of Higher Education, 52*(26), A31.

McCullagh, D. (2005). *Wiretap rules for VoIP, broadband coming in 2007.* Retrieved September 30, 2005, from *clnet News.com* at http://news.com.com/wiretap+rules+for+VoIP%2C+Broadband+coming+in+2007/2100-7352_3-5883032.html

The Meta Group. (2005). *First steps toward the data center of the future.* Retrieved July 1, 2005, from http://www.dell.com/downloads/global/corporate/iar/20041101_meta.pdf#search='meta20group%20white%20paper%2C%20first%20steps

Mickool, R. (2005). *The challenge of single sign-on.* Retrieved July 22, 2005, from http://www.campus-technology.com/print.asp?ID=9194

Reuter News Agency. (2005). *'Evil twin' fear for wireless net.* Retrieved September 10, 2005, from http://news.bbc.co.uk/2/hi/technology/4190607.stm

Rezmierski, V. E., Rothschild, D. M., Kazanis, A. S., & Rivas, D. R. (2002). Final report of the Computer Incident Factor Analysis and Categorization (CIFAC). *EDUCAUSE, 1,* 1-89.

Rhoades, G. (2005). Technology and the changing campus workforce. *The NEA Higher Education Journal,* 127-137. Retrieved September 10, 2005, from http://www2.nea.org/he/heta99/s99p127.pdf

Seeley, R. (2005). *Campuses make way for worldwide wiki.* Retrieved October 2, 2005, from http://www.campus-technology.com/print.asp?ID=11902

Sprague, G. (2005, April). *Regaining user trust in cyberspace – Is it already too late?* Presented at Security Professionals Conference, Washington, DC.

U.S. Department of Education. (2004). *Weaving a secure web around education: A guide to technology standards and security* (NCES 2003-381). Washington, DC: National Center for Education Statistics, National Forum on Educational Statistics.

Van Dusen, G. C. (1998, Spring). Technology: Higher education's magic bullet. *The NEA Higher Education Journal.* 59-67.

Villano, M. (2005a). *Organizational change: Model citizens* (from 12/12/2004 issue of *Syllabus)*. Retrieved August 21, 2005, from http://www.syllabus.com/article.asp?id=11881)

Villano, M. (2005b). *Organizational change: Model citizens* (from 10/1/2005 issue of *Syllabus*). Retrieved October 2, 2005, from http://www.syllabus.com/print.asp?ID-11881

Villano, M. (2005c). *Rich media: Get rich quick.* Retrieved August 10, 2005, from http://www.campus-technology.com/article.asp?id=11519

Villano, M. (2005d). *Rich media: Get rich quick continued.* Retrieved September 10, 2005, from http://www.campus-technology.com/article.asp?id=11632

Voss, B. D. (2004). *Evolving strategies for campus network infrastructure.* Retrieved September 10, 2005, from http://www.campus-technology.com/article.asp?id=9939

Voss, B. D. (2005). *Evolving strategies for campus network infrastructure.* Retrieved October 18, 2005, from http://www.campus-technology.com/print.asp?ID=9939

Voyles, B. (2004). *IT spending: Where's the value?* Retrieved October 18, 2005, from http://www.campus-technology.com/article.asp?id=10063

Wada, K. (2004). *Privacy and compliance: Better safe than sorry.* Retrieved June 17, 2005, from http://www.campus-technology.com/article.asp?id=10509

Managing Construction and Renovation in Residential Facilities

Mark D. Hill and Fred Fotis

People, programs, and property are the three components of college and university housing operations. The people component includes students and staff. The program component includes the student development, administrative, and customer service programs. And the property component takes in all housing and facilities operations. This may be the most obvious aspect of campus housing but not the simplest. Planning and executing new construction or renovation involves a complex cascade of events requiring rapidly changing knowledge.

History and Changes

The bulk of university housing constructed prior to 1970 fell into two categories: traditional residences of double and single rooms with shared bathroom and lounge facilities; or apartment-style housing which was reserved exclusively for families. University housing, built to last, meant 100-year concrete and masonry buildings with a typical 30-year debt service. Institutions didn't foresee two things, however: a profound shift in student expectations and ongoing maintenance, which reached a critical point during the financially trying 1980s and early 1990s.

Students began arriving on campuses with more than clothes, an electric typewriter, and a radio. They had music systems, personal computers, televisions, cell phones, and battery chargers. Suddenly, it was not only inadequate but it was unsafe for double-rooms to have two electrical outlets per wall. When they were originally built, most buildings did not include fire sprinkler systems.

The facilities didn't accommodate students with disabilities. And there was little thought that someday these buildings could house more than one gender.

Over the years students changed, expectations changed, technology of all kinds changed, accountability for institutions changed, but buildings and budget issues have not. Institutions with 50- to 100-year-old residential buildings, designed for students of generations past, are facing full-scale replacement of plumbing, electrical systems, mechanical systems, windows, doors, furniture, and elevators, along with the addition of new and ever changing life-safety systems. Most times, the renovations required were so extensive and costly that compliance with the new codes almost always required rebuilding rather than renovation.

Changing expectations were particularly unexpected. Students today will rarely "live with something." If the room is too hot, the window does not fully open or close, or a drawer sticks, students expect the problem to get fixed immediately. They also can struggle with the issues of shared space. Many of the students have never shared a bedroom with a sibling, let alone a stranger, and many arrive on campus having never had to share a bathroom.

Parents have equal if not greater expectations and are more involved in their students' college lives. This involvement extends to their expectations about the speed with which repairs are completed, the style of accommodation they believe is best suited for their student, and their desire to be the final arbiter on decisions that impact their children. If there is an item or service not provided, they may expect policy and practice to be altered to provide it or may themselves attempt to have the item or service provided. Some parents have actually been known to rent an apartment in town for several months at the beginning of their student's college career in order to make certain their (the parent's) wishes are met. In some cases, parents have actually brought in interior designers to assist in decorating a residence hall room, have brought in workers to install wood or ceramic tile floors in the room, and have had wallpaper installed (N. Dunkel, March 6, 2006). They remain undeterred by having to remove any added features and return the space to original condition. Times have certainly changed.

Building technology also changed over the years, as safety, codes, communication, and energy efficiency became more important and prominent. This was amplified by the desire of many institutions and colleges to be in the forefront of energy conservation and safety technology, especially as institutions became more accountable through state and federal legislation. The Americans with Disabilities Act, fire sprinkler installation, lead paint concerns, and asbestos issues, to name a few, may have been accelerated due to attention in the media. Priorities are a shifting landscape, often driven by internal or external pressures as opposed to real need. This presents a specific challenge to be knowledgeable and deliberate in all aspects of planning and budgeting for facilities management.

The challenge of overcoming deferred maintenance issues—necessary maintenance on a facility that can't be completed because of budget constraints or physical limitations—will require each housing operation to conduct a composite facility assessment in order to determine the prioritization of the needed repairs. According to the Association of Higher Education Facilities Officers (APPA) Facilities Cost Index (FCI is the ratio of a building's current Deferred Maintenance needs divided by the building's total Current Value: FCI=DM/CV), if deferred maintenance ratios cannot be worked down to less than 5% of the current value of housing properties, the ability to overcome the lack of funding decreases, and the properties will deteriorate to the point of needing demolition or major reconstruction.

Housing professionals must fully understand their facility maintenance needs. A professional audit of buildings is where many institutions start, but know that they require investments of time and money. Housing professionals are directly involved in setting the task and scope with the vendor, who may work from a template of general issues that will need adapting for your institution. That customization will be vital for making informed decisions. The audit must include electrical, plumbing, heating, ventilation, air conditioning, controls, finishes, windows, elevators, doors, floors, ceilings, roofs, and other building envelope components, to name the main ones.

Some institutions may choose to conduct an internal facility audit, a composite assessment of the condition of a building and all components. Again, the greatest challenge is to be careful and deliberate in determining the scope of the audit. The goal is an honest and careful self-appraisal that isn't swayed by any institutional preconceived notions.

Whichever route an institution takes, everyone must understand that for facilities with a history of deferring maintenance, audits may provoke discomfort among campus officials or others not prepared for sticker shock or bad news. If an institution undertakes an audit, therefore, all affected parties must also be braced for living with the results.

The assigned individual or assessment team will spend a lot of time walking and talking with the maintenance and facilities staffers who know the condition and history of the facilities. It is important that anyone who will be involved in the daily activities of maintaining the facility are involved in the design process—for obvious reason and also to ensure that future employee productivity, access, and ease of maintenance is taken into consideration, thereby saving operational costs.

To organize, prioritize, compile, and analyze the assessment information, they will select one of several proven assessment frameworks.

One framework is the Construction Standards Index (CSI: an industry standard reflecting a numerical list of all construction processes and materials), which the team will adapt to the particular facilities under scrutiny (Ramsey, Sleeper, & Hoke, 2000). Once the developed format matches the need of the facility, the assessment process becomes a matter of consistent evaluation and documentation. At first glance this process may appear less restrictive, but both require staff with technical knowledge of buildings, the systems contained within them, and their inter-working relationships.

The Association of Higher Education Facilities Officers (APPA) has developed an assessment and evaluation method called the Strategic Assessment Model (SAM). Many articles and publications are available as references from its Web site. SAM is an organizational excellence- and continuous-improvement model. In its third and newest revision, SAM combines features of two performance models: the Baldrige National Quality Program and the Balanced Scorecard concept, which Robert Kaplan of Harvard's Business School and David Norton of Renaissance Solutions developed.

SAM combines the features of the two models into three components: the Balanced Scorecard domains (financial, internal processes, learning/growth, and customer service), quantitative performance indicators, and qualitative criteria for determining levels of performance. The FCI is part of the financial section of SAM. When a facility manager considers the Capital Renewal and Deferred Maintenance (CRDM) model developed in managing the facilities portfolio, it becomes evident that inclusion of the FCI within SAM is a logical step. The book *A Foundation to Uphold* (Kaiser & Davis, 1996) is an excellent reference for application of the FCI.

Whether they operate as an auxiliary or receive funds as an institutional department, housing operations are sensitive to the impact of rent on the total cost of higher education. This stewardship drives housing operations to be increasingly frugal when developing budgets to cover annual operating costs and debt, with perhaps some money remaining for renovation projects and new program initiatives. To keep occupancy high, even with parietal rules, institutional housing departments often must market to students. They might emphasize tradition, lack of housing in the immediate vicinity, exceptional programs, value, and safety and comfort.

Alternative Approaches

Two approaches have emerged from these challenges to address present and future needs: Start over or invest in current housing stock.

In the first approach, existing buildings are demolished or repurposed. New, smaller buildings often go up using new building technologies, non-masonry construction with life cycles of 40-50 years or less. These buildings can be designed with the newest technology and often focus more on privacy and independence for the student. They typically are not double-loaded corridor style, instead emphasizing amenities that students may be finding in off-campus housing. These buildings may be done in partnership with a private developer and, depending upon institutional capabilities and lease agreements, may not require future debt.

LEED Certification

Leadership in Energy and Environmental Design is a certification that is given by the United States Green Building Council. The LEED program provides a complete framework for assessing building performance and meeting sustainability goals. Based on well founded scientific standards, LEED emphasizes state-of-the-art strategies for sustainable site development, water savings, energy efficiency, material selections, and indoor environmental quality. LEED criteria provide environmental benefits; reduce the impact on natural resources consumption; provide economic, community, health, and safety benefits; enhance occupant comfort and health; and minimize strain on local infrastructure.

Many campuses are including issues of Leadership in Energy and Environmental Design (LEED) certification into their new construction and renovation projects, for the savings and reduced environmental impact they offer. In addition, changes in the American Society of Heating, Refrigeration and Air Conditioning Engineers (ASHRAE) standards, Sheet Metal Manufacturers' and Air Conditioning Contractors' National Association (SMACNA) standards, and government mandates reduce air infiltration into building envelopes. This may require a mechanical means for increasing fresh air exchange. In order to have these competing systems function in concert with each other, installers are required to conduct physical inspections of each piece of equipment in order to verify proper function, certify that installation meets specifications and design intent, and establish a baseline documentation for future reference.

In the future, campuses with land limitations may choose or even be restricted from growing horizontally so high-rise construction may begin to proliferate. This choice brings a unique set of operational and physical issues.

The second alternative is for institutions to invest in their existing properties. This is particularly prevalent on campuses with heritage or historical residential buildings that simply should not be replaced. Many times the historical value may help garner interest in renovation.

If a building is classified as historic, which buildings on campuses that are primarily 50-plus years old tend to be, it is grandfathered into *historic* classification and subsequently is subject to review and approval by historic preservation entities. These will generally require buildings to maintain the features that define its historical era, a very subjective notion. The United States Department of the Interior has established a reference of minimum standards for the preservation of historic buildings. Added to those are specific geographical region minimum standards. What may work in Phoenix will not necessarily work in New York City.

Historic renovation is tricky in other ways. Without question, renovators will encounter asbestos and lead paint remediation. Changing footprints or meeting new codes are tougher in a building with a rock-solid structure. These facilities quite likely were not designed or constructed to handle increased interior building air pressures of modern mechanical systems. When the envelope is upgraded with new windows and doors, the potential exists foor poor indoor air quality to rear its head, and this must be addressed.

Costs and logistics begin to multiply exponentially when a housing operation decides to or must upgrade all building systems. There are physical issues such as fire proofing, shaft wall construction required for fire rating, vertical pipe and duct chases, and shaft effect-driven air flows. These renovations often go hand in hand with major renovations of food service facilities within residential buildings. It's easy to see why new construction is more cost effective. There is a fine line that campus housing operations must walk regarding how high housing fees can go before students opt to live off campus or decide on other campuses altogether.

The following is a series of questions that may help provide focus on which approach to utilize:

- Is there institutional will for new construction or renovation? Is there a preference?
- What are enrollment and occupancy projections?
- What must be done to effectively renew the residential campus? Is a particular type of housing needed?
- Does the building location affect the design due to the surrounding historic buildings, and will it affect the character of the campus?
- What are the impacts of the renovation or new construction on the existing occupancy?
- What is the estimated cost of the new construction versus renovation?
- What new codes will come into play?
- What is the capacity for debt? If there is little capacity, must private partners enter the picture?
- What changes in student needs must design accommodate?
- What changes in institutional needs must design accommodate?
- What cost saving, efficiency, or *green building* options are available?
- How does the plan for construction or renovation impact the academic calendar?
- What is the best way to consult different constituencies in the design process?
- Should the new or newly renovated structures strive for 20-year or 50-year viability?
- Will there be any impact on town-gown relationships?

This latter consideration is one that can not be overlooked. Campus growth and renewal has an impact on the surrounding community, and housing must be cognizant of how widespread the consequences of its decision can be. The economic impact of campus renewal is better recognized and valued if housing adopts a good-neighbor policy that adds value (i.e., in services, advice, events, etc.) back to the community. Sometimes the interplay between campus and town is purely logistic. Do any local zoning laws impact campus growth? Or is a high-rise building untenable because the local fire department doesn't have appropriate fire vehicles? Will a campus building too close to adjacent homes result in conflicts down the line?

Campus Involvement

One of the biggest challenges for the housing professional is even to be included in the broad campus-wide master planning discussions about new residential facilities that will allow input and involvement in the design, development, and construction of those same facilities. As many housing operations show, inclusion in future housing decisions is not always automatic. This can be problematic for any number of obvious reasons, not the least of which is having certain standards imposed on campus housing. Many times these standards are excessive for the residential construction needs for housing entities, which end up with increased project costs and or decreased scope to cover the cost of standards within an established budget. These increased costs may cause the floor space and the needed amenities to be reduced or possibly sacrificed completely. Campus housing facilities managers must be prepared to offer alternatives that are less expensive and equally as functional. It may take several years of discussions and work before the campus or local municipality accepts a housing standard, but the end result is a tremendous budget savings. The following is a list of potential housing standards versus possible campus standards:

- Specification grade outlets and switches versus hospital grade
- Nylon outlet and switch covers versus stainless steel
- Domestic and heating hot water lines insulated with fiberglass versus foam glass
- Using one Category 5e for data outlets versus requiring three or four per outlet
- Standard lay-in troffer fixtures versus fixtures with damage-resistant lenses
- Plug-in breakers versus bolt-in breakers
- Wainscot tile or ceramic cove base with epoxy paint versus full height ceramic tile
- Stick-built versus concrete and masonry
- No central air conditioning versus central air
- Space dedicated to study rooms and lounges versus all the space dedicated to student rooms

- Group plumbing shut-off valves versus shut-off valves on every fixture
- Plumbing clean-outs in each plumbing "stack" versus clean-outs placed on every floor
- Above-ground utilities versus underground utilities
- Utility lines placed in trenches or pipes versus utilities in an underground vault
- Garden-style ground-oriented facilities versus high-rise housing units
- Not meeting LEED standards versus imposed LEED standards

Knowledge of Code and Construction Changes

The previous list of possible variations in standards points to an important component of building and renovation: knowledge. The foremost task of housing and residence life staff embarking on construction projects is becoming and staying informed.

Housing and residence life professionals must start by knowing the goals of the institution, the needs of their residents, and the issues that operation and maintenance will encounter. From there, they must tackle the issues of building and renovation, which change rapidly. Staffers also must be prepared to sell new ideas to a campus community steeped in a "this is the way we have always done it" attitude.

Code changes are one of the most challenging areas. Being universally code literate is not an easy matter. The national codes are revised every three years, and if they are not in a revision year, they are being reviewed, adjusted, or in the process of formal adoption or codification. Unfortunately, not all codes are revised in concert with each other, and therefore it is quite a challenge for designers and construction managers to keep up to date. Often by the time the project begins, it is being permitted under a new and more stringent code. This can potentially lead to change orders that reduce quality, quantity, and value and add time to the construction schedule.

The authors have often found the variety of responses interesting when asking the question, "What codes do we currently design under?" There may be as many as three different answers from three seemingly qualified sources. The architect might identify some but not all that they are using. The engineer might be specific about only the codes in the engineering realm, and the project manager might cite some of both and the institution's standards. All are marginally correct. It is important to involve a code enforcement authority to keep the design team informed about the current codes and any potential code changes that might come about prior to the bidding and contract award process. If an institution is using a construction manager (an entity that provides administrative oversight for the construction of a facility) and negotiating a guaranteed maximum price (a price that is provided by the construction management entity as a "not to exceed" price to construct the building), the person in charge should make certain that the code compliance issues are addressed with every GMP draft submittal.

Work with the local code enforcement group on campus, even if it is just a meeting to be updated on what code changes are in the works and how they may affect buildings. This will help to budget accurately for the upcoming years. Have someone who is charged with keeping code current, and charge him or her with briefing others. Have that person attend code review classes offered in your area, and keep staff members on the leading edge of technology so they are more efficient.

Staff members must also diligently keep up with technology advances. Sometimes this simply means knowing which questions to ask of which design professional. When one considers that someone, somewhere has probably already built or used every available construction system, it seems prudent to ask questions of others in the profession and be willing to share experiences. It will be imperative that campus housing facilities managers bring to the table well studied cost benefits for various options that will come up. There are always new products and procedures being developed, and not all are applicable to every situation, so it is important to encourage technology compatibility as well as standardization.

A good example is variable frequency refrigerant compressors. Although this technology is new to the United States, it has been tested, proven, and used successfully in Japan and South America for years. This technology could replace the use of chilled water for air conditioning and will additionally reduce various issues of indoor air quality and maintenance connected with chilled water-heating-hot water-air distribution systems. Direct digital controls connected to and managing this system will enhance energy conservation. This system, coordinated and combined with digitized monitoring of electrical distribution systems, will enable building managers to allocate energy usage to the individual room level if desired. It will be important, however, that the design team is required to provide documentation about compatibility with existing technologies, true energy savings, personnel capable of operating and maintaining new types of systems, and whether such an innovation might pay for itself in part by the marketing value it brings.

Professional Development

A housing and residence life budget that includes funds for staff members to attend Association of College and University Housing Officers-International (ACUHO-I)/APPA facilities workshop will pay itself back in the smart, cost-effective decisions these staff members will be prepared to make. They'll gain knowledge from the course content as well as networking with those who have already been through the various processes.

Some institutions conduct informal "Lunch and Learn" information sessions on facility-related issues that could provide invaluable insight. These sessions are somewhat common among physical facilities groups where vendors provide lunch for a group of staff that attend a session presented by the vendor in order to inform the campus staff what products they have available. Hundreds of new products are discussed and displayed, and, even more important, you will meet contacts for future references and inquiries.

Those who possess more than a basic knowledge of facility standards should consider initiating a standards review process of housing facilities. Even if a campus cannot undertake such a process, learning the details of what are involved in the process and what types of changes have resulted from other campuses undergoing standards review will provide valuable insights.

Housing professionals should also get involved with the utility infrastructure maintenance and improvement processes on campus. This process is usually managed by the physical plant departments and involves the scheduled upgrading of utilities. This will allow you to know when and if the utilities that serve your facilities will be upgraded. Knowing this will give you more information about the potential timing of your renovations and/or new construction. Most campus facilities groups have up-to-date Web pages with project listings and their proposed time frames and impacts. There may be a cost savings in joining with other campus projects.

The Future

Can we adequately plan for the future? The discussions are happening within ACUHO-I as evidenced by the ACUHO-I 21st Century Project, an ongoing program that has brought a variety of housing professionals together to discuss what form the college residence hall of the future might take.

> It is very difficult for housing professionals to visualize what type of facility and associated amenities will be needed in future residence halls. Several ACUHO-I members developed the idea of bringing together individuals from many aspects of college and university life to design the prototype residence hall of the future. During the spring of 2006, ACUHO-I held the 21st Century Project in Chicago, Illinois. This was a multi-phase initiative which will lead to the construction of a new state of the art residential facility for colleges and universities. In addition to creating one or more prototype residential facilities on a few campuses, the project assists colleges and universities more broadly in designing new residential facilities that better accommodate the ever-changing roles that residence halls play in the collegiate experience and in institutions of higher education. (ACUHO-I, 2006, p. 1).

When you think about how far society has progressed technologically over the past 100 years and the incredible speed at which it has progressed in recent decades, it is inconceivable to predict the future. We now see the earth's limits more clearly every day and understand that the rules established at the beginning of the 20th century will be useless to sustain us into the 22nd. We need to make the bold move beyond our attempts to simply institute new ideas and instead concentrate on theoretical and technological ideas that will challenge the students today to be the leaders and innovators of tomorrow (Lewis, 2005).

It is time for campuses and housing professionals to take a more serious role in preserving and saving our environment. An example of a facility in another country that establishes a high sustainability standard is the Next 21 project. In 1993 the Osaka Gas Company, in cooperation with several other Japanese entities, developed the project called Next 21. It placed a six-story, 18-unit apartment building in the middle of downtown Osaka that contained underground parking; gas-fired boilers that create steam to drive electrical generation and chilled-water equipment; self-contained refuse disposal and sewage treatment; a reuse water/gray water/rainwater collection system; solar heat and electrical generation systems; and a contemporary design. The facility was constructed as an experiment to consider a new relationship that mankind could have with the environment and to define what complications it would present (Osaka Gas Company, 2002). The extent of this project is probably far greater than colleges and universities are currently prepared to achieve; it is an example of what can be done to save the environment.

The housing professional must keep in mind cradle-to-cradle sustainability costs when designing facilities that will last into the next decades and beyond. Technologies exist that might be expensive to implement but provide significant cost savings in operations from year to year. Certain innovations don't yield immediate results but still are warranted for the future savings they'll engender. We need to make sure the design team provides the information to the owner that takes into full account the life-cycle costs of the proposed systems and encourages the long-term planning strategies. It will be important to set realistic expectations, of course. This aspect may also require the design team to provide a certain amount of education to the owner.

It's been said that people react to their environment based on the way they perceive it. It is incumbent on any staff in the area of housing facilities management to increase their knowledge, follow the codes and their changes, and continue active research for new products. By fulfilling these approaches, the facilities manager will be in a much better position to make accurate knowledge-based decisions. With initiatives like the ACHUO-I 21st Century Project and the Osaka Gas Next 21 project, we can see that our level of knowledge and skill must go well beyond the basic concepts of concrete, steel, and pipe.

References

ACUHO-I. (2006). *21st century project: A compilation of the team reports and plenary reflections of the participants.* Columbus, OH: ACUHO-I.

APPA. *The strategic assessment model.* Retrieved March 8, 2006, from http://www.appa.org/Research/SAM.cfm

Briselden, D., & Cain, D. (2001). The facilities condition index: A useful tool for capital asset planning. *Facilities Manager,* 17. Retrieved March 8, 2006, from http://www.appa.org/FacilitiesManager/index.cfm?ItemNumber=204

Kaiser, H., & Davis, J. (1996). *A foundation to uphold.* Alexandria, VA: APPA.

Lewis, G. (2005). Special column: Designing cradle to cradle. *ASHRAE Journal,* 17, S39.

Ramsey, C. G., Sleeper, H. R., & Hoke, J. R., Jr. (2000). *Architectural graphic standards* (10th ed.). New York: John Wiley.

Osaka Gas Company (2002). Next 21: *Osaka gas experimental housing.* Retrieved March 8, 2005, from http://www.arch.hku.hk/~cmhui/japan/next21/ next21-index.html.

Privatized and Off-Campus Housing Relationships

Jim Short and Christi R. Chisler

T he advent of privatization in campus housing is steeped in fears and myths, which makes it a hot topic in the university community. Although it is more widely accepted now than in the past, allowing private companies to be involved in housing that universities traditionally operated still makes some institutions wary.

Privatized housing can take many forms. It can be on- or off-campus. It can be carried out by working as partners or competitors with an educational institution. A private company can manage campus-owned housing. Campuses can manage privately-owned housing. Or the two can coexist (peacefully or not) on the same campus.

What factors drove the need for this industry to develop? What companies are involved? What is the effect on campus housing? This chapter examines the history of contemporary privatized housing models evaluates why institutions turn to it defines the most common ownership structures details procurement procedures examines the effects on professional staff and students and identifies factors to consider in determining if privatized housing will work for a particular institution.

History

For many housing professionals, privatization in student housing is a relatively new phenomenon. However, the roots of privatization in colleges and universities date back at least to 1964 when the diversified real estate manager and developer firm Allen & O'Hara, using equity capital from the Northwestern Mutual Life Insurance Company (NML), developed, built, and managed Granville Towers at the University of North Carolina at Chapel Hill. According to Paul O. Bower, chairman, chief executive officer, and president of Allen & O'Hara, the management scope included residence life for 1,400 students, mostly freshmen. Northwestern Mutual Life, with Allen & O'Hara and other partners, went on to develop 24 off-campus projects and also teamed with 18 universities to finance on-campus residence halls (P.O. Bower, personal communication, May 2005).

In 1969, Portland State University (PSU) needed student housing at the same time the city of Portland was about to demolish some condemned apartment buildings near campus. PSU students in an urban studies class proposed, and were ultimately allowed, to renovate the buildings for student housing. A nonprofit entity, Portland Student Services Inc. (PSSI), was created to serve as owner of the housing. PSSI was the predecessor of the current College Housing Northwest (CHN) that now owns or manages all PSU campus housing. According to CHN chief executive officer Gary Meddaugh, CHN remains a nonprofit entity, making it unique in today's privatized industry (personal communication, May 2005).

A central element of today's typical privatized transaction is a ground lease where the institution leases institutional-owned land on which housing is constructed to the developer or nonprofit entity. One of the first developers to use the ground lease concept was Clarence T. Bach, a principal in Bach Development. He entered into a ground lease with the University of Texas at San Antonio (UTSA) in 1983 to open and manage the 500-bed Chisholm Hall, a traditional residence hall, in 1985. Chisholm was UTSA's only student housing at the time. In 1994, Bach sold his ground lease interest to Century Development, a transaction initiated by UTSA.

Century became the first developer to make a national program of the ground-lease structure for developing on-campus student housing. In 1990, Century opened its first project under a ground lease on the campus of the University of Houston. In the ensuing 10 years, Century completed 22 ground lease projects for a total of 9,500 beds, all apartment-style.

All the Century transactions referred to above were financed with taxable bonds. In 1995, Capstone Development, which previously had only developed off-campus student housing, created a ground lease model of finance using tax-exempt bonds for on-campus housing projects. For reasons discussed in a later section, the tax-exempt model proved to be more popular with most institutions and is now the prevalent model for on-campus privatized housing development.

Because of the recent need for more or updated student housing, there has been a boom in construction of housing facilities on and off campus. There are currently 15 or more companies, of varying degrees of experience and focus, vying to develop on-campus housing. The most recent trend is for these companies to partner with a financial entity, merge with a financing arm, or raise additional capital for expansion. Specifically, in 2004 and 2005, three student housing companies — American Campus Communities, Allen & O'Hara, and GMH (dba College Park Communities) — have had initial public offerings on the New York Stock Exchange and are now public companies.

An interesting side note in the history of privatized student housing involves institutional consultants. In the late 1980s and early 1990s, a Washington, D.C. firm, MPC Associates, specialized in consulting and project management for higher education. MPC ultimately disbanded, but some MPC alumni continue to provide higher education consulting services.

Why Privatization

Why have or why should universities undertake privatized housing? In this period of rapid growth in enrollment, sometimes there is not enough time for expensive and time-consuming state design and capital outlay procurement processes. Because privatized housing companies are not bound by the same constraints, universities often consider them a good alternative. Funding is a second factor – whether it is reduced state funding or lack of debt capacity. The increased awareness of privatization among legislators, trustees, and senior administrators increases the pressure beyond economic and timing factors into the political realm.

Another consideration is competition. As colleges and universities must vie with one another, students' expectations for services and amenities have grown considerably. The challenges these expectations present to planners, operators, facilities, auxiliaries, and student life professionals have become increasingly complex, including

- Evaluating the degree to which facilities contribute to the mission of the institution
- Evaluating the impact of services on recruitment
- Examining issues surrounding competition among on- and off-campus venues
- Evaluating the degree to which individual facilities must be self-supporting
- Involving the campus community in the effort to face the challenges presented to provide housing that meets the mission, academic benefits, and convenience of on-campus living.

Turning to a private developer often assists universities in meeting these needs in a timely and financially beneficial manner.

In the 1960s and 1970s the increasing number of baby boomers drove a corresponding campus housing boom. Today, another surge of campus housing is occurring because those '60s and '70s structures are in need of renovation or replacement. In addition, a baby boomlet is in force. Every year until 2009, the number of students graduating from high school will increase. Add to that trends showing higher percentages of those students attending college, as well as a need and desire of some two- and four-year institutions to move away from a commuter image by housing more students on campus (National Center for Education Statistics, 2005). The amount of funds institutions have or are willing to allocate for housing is often insufficient relative to the need.

On the business side of institutions, there are two issues that significantly affect how the funds for new housing are obtained. The first is debt capacity. All institutions have limits on their debt load. Subject to a number of accounting rules, ground lease transactions can usually get new or renovated housing for an institution without the related debt being included on the institution's balance sheet. This leaves coveted debt capacity for other projects (student centers, parking decks, etc.). The second issue is the rating for institutional-issued bonds. The higher the rating on bonds, the lower the interest rate required, and a higher value of bonds issued drives the rating down. Thus, institutions aggressively protect their bond ratings. Rating agencies (Standard & Poor's, Moody's Investors Service, and Fitch Ratings, for instance) will consider all of institutional-issued bonds when rating future bond issues. But the agencies will include only a portion of the bonds issued in privatized transactions, which should result in a higher rating for future bond issues.

Both of these issues are affected by the amount of control the institution retains in a privatized transaction. Control includes such issues as living policies, rate and budget approval rights, and overall management. The more control a campus retains, the more likely the debt will be included on the institution's balance sheet and the higher the percentage of the bond issue that will be considered by the rating agencies. Thus, while it is not a requirement that the developer manage the project once constructed, most do to help keep the privatized project debt separate from the institution's debt.

A secondary reason that institutions consider privatization is the time and cost required to construct buildings through the state capital outlay process. It is not unusual for a developer to build more quickly and for a lower cost than an institution can. Further, because the project owner is an entity other than the institution, state- or board-mandated building standards may not apply. If the institution desires, a private firm can build a 40-year structure (wood frame) instead of a 100-year structure (concrete or steel frame). Many institutions question the need for 100-year buildings when they have buildings that are 40 years old that are functionally obsolete and renovation cost estimates exceed the cost of new construction.

A third reason that some institutions are interested in privatized transactions is that the institution can require the developer to guarantee that a project will be delivered on time and on budget, and a portion of the developer fee can be withheld as insurance accordingly. The guarantee allows the university to share or reduce the risks associated with building housing.

Ownership Structures

The two ownership structures for privatized housing are developer-owned taxable and nonprofit tax exempt. Taxable transactions are somewhat complex, and tax-exempt transactions are even more so.

Both structures utilize a ground lease by which the institution allows the private developer to use the institution-owned land for a specified period of time. Technically, what the owner owns is a leasehold interest but not the land itself. Ground leases for privatized housing are typically for 30 to 40 years. At the end of the ground lease term, the institution regains the right to use the land and anything that remains on the land.

Taxable transaction

In a taxable transaction, the developer owns the leasehold interest and issues the bonds. When the improvements (buildings) are completed, the developer typically deeds over the improvements to the institution, leaving the bonds secured by the leasehold interest only. This reduces or eliminates the amount of property taxes the developer owes each year.

The ground lease requires the developer to pay rent. Usually the rent comprises a minor fixed annual amount (say, $100) and a share of the annual profit from the operation of the housing project. The institution's share is negotiated, but usually ranges from 25% to 50% of the profit. "Profit" is defined in the ground lease but is usually the net cash flow after paying operating expenses and debt service and setting aside reserves.

The developer assembles the team necessary to complete the development, typically including an investment banker (to market the bonds), architecture and engineering firms, a contractor, and a bond trustee.

Because the developer issues the bonds and ultimately is responsible for the repayment of the bonds, the developer retains a certain level of control over financial issues such as rental rates and budget. For the same reason, the developer usually manages the project. As a result, this financing structure will have the least impact on the institution's balance sheet and bond ratings.

Tax exempt

The Internal Revenue Code (IRC) prohibits a for-profit company from issuing tax-exempt bonds. It also does not allow a for-profit company to have an ongoing, long-term interest in the profitability of a project financed with tax-exempt bonds. Therefore, the owner of the leasehold interest must be a nonprofit entity, usually pursuant to IRC section 501(c)(3).

The nonprofit entity can be owned by the institution's existing foundation, a national student housing 501(c)(3) such as Collegiate Housing Foundation, or some other independent nonprofit entity. In all cases, the nonprofit will be created for the sole purpose of being the leasehold owner and typically has no staff and other assets or operation.

After the ground lease is executed with the nonprofit, it enters into separate agreements with the developer and the post-construction management entity. The management entity can be a developer-owned management company, a third-party company, or the institution itself (for "self-operation"). The nonprofit entity also enters into contracts with the investment banker and bond trustee. The architecture/engineer firms and the contractor can contract with either the nonprofit entity or the developer. All of these entities will have legal counsel.

Since the nonprofit entity is normally already exempt from property taxes, it usually retains ownership of the improvements. At the end of the ground lease term, the institution will get ownership of the improvements as well as regaining the use of the land. As in taxable transactions, the ground lease still requires rent to be paid to the institution. In addition, the institution typically will get all of the profit.

Because the developer has no ongoing financial interest in the project (developers enter into these transactions in order to earn development and construction management fees), it is less concerned about what is built. As a consequence, institutions have much more control over program and design. However, there will not be any developer equity in the project and usually no institutional support. Thus, the cost to finance, build, and operate the project directly affect the rental rate that will be charged to the residents.

Because of the absence of the developer, tax-exempt transactions are more likely to affect the institution's balance sheet and bond ratings.

A variation possible under tax-exempt transactions is that the developer can secure land under an option contract, which allows the land to be acquired by the nonprofit entity at the bond closing. Then when the bonds are paid off, the land and improvements transfer to the institution, and the institution's land holdings grow as a result of the transaction.

Preparation

Privatized housing is not a panacea for every institution – but neither is it the ruination of student housing. Each institution must assess its mission and institutional culture to determine the impact. An institution's desire to be in control of the direction and operational priorities may not make it a good partner for private development, but if the institution is open to privatization, best results occur when it is well informed beforehand. Assessing the impact on support departments is one of the first steps.

The complexity of the process requires input from many areas. Bringing departments into the process early ensures alignment with the missions and goals of all stakeholders. Understanding the legal, ethical, and financial ramifications—such as the level of risk and potential liability, potential conflicts of interest, tax considerations, and the power of the contract—require input from both the institution's legal counsel and controller.

Understanding how other departments augment the project is also essential to the success of the endeavor. Will the facilities department oversee construction? Will the institution's foundation be asked to procure the developer or obtain funding? Will the enrollment management office have a role in filling the project?

Including senior administration in the planning process provides buy-in from the top. Additionally, utilizing staff from housing, including the director and senior staff from departments of facilities and residence life, ensures that the privatized project fits with the overall housing program and helps identify potential disconnects. The housing department staff also provides historical perspective, which helps clarify how the project fits into the institutional and housing missions. Biases of staff, if present, can be overcome if their input is valued. More importantly, allowing stakeholders to have information and input from the beginning will help to build consensus and allow time needed to plan for resources.

Another useful tool in ensuring the success of the undertaking is the utilization of an outside consultant. Consultants offer an objective perspective and can often help the team work together and communicate more effectively. They bring experience from similar projects, reducing time the institution would otherwise spend researching and informing its members of current practices.

Once the stakeholders are together, defining the project in the following terms is the next step.

- Inputs: money, staffing, capital resources
- Activities: filling beds, uses for community spaces, and retail and service offerings
- Outputs: management, residence life programs
- Outcomes: what the institution hopes to achieve short- and long-term.

Another significant step is agreeing on the most important goal of the procurement—money, service, timing, product, or a combination of those. A lack of internal agreement diminishes the chance of getting the desired project. Depending on the time before bids go online, either subsequent to or concurrent with the definition of the project, the procurement process can start.

Procurement

Becoming knowledgeable about the current players and processes in the industry is the most important step you will take and the foundation of success. A consultant familiar with the industry and the players can facilitate building a strong foundations.

In this information-gathering phase, collect and use data to help refine the project and to begin to build consensus among stakeholders and committee members. The data can be gathered, either informally by contacting other colleges and universities and qualified developers or through a formal Request for Information (RFI) process. This step is particularly critical if the university community is not in agreement or if this is the institution's first privatized project.

After the project is defined, the institutions should put out a Request for Qualifications (RFQ) to solicit formal information about each interested vendor's experience, history, qualifications, and performance. Responses to the RFQ aid the university in identifying interest ina project, determining who the players are, and defining where and what types of projects are being built. Depending on procurement rules, this process may be the first step of a two-step process to short list or identify qualified bidders who will respond to the Request for Proposal (RFP) or may be used to identify a vendor with whom the university can enter into negotiations.

According to Biddison Hier, a consulting firm for higher education, in its white paper *The RFP Process, A Primer,* the RFP requests a specific set of services from vendors qualified to provide them, with background information about the project's parameters, constraints, and desired outcomes and a clear, concise statement of the expertise and experience based on your parameters. The paper stresses the importance of "requesting the right information to provide context for the project without limiting the creativity of the bidder." (Biddison & Hier, 1999). The RFP should also prescribe the submittal format to allow for ease of comparison and the selection criteria.

A mandatory pre-bid conference is critical, whether as part of the RFQ or RFP. The conference gives the university the opportunity to answer questions from developers, clarify any specifications, and gain a sense of how successfully the document set out the parameters (allowing time for addendums to be issued if necessary). It also gives the bidders an opportunity to clarify their understanding of the parameters, better understand the university's goals for the project, and see the site and surrounding campus community.

If the selected developer will be asked to manage the finished project, make certain RFP specifications clearly ask for a management plan and philosophy, including details about maintenance, housekeeping, residence life, assignments, judicial affairs, and security. Commonly this area only gets secondary attention during the evaluation process, although the relationship with and understanding of the campus culture can really make a difference in the continuing success of the project.

An essential issue to remember in a management component of the project is how the length of the relationship will affect the institution legally for rating and tax purposes. Bond counsel can advise the institution on the most appropriate length. Although this relationship does not last as long as bond terms, it typically ranges from 3 to 15 years.

Whether the team elects to use an RFQ, RFP, or both, include site visits as part of the process. To get a complete picture of how well the project meets the university's needs, prospects can visualize the process and talk with any staff, students, and faculty who are, or will be, involved or affected.

Prior to the review of proposals, spend time with the evaluation committee clarifying the evaluation criteria as well as standardizing the scoring method for choosing the final company. Otherwise there may be wide variation on how criteria are defined. By defining four or five factors for each criterion and asking members to utilize a common scale to rate each of the factors, the scoring becomes more defensible if the outcome is challenged.

The utilization of additional reading teams can help discover potential problems not readily apparent to all and can bring to the evaluation competencies that are not present in voting members. Reading team members should consist of experts from around the campus such as the central heating and cooling plant engineers, the information technology and telecommunications staff, or others who may hold expertise that is valuable to the success of the project. These reviews go a long way in ensuring that all aspects of the process have been properly considered, including construction schedules, constructability, utility conflicts, the presence of required program elements, site considerations, viability of service roads for deliveries, fire-truck access, and move-in and move-out. These reviews not only help the evaluation team compare and evaluate solutions presented but also help develop questions for the next phase of interviews.

Interviewing the top teams provides answers to questions, clarifies the process that went into the submission, and opens up discussion of alternatives. Once the submissions are fully understood, it is time to select the project and team that best meet the needs of the university.

The differences between the university and corporate cultures are not as evident in the pursuit of the project as they will become in the delivery of it. Thus, for the venture to be successful, build in leeway for making changes to the proposed design, schedule, university involvement in selection of finishes, and response time available to make decisions.

Another factor to include in contract negotiations is what the developer will pay if the project is not delivered on time. The contract should allow for actual damages related to putting students in alternative housing, providing meals if the units have full kitchens, and providing transportation to and from campus if the alternative housing is not within walking distance.

Contract Management

Unlike the traditional design-bid-build process, the privatized model of housing places heavier responsibility on the institution up front in the development of the RFP and evaluation of proposals. Once the firm is on board, the responsibility shifts from the institution to the developer—which contracts with design and construction firms—for accuracy of design, cost control, construction quality, and schedule adherence. Nevertheless, it is still important to have a specific person assigned to oversee the process from design through construction.

If the institution does not have the resources or capability for oversight, the institution should retain an outside consultant to assist in all areas from negotiating the developer's contract through delivery of the project. This individual oversees design, helps with submissions to the state agencies, ensures that responses to state review comments are complete, acts as the single point of control through which all comments and directions from the university funnel, and ensures that the quality of the project is as specified and promised. If there are issues to be resolved, however – whether they are design- or construction-related—it is not the responsibility of the institution's representative to resolve them but rather the developer's. Change orders, other than owner-initiated ones, should be virtually nonexistent because the development team is responsible for the entire process.

A development team made up of the developer, architect or engineer, and contractor who have worked together on similar projects in the past will have an advantage over a newly formed team and will help avoid misunderstandings that can affect the viability of the project. In one instance on a newly formed team, it became apparent after the submission and selection process but before the contract was signed that an error occurred in determining the net-to-gross ratio of the project, an error that would either increase the cost of the project or force the elimination of some of the desired elements. Had the team been experienced in working together, the likelihood of the error would have been minimal.

Challenges for the Profession

Depending on the structure of the deal, the university may have more or less involvement in the management of the housing. Whether there is a close affiliation between the university's and the private developer's housing or not, the public perception in the end is that they will still be your buildings, with your students and programs in them. Any issues will likely require university involvement.

The challenges for university housing staff can vary from phone calls regarding roommate and assignment issues in the privatized housing to contractual requirements that students be referred to the privatized housing first, putting strain on filling university beds. Private developers who take on residence life may not assign staff with education and training in student development, and they may view their role more as recreation directors than as providing activities that guide the students through the various stages of maturity and educational enrichment.

According to *Public Private Partnerships for Student Housing* (Coakley, 2000), "Partnering with a private firm brings another player to the decision-making process, and this can be difficult for an institution to adjust to. There is also a learning curve that is necessary for the private firm to truly understand the role of housing to the mission of the university beyond a revenue stream." The university may have to spend time educating the developer on the role of and need for staff from resident advisors to area coordinators, community space (especially in apartment complexes), and differences between property management and residence life (Coakley, 1991). But these issues do not need to scuttle the entire arrangement and can be avoided through the careful construction of the RFP and management agreement.

Cautions

As in many processes, the procurement of privatized housing may highlight conflicts in institutions. Resolving the conflict often means that one department's values feel trampled by those of another. Mitigating risk and preserving debt capacity may be important to senior administration, the lowest interest rate may make the project viable or competitive for housing staffers, and maintaining the architectural integrity of the campus may be important to the facilities department. There are no right or wrong answers to resolving conflicts, but having internal discussions to air the issues and come to an agreement is vital to the success of the project.

Depending on the type of deal and on individual state regulations, more state involvement might result than originally envisioned. Meeting with state officials in advance allows time to understand the requirements and convey them in official proposal requests and informal meetings. The ground lease may require approval from the state attorney general's office, treasury board approval may be required for the bond sale, and, the management agreement may be affected by the financing structure because buildings funded by tax-exempt bonds have limitations on revenue-producing activities. If the building is going to be turned over to the state at the termination of the lease period, the art and architecture review board may have to approve the design, and in all cases state or local building officials will need to review the plans for code compliance.

Facilities and housing staff often are concerned about the loss of control in constructing and managing privatized housing. Questions regarding the quality of construction (institutional, commercial, or residential quality), the tie-in to campus infrastructure, and oversight of projects must be resolved internally for facilities to fully buy in to the project. For Housing staff, the questions center more around operations and accountability: How will the developer provide management of student housing in the best interests of the university if they are driven by different values? What will happen if the services are not provided as the university desires? Some institutions resolve these concerns by providing university-employed resident-assistant or training the developer's staff. Housing assignments policies mayalso be affected by contract terms.

Cases to Consider

As with Wright State University in Dayton, Ohio, which exploited the advantages of privatized housing to boost enrollment when other campuses were experiencing trouble keeping up (Coakley, 1991), George Mason University (GMU) in Fairfax, Virginia, has had great success in the management and development of privatized housing, although not without some trials and tribulations.

Beginning in 1995, GMU first privatized management of all university-owned housing. After refining the process and moving to a second management company, housing occupancy soared, housing's financial position strengthened, deferred maintenance lessened, and faculty involvement in the residence halls increased. GMU's housing has gone from declining occupancy to an aggressive building program that includes a developer-built project.

The advantages are still there – timing, debt capacity, land, expertise, state regulations, and risk sharing. To build successful in-house or privatized housing project, institutions must bring all the pieces of the puzzle together. These include historical perspective, an understanding of institutional missions, the right team, an outside consultant, qualified providers, clear goals, clearer specifications, and a solid relationship.

Once the contract is signed, it is important to stay involved. The institution's willingness and ability to contribute can drive the developer's effectiveness. Share information with the developer, and help it to understand your culture. Be a willing partner to make it a good situation for both parties.

References

Biddison, G., & Hier, T. (1999). *The RFP process: A primer* [White paper, SL5]. Washington, DC: Biddison Hier.

Bryson, Charles V. (1997, Feb). Learning from post privatization at Virginia Commonwealth University Staunton, *The Journal of The National Association of College Auxiliary Services* http:/128.174.220/news/vcuart.htm. Retrieved 9/9/97.

Bumgardner, D., McKinney, D., Needham, J, Ripper, H. & Wysocki, A.J. (1997, March 14). *Privatization: Lessons learned by state and local governments* (Letter Report, GAO/GGD-97-48). Retrieved September 9, 1997, from http:www.access.gpo.gov/cgibin/getdoc.cgi?dbname=gao&docid=f:gg97048.txt.

Coakley, M. (1991). To use or not to use private developers....That is the question. *Talking Stick* 9(4), 10-13

Coakley, M. (2000). *Public private partnerships for student housing,* Retrieved 5/12/06 from www.reslife/net/html/facilities

National Center for Education Statistics (2005). *Projections of education statistics to 2014* (NCES 2005-074, pp. 47-57). Washington, DC: Institute of Education Statistics, United States Department of Education.

Ryland commentary. (1993). Contract management or self operation: A decision-making guide for higher education. *CAUSE/EFFECT, (16)*3.

Van der Werf, M. (2000, April 7). How the University of Pennsylvania learned that outsourcing is no panacea. *The Chronicle of Higher Education,* A38-A39

Wertz, R. D. (1997). *Outsourcing and privatization of campus services: An overview and guide for college and university administrators.* Staunton, VA: The National Association of College Auxiliary Services.

Part III

The Politics, Budget, and Accountability of Housing Operations

ousing operations do not exist in a vacuum. No longer ancillary services, they are becoming a much more integrated part of the higher education system. And, as with any system, change is driven by a host of factors that include both internal and external elements. Part III explores changing operations as well as the influences that are likely to emerge in the future.

There are a myriad of influences that drive operations, and they come from both internal and external sources. There is the demand for accountability and, of course, everyone is feeling the weight of rising financial costs. The authors look at these topics and search for ways to not just survive, but thrive under these different pressures. And when the book concludes with a discussion on emerging trends and strategies housing officers can utilize, it will help ensure that the foundation of collegiate housing will remain strong into the future.

The Changing Nature of Housing Operations

Alan Hargrave, Ed.D.

T he professional lives of housing and residence life officers have changed significantly through 2005. The days of relaxing summers and clearly defined intra-institutional boundaries have given way to campus environments that rarely provide time for reflection and where collaboration and blending of service resources have become more common. "The activity of management is viewed as making what is going on in the organization meaningful and sensible to the organizational participants, and furthermore developing a social consensus and social definition around the activities being undertaken" (Pfeffer, 1981, p. 18). While housing and dining operations have already adjusted to external and internal changes, future challenges still lie ahead.

Student Expectations and Demands

Howe and Strauss (2003) provide an exhortation to college administrators regarding the Millennial generation students who are beginning to enroll in colleges and universities.

> The years ahead can be a new golden age for America's colleges and universities. So too will they be years of increased stress, scrutiny, security, accountability, tuition relief, and—very likely—mainstream political activism of a kind that will seem oddly unfamiliar to most veteran Boomer activists.
>
> It will not be an easy time. The nature of every college function from admissions to campus life to the classroom to career counseling will change dramatically. The

doctrine of *in loco parentis,* thrown over by rebellious Boomers 40 years ago, will reemerge in a new community guise as the Boomers' own children fill dorm rooms. (p. 3)

It is important to learn as much about residence hall and apartment residents as possible. While there is considerable documentation on the increasing numbers of non-traditional students entering higher education, the vast majority of students living in residence halls and university apartments are traditional-age college students. The generation of students who will inhabit university housing stock for the next 20 years are described as "smart, ambitious, incredibly busy, very ethnically diverse, and dominated by girls" (Howe & Strauss, 2003, p. 4). Additionally, more students are arriving at university housing operations with serious mental illness than in the past. Some of these students require close observation and significantly impact hall communities. This generation also demonstrates close relationships with their parents (Forbes, 2001, p. 13). In fact, anecdotal evidence finds that parents are more involved in their students' lives than ever before.

As products of a consumer-driven society, Millennial generation students and their parents often view higher education as a product that is investigated, purchased, and then put to use. They are aware of their abundant choices and shop around for the perceived best value. "Confidently, with generosity and grace, most parents let their children grow up. But this truth is often swept aside by the notion that college is just one more commodity to be purchased. Their sense of entitlement as consumers, along with an inability to let go, leads some parents to want to manage all aspects of their child's lives" (Forbes, 2001). Many students are used to having their own bedrooms, a wide array of electronic and technical equipment, high degrees of convenience, multiple choices, and security. This is also a generation increasingly stratified between those who are from families that are economically comfortable and those from families who struggle (Karen, 1991). "Harvard University's president, Lawrence Summers, recently told a group of college presidents that the gap in opportunities for children from different economic backgrounds is the 'most severe domestic problem in the United States,' and he called on colleges and universities to take steps to ameliorate it" (Ehrenberg & Rizzo, 2004, p. 2).

Responding to the expectations of students and their parents has not been easy. Facilities and technology upgrades, service improvements, safety and security enhancements, and an increasing pressure to keep room and board rates within bounds challenge housing professionals to be creative, collaborative, and politically savvy.

External and Internal Pressures

Increasingly, critics both within and outside higher education have expressed alarm about the cost of attending college. Governing boards, students, parents, and politicians indicate growing concern that the cost of attending college has increased more rapidly than the median family income, leaving some to hypothesize that students and parents may be unwilling to assume additional debt to pay for a higher education (Campaigne & Hossler, 1998). "Over the past two or three years, states have drastically reduced funding for higher education, and the situation probably won't be getting much better any time soon" (Smith, 2004, p. 4). "Today . . . nearly two-thirds of Americans say students and their families should pay the largest share of a college education" (Selingo, 2003, p. 5). In the 1960s, Americans thought that it was the responsibility of the government to pay the majority of higher education costs. In 2002, students at public colleges and universities in the United States paid $4,694 in tuition on average, which was a 14.1% increase over the previous year. Some institutions have implemented tuition increases of 40% to help offset reductions in state appropriations (College Board, 2003). It is not uncommon that in times of financial stress, institutions look inward to sources of income that were previously left alone, such as auxiliaries like housing and dining services. Schuh & Shelley (2001) indicate that despite pressures to keep room and board rates low, there are numerous factors affecting costs that are beyond the control of a housing officer such as utilities, food costs, health care costs, institutional overhead, and prior debt service. "Private institutions of higher education face exactly the same challenges, perhaps only from different sources" (Rowley, Lujan, & Dolence, 1997, p. 4).

The location of an institution also presents housing officers with particular challenges. Urban institutions often find themselves landlocked and unable to expand to provide convenient housing options for students when enrollments grow. Some institutions in the Midwest and Great Plains sections of the United States may find that they have more housing stock available than current and future enrollments can support while housing officers in the Sunbelt often scramble to build housing rapidly enough to accommodate bulging enrollments (Ratcliff, 2004).

Shifting leadership patterns within higher education also add to the pressures on housing officers. "Now, more than ever, higher education is facing significant challenges on its campuses. . . . During the past five years, over 50% of colleges and universities in the U.S. have appointed a new president" (Segal, 2004, p. 1). The average tenure of a university president is relatively short, creating an almost constant state of change regarding the basic institutional mission as well as strategies to achieve the mission. Presidential leadership change often precipitates changes in other top level administrative positions. While state governments tend to be less inclined to support public higher education financially, they are becoming more vocal about how colleges and universities are addressing the postsecondary educational needs of their citizens. Michigan governor Jennifer Granholm called upon her state colleges and universities to "do a better job helping students complete degrees or certification, to make it easier for students to transfer from one higher education institution to another, and to bring larger numbers of adult workers who have earned college credits in the past back to campus to finish their degrees" (Michigan Commission on Higher Education and Economic Growth, 2004, p. 2).

"Business as usual is no longer acceptable to the taxpaying public, the business leaders, and the other laypersons who sit on governing boards" (Gardner, 1995, p. 10). Learning to adapt quickly to the institutional and state political landscapes compounds the stress of housing officers, not only in terms of job security, but also in terms of maintaining the relevance of their operations.

Student as Customer

Much debate has occurred within higher education about treating students as customers. Some consider the concept to be the antithesis of an educational environment, while others believe that the relationship between an institution and its students has customer service components that should not be ignored. While few within the profession of housing and residence life would argue against the notion that considerable contributions to learning are provided by residential life operations, the successful housing professional must learn to distinguish those services, procedures, and policies that are primarily educational in nature from those that are mainly customer service functions. This delineation is a cornerstone to effective management of a housing and residence life operation that serves students well. It is also important in helping to clearly explain a department's services and philosophy to students, parents, governing bodies, and other educational administrators.

It is not enough for housing professionals to understand when residents are treated as students and when they are treated as customers: One must be able to clearly articulate this difference to students and parents. A great deal of time can be spent addressing student complaints, concerns, and frustrations. Much of this time spent reacting to these issues results from poorly communicated expectations, a poor understanding of student needs, and a failure to regularly evaluate the effectiveness of programs and services.

Know Your Student Customer

One basic mantra of modern business is to know your customer. What are the services, amenities, and facilities that interest them? What are they willing to pay for such services? Is there enough interest to make the service feasible? Much of the Western world contains data-driven societies, and housing officers must collect appropriate evidence upon which to make defendable decisions. Having access to individuals who have skills in conducting market studies, organizing focus groups, and analyzing data is crucial. It is also often important to be able to gather and interpret that information quickly. Interests, fads, and trends change quickly, therefore causing housing professionals to adapt more rapidly than they have in the past.

Businesses have emerged that focus solely on providing quality, timely information to higher education about who their students are and what student perceptions are about the quality of their experiences. "Too often, information is collected from students, through surveys and questionnaires, but is rarely fed back to them for purposes of discussion and insight as to potential action and understanding" (Strange, 1991, p. 189). "Trying out different approaches will force others to think more carefully about what they are doing and may help to identify policies and practices that are antithetical to what is desired" (Kuh & Whitt, 1991, p. 65). Because of the rapid rate of change, today's housing professional must be adept in utilizing data, accurately identifying trends, reallocating resources, and creating services that students perceive have utility.

In their popular study of successful U.S. businesses, *In Search of Excellence,* Peters and Waterman (1982) described eight characteristics that were commonly held by these companies. While this study is more than 20 years old, the qualities described endure.

1. Hold a bias for action. Leaders must be decisive and move the organization in a manner to keep it vital and relevant.
2. Listen closely to consumers. Those who utilize your services are in an excellent position to provide quality feedback and suggestions for improvement.
3. Encourage autonomy and creativity. People should be allowed to utilize their skills to their fullest. Risk taking and creativity are nurtured.
4. Implement Theory Y of work. Pay attention to your human resources. Encourage staff to develop their skill sets. Show you appreciate their contributions, and acknowledge their importance to your department.
5. Transmit a message of value. Your mission and your messages must be congruent with one another.
6. Stay with what you know. Understand your core mission and do not get sidetracked with products and services that are outside of that core mission.
7. Simple organizational structure. The current term for this concept is a "flat organizational structure," meaning few layers of bureaucracy, and keeping staffing levels lean. This does not mean to operate with fewer people than are necessary to provide quality service.
8. Simultaneous loose-tight properties. Staff are empowered to do their jobs and make decisions, but there are controls in place to correct problem performance as necessary.

Strategic Planning

Strategic planning should ideally change the way we see things. It should help to focus resources toward carefully targeted priorities. While many people will claim to embrace change, few in fact do. Most people will at least mildly resist it, and considerable energy must be expended to move a group toward needed changes.

There is a difference between organizational resistances to change with organizational resistance to arbitrary change. In fact, organizations adapt routinely and easily to their experience, though they rarely do exactly what they are told to do by proper authorities or managers. They follow rules that are contingent on the environment in such a way as to produce large changes without great difficulty" (Cameron, 1983, p. 126). Rosser and Penrod (1991) indicate that change in higher education primarily results from three conditions: a major crisis, outside pressure, or a vigorous and farsighted leader. "Clark Kerr (1982) once observed that the major test of a modern U.S. university is how wisely and how quickly it is able to adjust to important new possibilities. It is risk, not replication, that drives this active stance. (Rowley, etal., 1997, p. 25).

Kotler & Murphy (1982) indicate that an environment audit should be one of the first steps of a strategic plan. They suggest looking at major trends and implications of the trends and identifying opportunities and threats. Five different components of an organization's environment are described:

- Internal environment (board of directors, administrators, faculty, and staff)
- Market environment (traditional students, nontraditional students, alumni, source of funds, employers, and graduate schools)
- Public environment (financial, media, government, activist, local, and general public)
- Competitive environment (direct, type, and generic)
- Macroenvironment (demographic, economic, technological, political, and cultural)

Most colleges and universities have strategic plans. However, housing and residence life programs often are not a primary focus of the plans. Housing officers may be well advised to utilize their institutional plan to help guide the development of a departmental strategic plan. It probably would be unwise to be unable to link to the specified outcomes of the institutional plan. Strategic planning helps housing officers develop long-term goals and provides a framework for staff to begin making long-range decisions instead of short-range ones. Strategic planning is also one tool to help housing officers protect their budgets— encumber the money for meaningful and indispensable endeavors. It isn't uncommon for housing professionals to reflect on some shortsighted decision of their own or another administrator that burdened their operations for years.

Learning to think strategically is different from strategic planning. Planning is a process that helps identify opportunities and threats and to prioritize resources to bring an organization to where it desires to be. Teaching others to think strategically should infuse their entire professional identities. It takes strategic planning from a specified period of time or exercise and makes every hour of every day an opportunity to advance the department. It provides a lens to view the environment as a constantly evolving landscape and to identify the mega issues, those issues that are tremendously important, affecting your organization.

Responding to Institutional Needs and Expectations

Competition for the most academically gifted students is great among institutions of higher education. As students and their parents continue to compare scholarships and financial aid packages and academic reputations among colleges and universities, they also are comparing social opportunities, safety and security features, and living accommodations. There exists a paradox that the residence halls that were acceptable to the parents when they were students are not as acceptable for their children. This has led to the largest investment in renovation and building in university housing since the 1960s. University administrators are recognizing that the attractiveness of their residence halls impacts the admissions yield of the institution. This has provided additional support and pressure as housing operations assume large amounts of debt to fund the improvements and may be pushing construction of housing facilities that are more expensive than can be afforded. Concurrently, as general fund revenues are stressed, some colleges and universities are requiring housing and dining operations to commit a portion of the room and board budgets to general campus overhead costs.

The kinds of space and amenities that students desire are frequently not in line with what they are willing to pay for such services. There is also debate among housing professionals about the appropriateness of some building configurations as they relate to issues of community and student development. Students desire more privacy, are more likely to request a single room, want more space, the best technology available, vigorous security measures, high degrees of convenience, and freedom from rules they consider archaic.

Building and renovation costs have skyrocketed. The average new construction cost per suite-style bed in 1999 was $32,314 (Grimm & Dunkel, 1999). In 2003 those costs increased to $45,639 per bed for suite-style new construction (Dunkel & Grimm, 2003). Students are no longer satisfied with the cafeteria lines in food services and demand more choices, longer serving hours, and flexibility in how they spend their dining accounts. The cost for building dining centers for these types of dining programs is substantial. Balancing room and board rates and occupancy levels to pay interest payments on this debt and still maintain enough reserve dollars to cover maintenance on other facilities requires skill on the part of the housing officer and support from other university administrators to resist reallocating auxiliary funds.

The reemergence of living-learning programs or learning communities provides the opportunity for housing and residence life operations to partner with academic programs to enhance student learning. Research has shown that students involved with learning community programs are more likely to be involved than students not living in learning communities, and students in learning communities achieved higher gains in general education, greater positive day-to-day behavior effects, and higher scores on the integration of course information (Pike, 1999). Hart (1991) stated, "Colleges and universities wishing to improve the quality of their residence life program and improve programming for first-year student success should strongly consider the development of programs linking academic and residential student life" (p. 54). Learning communities also have the potential to positively affect campus culture (Kuh, 1996; Schroeder & Hurst, 1996). Bringing faculty and student affairs professionals together to discuss learning helped to refocus university energy toward educationally purposeful activities (Boyer, 1990; Pascarella & Terenzini, 1991). Blake (1996) indicated that the separation between faculty and student affairs professionals on most campuses was pervasive. However, learning communities provide structures to create greater understanding between residence life professionals and faculty members as they collaborate on student learning (Hargrave, 2000).

As colleges and universities focus on undergraduate education, learning communities continue to emerge as an attractive option. Residential life staff may have to be trained about how students learn and how to effectively work with faculty members to create the best learning environments for students. They can also be another line item in a housing budget. While institutions find learning communities attractive, many do not have discretionary general fund dollars to support the initiatives. Housing, as a partner in the learning community enterprise, may find that it is financing activities that are beyond its core mission. Particular care should be taken when establishing these academic partnerships about which entity should pay for which program or service. Few would argue about the benefits to students of a learning community program that is successfully designed and operated. However, if the parameters of the program are not clearly articulated, there may be frustration on the parts of both housing and academic administrators.

Personnel

Perhaps one of the greatest responsibilities of a successful housing officer is the hiring of staff. Staffing needs for housing operations have changed even though the actual patterns of staffing have not evolved substantially. There were cycles in the late 1900s and early 2000s when it was difficult to fill various positions within the profession, notably resident assistant and residence hall director positions. Resident assistant positions became more demanding during that time as a result of a tendency of housing officers to assign additional tasks to this group of employees, often without taking away other responsibilities.

The significant and time-consuming work of paraprofessionals, as well as the rigors of supervising peers, has led to the perception of some students that these roles are not worth the compensation. Successful housing operations must provide adequate support, salary, recognition, and proper supervision to this group of staff members. It is also important to market the skill development and personal rewards these positions provide to students. One must remember that resident assistants are students, not full-time employees. Job descriptions and expectations for performance must be reasonable.

Various staffing patterns with graduate and professional live-in personnel exist within the profession. Traditionally, live-in staff members were expected to possess prior residence hall experience. Some have begun to question this assumption and have recruited staff with other backgrounds such as human resource management, teaching, social work, or business. Others have looked for experience with specific subject matter as it might relate to a particular learning community. The most successful live-in staff are able to relate in a meaningful way to others, are organized, and are willing to spend time with students to build strong communities.

Mid-level and upper-level management positions are critical to most operations. Certainly, a strong past performance in a residence life position provides a strong predictor of success for a position with greater responsibility. But that cannot be the sole determinant. Institutional fit and the similarity of roles are also important to consider. For housing operations with self-operated custodial and maintenance functions, it is beneficial to recruit staff with backgrounds in building maintenance, construction, housekeeping supervision, and related areas. Building systems are more complicated today, and new materials are constantly being introduced in the marketplace. Someone without knowledge of these areas could require extra time to become familiar with the terminology and to understand the details of electrical, mechanical, or building systems. With the increased number of construction and renovation projects, a lack of this basic knowledge could lead to higher costs as well as systems that are difficult to maintain.

It is often challenging to hire individuals with appropriate technology skills for the compensation offered by housing operations. However, it has become necessary in many situations to have persons with computer programming skills and others who are skilled with computer networks and hardware. Some housing officers are able to contract some of these particular services, while others find it more efficient to add these individuals to their staffs.

Campus Partnerships

It is worthwhile to remember that a partnership describes a relationship in which two entities share the responsibility for planning and implementing an endeavor.

It does not accurately describe a relationship where one entity provides all of the money but is not engaged in the development and implementation of the endeavor. Student affairs in general, and housing specifically, tended to have had a bit of an inferiority complex when dealing with other areas of their institutions. To be a true partner, housing officers must enter relationships with their colleagues in business affairs and academic affairs as equals. The contributions to student learning and success that are made by housing professionals are laudatory and must not be diminished by allowing others to assume that these contributions are insignificant.

Developing meaningful partnerships across the college and university landscape is an important way to improve the campus environment for students and to help establish housing and residence life operations as a vital component in the learning process. In fact, it is critical for the long-term health of a housing operation to be closely partnered with a variety of offices and programs throughout the college or university community. When considering a partnership, the following questions should be addressed:

- How does this initiative improve life for students?
- Does the partnership advantage on-campus students in some way, or is it a way to shift the cost of advantaging all students onto the backs of on-campus students?
- Is it consistent with the core mission of the department?
- Does the partnership advance the strategic plan of the department or institution?
- Is the cost-benefit worth the investment?
- Are there available resources to make the initiative successful?
- Are there data to support the initiative?
- What are the political ramifications?

Professionals in housing and residence life are generally a gregarious and helpful group of people. These qualities can be assets in building campus relationships and partnerships. They also can be impediments. If one too readily tries to be helpful without considering the full range of potential outcomes, then a department may be mired in unproductive situations or, worse, exploited for financial advantage. One of the icons of the housing profession, Jim Grimm, exhorted young chief housing officers to "Protect the money!" He knew that housing and dining budgets were attractive targets for all manner of special projects that originated outside the residence life department. That being said, creating collaborative environments throughout college and university structures is healthy and is becoming a necessary endeavor. These types of communities help to create the "seamless learning environments" stressed by Kuh (1996), which students desire and in which they thrive.

Needs and Priorities

Assessing student needs is different from assessing student wants. This is a dilemma for housing professionals. Many operations utilize benchmarking services to ascertain student satisfaction and make decisions about how to best spend room and board dollars. For example, enhancing training for staff may help improve student satisfaction in a more cost-effective manner than spending on facility upgrades. Without data, one is guessing, sometimes correctly, about how to best improve the living environments for students.

Technology has transformed survey data collection. It is now as affordable to survey an entire residence hall or apartment population as it is to survey a sample population. The larger number of returned surveys one receives, the greater the validity of the study. Focus groups also can be an excellent method to gather evidence and to help refine survey questions before asking the questions of an entire population.

Using a forced choice format can help housing officers divine the difference between need and want. This format also helps to determine the extent of want. An example of this methodology would be to show a group of students a list of desired amenities to incorporate in a new residence hall. The list may include air-conditioning, wireless Internet, single bathrooms, single bedrooms, stackable furniture, carpeting in student rooms, floor lounges, study lounges, laundry facilities, and recreation space. Students would be required to choose only five of the features. This forces them to prioritize what is most important to them. A variation of this format would be to show students a variety of room configurations, such as single bedroom apartment, single room with private bath, or double room with semiprivate bath. For each type of room, students would be asked what would be the upper limit they would be willing to pay for each room type. This information is valuable when planning a new or remodeled hall to help determine what students and their families can afford to pay. The housing officer needs to have done homework in advance of such exercises so that he or she knows an approximate cost.

Many desired new services result in higher room and board charges to cover the increased cost. Residence hall student organizations are often excellent barometers of student opinion. They are also excellent ambassadors when given accurate information and permitted to participate in decisions. An illustration of this would be a desire for weekend housekeepers to clean restrooms. The housing officer estimated the number of hours it would require to clean hallways and restrooms, multiplied that times the number of weekends per year, and then divided that number by the number of residents, and it was determined that room rates would have to increase by $25 to cover this service. This information is then presented to focus groups, residence hall groups, or in a survey format such as, "Would you be willing to have your room rate raised $25 a year to have custodians clean your hallway and restroom on weekends?" The advantage to the housing officer is that, regardless of the results of the survey, data is present to support the decision.

Students are being more vocal about service hours for meals and recreational services. It is expensive to keep dining operations open, and many recreation centers require staff present because of liability concerns. The Millennial generation is described as overly scheduled. Millennials are used to being busy. Classes often require additional lab hours, community service components, or group work, thus forcing students to eat whenever their schedule permits. Utilizing meal counts as data helps to determine if there would be enough business to keep a particular operation open later at night or between more traditional meal hours. While it is not uncommon to hear that students want particular dining options available to midnight, it is rare to have enough business transactions to make that service financially viable. Helping students learn how their requests affect their housing and dining costs should be a part of each housing officer's educational and marketing plan.

Marketing the Residential Experience

With the demands from internal and external constituencies about the quality of campus housing, clear and attractive messages must be crafted and delivered regarding what is promised, what is expected, and where to express concerns or ask questions.

Student and parent expectations are usually high but rarely unreasonable if given adequate information about the housing program. A successful marketing plan begins with a succinct departmental mission that is congruent with the institutional mission. This provides boundaries and guidelines for the types of services that are offered.

The next step is to map the various programs and services that are provided and accurately describe each one. List the pros and cons of the most notable ones, and talk with staff about how the list of cons could be reduced and the list of pros enhanced. What is there to be proud of? What could be changed about the operation? Then, look again at programs and services and decide what promise can be made to the markets. The promise statement indicates the organization's values and attributes and describes to others what they can expect.

After crafting a promise statement, develop a compelling message about the services in which you have the most confidence. Lead with your best, but don't paint an unrealistic picture of your challenges. Most people understand that nothing is perfect, but if it's presented as perfect, unreasonable expectations are being developed that can cause a disconnect between the student or parent and your operation. Clearly crafting your message and your promise also assists other college or university administrators to be supportive of your efforts. Admissions counselors need accurate information upon which to help students make selections. Most colleges and universities are complex bureaucracies, and your message will be delivered by a number of individuals from a variety of offices. Try to anticipate this and make sure they have accurate information.

Technology is not a substitute for human interaction. It should be used as an enhancement. With that said, students of today heavily use the World Wide Web, and your marketing is enhanced by utilizing it wisely. Does the Web design convey the messages you want conveyed, both in print and in layout? Is the front page cluttered with unnecessary or confusing links? Are students invited to explore the site, and is it intuitive for users? Can they find the information they seek?

Peers still heavily influence students. Employing current students to speak to prospective students about their experience can be successful. The caveat to this prior statement is, *if they are properly trained and supervised.* Once the messages from your department have been crafted, it is important that representatives stay on point with those messages. It is easy for new or prospective students to get overwhelmed with information during the college selection process. We often are not helpful when we barrage them with jargon and acronyms with which they are unfamiliar. When we add to that confusion with inaccurate or incongruent messages, we do a disservice to our operation, our institution, and the prospective students.

College and university admissions offices are being more closely linked to communications or media relations departments. There is a belief that the messages from the institution must be carefully scripted. This approach often flows to any office that sends materials to an external constituency such as a prospective student. There are understandable reasons for this. Students delay decisions about admissions as long as they can. Summer orientation sessions that used to be a confirmation process are now viewed as another step in making an admissions decision. Many students travel to two or three summer orientation programs at different institutions. Housing and residential life marketing materials and processes come under scrutiny regarding whether they assist or detract from admissions yield initiatives. Timing of hall assignment letters, where students are housed for orientation, and how roommates are assigned are all of interest to other university administrators who may have legitimate reasons to be involved.

Challenges to the Profession

The ability and willingness to rapidly adjust to future changes will be important to housing professionals, whether that is arranging for a new service or adapting to a new institutional strategic plan. These are not new situations to the field. The rate of change is what is becoming shorter. Trends and fads are changing more quickly. Most of our financial models are developed around 15- and 30-year assumptions, whereas student demographic trends may require more frequent and dramatic renovations, pressuring housing officers into unstable or unsupportable business or financing plans.

Keeping abreast of upcoming trends and demographic information provides evidence upon which to make changes to strategic plans. Strategic plans, in turn, help to focus priorities and spending. They also can help protect budgets and reserve accounts from those who covet the funds for short-term gain.

Conducting regular assessment of existing programs to determine viability and having the determination to sunset programs that are not able to demonstrate appropriate cost and benefit is just good management. Know what students want and what they need by utilizing needs assessment. Keep data current, and use data and evidence to guide departmental decisions.

Maintain a lean staffing structure that allows the department to respond quickly to changing needs but also provides a level of service to students that adds value to their experiences. Housing and residence life operations are personnel-intensive for a reason. It is expensive to provide the staffing levels adequate to manage living-learning environments for large numbers of students, just as it is expensive to provide lower teacher-to-student ratios. The evidence is clear that lower ratios are more effective. Establish effective and appropriate collaborative relationships across the institution. Partnerships that make sense for residents should be encouraged, and ones that are simply ways to shift a financial burden onto the backs of on-campus students should be avoided or reevaluated.

Trends and issues tend to cycle through higher education. With the many changes in society, not the least of which is technology, these changes or cycles tend to be occurring more frequently. What we can expect is the demand to rapidly adjust to these trends as they emerge. If we look back to the 1950s when American society was relatively stable and campuses were traditional and relatively peaceful, there are many similarities to today. Students today are more traditional in their political and social behaviors than students of 30 years ago. The divorce rate is declining, and there are increased pressures to act *in loco parentis*. The 1950s were followed by the more tumultuous 1960s in which students rebelled against the conventional social forces of their parents. Can we expect a shift as dramatic as the ones of the 1960s? Certainly! The changes may not mirror those exactly, but we can be assured of societal changes that will force us to retool and reengineer our operations to meet new demands.

Adjusting to the future is the only choice for housing professionals who want to remain relevant. The competition for student housing and dining dollars is intense, and there we no longer have a monopoly in most places. Our challenge is to remain relevant, to provide value, and to assist future generations of learners in higher education.

Conclusion

Students entering colleges and universities today bring increased expectations and demands for service, quality, and affordability. Housing officers must equip themselves to address these expectations competently managing their operations, understanding student needs, and by marshalling resources strategically with realistic plans. Staff must be selected and nurtured to fulfill their reasonable duties with an emphasis upon excellent service and quality interactions.

The constant change can be stressful to staff. Finding ways to facilitate change, encourage participation, and recognize substantial accomplishments and contributions can help reduce reluctance to ongoing modifications.

References

Blake, E.S. (1996). The yin and yang of student learning in college. *About Campus,1*(4), 4-9.

Boyer, E.L. (1990). *Campus life: In search of community.* Princeton, NJ: The Carnegie Foundation for the Advancement of Teaching.

Cameron, K.S. (1983). Organizational adaptation and higher education. *Journal of Higher Education, 55*(2), 122-144.

Campaigne, D.A., & Hossler, D. (1998). How do loans affect the educational decisions of students? Access, aspirations, college choice and persistence. In R. Fossey & M. Bateman (Eds.), *Condemning students to debt: College loans and public policy.* New York: Teachers College Press 88-104.

College Board. (2003), *National report.* New York: The College Board.

Dunkel, N., & Grimm, J. (2003), *Campus housing construction.* Columbus, OH: Association of College and University Housing Officers-International.

Ehrenberg, R., & Rizzo, M. (2004). Financial forces and the future of American higher education. *Academe, 90*(4) 38-41.

Forbes, K. (2001, September/October), Students and their parents: Where do campuses fit in. *About Campus,* American College Personnel Association,.

Gardner, D.P. (1995), Managing transitions in a time of acute modernity. *Trusteeship, 3*(4), 10-15.

Grimm, J. (1999), Presentation to participants in the ACUHO-I new CHO Institute, Pingree Park, CO.

Grimm, J., & Dunkel, N. (1999), *Campus housing construction and renovation: An analysis of cost and design.* Columbus, OH: Association of College and University Housing Officers-International.

Hargrave, A. (2000), Faculty and student affairs staff involvement in learning. *Journal of College and University Student Housing, 23*(2), 24-30.

Hart, D. (1991). *Residence life programs and the first-year experience: The freshman year experience* (Monograph series No. 5). Columbia, SC: National Resource Center for the Freshman Year Experience. (ERIC Document Reproduction Series No. ED334884)

Howe, N., & Strauss, W. (2003). *Millennials go to college.* Washington, DC: American Association of Collegiate Registrars and Admissions Officers and LifeCourse Associates.

Karen, D. (1991). The politics of class, race, and gender: Access to higher education in the United States, 1960-1986. *American Journal of Education, 99*(2), 208-237.

Kerr, C. (1982) *The uses of the university* (3rd ed.), Cambridge, MA: Harvard University Press.

Kotler, P., & Murphy, P.E. (1982, September/October). Strategic planning for higher education. *Journal of Higher Education, 52*(5), *470-489*.

Kuh, G.D. (1996) Guiding principles for creating seamless learning environments for undergraduates. *Journal of College Student Development, 35*(2), 135-147.

Kuh, G.D., & Whitt, E. (1991). Organizational theory: A primer. In T. Miller & R. Winston (Eds.), *Administration and leadership in student affairs* (2nd. ed.), Muncie, IN: Accelerated Development, Inc, 37-40.

Michigan Commission on Higher Education and Economic Growth (2004). Available online at www.cherrycommission.org

Pascarella, E., and Terenzini, (1991) *How colleg affects students: findings and insight from twenty years of research,* San Francisco: Jossy Bass.

Peters, T.J., & Waterman, R.H. (1982). *In search of excellence.* New York: Harper and Row.

Pfeffer, J. (1981). *Power in organizations.* Marshfield, MA: Pittman.

Pike, G.R. (1999). The effects of residential learning communities and traditional residential living arrangements on educational gains during the first year of college. *Journal of College Student Development, 40*(3), 269-284.

Ratcliff, C. (2004). Lessons learned: Reflections on the evolution of higher education student housing patterns. *Journal of College and University Student Housing, 32*(2), 11-13.

Rosser, J.M., & Penrod, J.I. (1991). Strategic planning and management: A methodology for responsible change. In J. Williams II (Ed.), *Strategic planning in higher education.* Binghamton, NY: Haworth Press, 9-34.

Rowley, D., Lujan, H., & Dolence, M. (1997). *Strategic change in colleges and universities.* San Francisco: Jossey-Bass.

Schroeder, C.C., & Hurst, J. C., (1996) Designing learning environments that integrate curricular and cocurricular experience. *Journal of College Student Development, 37*(2), 174-181.

Schuh, J.,& Shelley, M. (2001). External factors affecting room and board rates: How much influence does the housing director have? *The Journal of College and University Student Housing, 30*(1), 41-47.

Segal Company. (2004). Web site http://www.segalco.com/higher_ed/index.cfm

Selingo, J, (2003, May 2). What Americans think about higher education *The Chronicle of Higher Education, 49*(34), A10-A17.

Smith, M. (2004, July/August). Growing expenses, shrinking resources: The states and higher education. *Academe* 90(4) 32-35.

Strange, C. (1991). Managing college environments: Theory and practice. In T. Miller & R. Winston (Eds.), *Administration and leadership in student affairs* (2nd. ed.), Muncie, IN, Accelerated Development 159-199.

External Pressures to Higher Education and Housing

James F. Conneely, Ph.D. and Claire Good, Ph.D.

C olleges and universities range from small, private, religiously affiliated institutions to large, complex, state-funded research institutions and most every variation in between. Regardless of the type, all colleges and universities are subject to external pressures that influence, impact, and, at times, mandate how the institution is going to operate or, at the least, react.

Pressures come in many different forms. Some may be subtle and low key, such as a parent calling on the phone to ask simple questions, while others may be more formal, such as a legislative directive. From the colonial times to the present, outside forces have influenced higher education whether through war (either at home or on foreign soil), federal legislation (the Morrill Act or the Clery Act), or the national economy (The Great Depression or time of an energy crises). Other pressures that have had an effect on higher education are enrollment trends, local and state economies, and local and state legislation. All of these may influence how the institution conducts its affairs and, by association, how they make their presence felt within the campus housing programs as well.

Enrollment Projections

Total enrollment in colleges and universities rose by 23% between 1989 and 2002. According to Hussar (2005, section 2), colleges and universities can expect an increase in enrollment of close to 17% between 2002 and 2014. Men's enrollment is expected to go up by 12% and women's, by 21% during that same time. Undergraduate student enrollment may rise by up to 16% as well as 21% for graduate students. The total number of high school graduates increased 6% between 1988 and 2002 and is projected to grow an additional 10% through 2014. Meanwhile, other enrollment projections include an increase of 16% for 18- to 24-year-old students and of 5% for students 35 and older. All of these factors will likely trigger a need for more residential space on campus.

To face this increased demand, housing officers will have to consider expanding the use of current facilities (fewer double rooms used as singles) so that all residence halls are used to capacity as well as constructing more residence halls or utilizing privatized off-campus housing options. Some universities with freshmen residency requirements already have been balancing their commitment to house freshmen with the successful residential communities that keep students in the halls even after they are freshmen. If the numbers of 18- to 24-year-old students entering colleges and universities grow larger, as predicted, housing and residence life programs will face difficult decisions.

How do housing programs incorporate the best of both worlds? Can there be adequate space on campus for entering freshmen as well as more space set aside in apartments and suite arrangements for upperclass and graduate students? Graduate students have different expectations for housing programs. Experience has shown that graduate students value their privacy so much that single rooms are a minimum requirement – even if they must share bathrooms. Depending on the requirements of a particular graduate program, housing programs might be called on to offer more transitional housing for those students coming to campus for one or two days a week. Summer occupancy numbers easily could balloon if graduate programs target people such as educators, who typically have those months free,

According to the 2005 almanac of *The Chronicle of Higher Education*, women comprise 56.6% of current enrollment at the nation's 4,236 public and private institutions of higher education. Minorities make up 29.4% and foreign students, 3.6%. The increasing diversity of college students requires a comprehensive or holistic approach to the educational experience. Institutions should research their students to know who they are (demographics, geographies) and what their needs are as individuals (when practical to do so), especially as members of subgroups. Gender, sexual orientation, and ethnicity should be considered. However, culture, heritage, and familial experience are less tangible factors that also directly play into a student's probability of success on campus.

International Student Populations

An article by Johnson (2003) in *The Chronicle of Higher Education* states, "foreign students bring important and growing educational benefits to American colleges. They add diversity to the student body, they provide the first opportunities that many Americans have for close and extensive contacts with foreigners, and they fill perennially underenrolled science courses that colleges would otherwise find difficult to offer" (p. 1).

More than half of all international students in the United States enroll in doctoral degree-granting and research universities. The Institute of International Education (2005) reports that in 2004-'05, these universities were the only higher education institutions to show a decline in international student enrollment. However, "this was partially offset by increases reported by other types of institutions (master's, baccalaureate, associates and specialized institutions)."

Housing international students can present numerous issues for consideration. Should international students room together? Should space in residence halls be set aside and held for late enrollees since it is often difficult for students from other countries to obtain visas in a timely manner?

Faculty and others who work directly with international student programs may expect housing staff to make exceptions for international students who do not want to live or eat on campus. Family culture may be cited as a reason to allow a young female student from Vietnam to reside off-campus with her 18-year-old male cousin. This living arrangement is fraught with potential problems, not the least of which is the inability of the student to connect with the campus community. Parents who live thousands of miles away can easily dismiss the developmental advantages of living on campus.

Higher enrollment of 17- to 19-year-old students from underdeveloped countries increases the need for housing administrators to learn more about the cultures of the students they intend to house. Family housing, or housing for nontraditional students, will no longer be adequate for the growing number of international students. Many international graduate students bring a spouse and children to live with them in the United States. While the student is in classes, the spouse and children remain in on-campus housing, with little or no understanding of the English language or the American school system. The housing staff find themselves acting as social workers to arrange appropriate resources for family members trying to assimilate into life in the United States.

Housing staffers learn quickly that gender and culture have a significant impact on the level of assistance they are able to offer international family members. In the past, housing staff could expect international student families to take on the characteristics of their U.S. neighbors. Today, many international students look to retain the customs of their homeland. For example, Chinese families often raise their children with the help of an extended network of close family members. Housing staff must understand that a Chinese mother may not comprehend why she cannot leave her small children unattended.

In the November 28, 2003, issue of the *Chronicle of Higher Education*, a special report authored by Schmidt indicated that the largest minority group in the United States was Hispanics. Schmidt (2003) stated, "Hispanic students are having a profound influence" (p. 1) on college campuses. College housing programs may be faced with a need to reevaluate family housing policies to provide for extended family presence. Citing a report by the Pew Hispanic Center, Schmidt notes that "an emphasis on close family ties is one characteristic shared by most Latinos regardless of national origin or income, and among Latino immigrants this often translates into an expectation that children will live with their parents until they marry" (p. 5). Geographic proximity of Latino family members may distract the student from academic achievement when family needs are prominent.

The enrollment trends that will influence universities and college housing programs also will affect the economic picture of higher education. The concern about the cost of attending college continues to present challenges for the academy.

Economic Aid

According to Hall (2003), with the influx of a more diverse student population entering higher education, the most important action colleges and universities can take is to offer grants to students from low- and moderate-income families. This may require housing operations to become more involved in university financial aid by looking at creative ways to provide housing to low-income individuals. As costs rise on campuses, housing operations could be asked to contribute a higher rate than in the past to scholarships and grants in aid. The self-supporting operations are going to need to examine the effect of this request on the housing costs for all residential students. There continues to be a call for better financial support for needy students. Colleges that strive day in, day out to provide educational opportunities for all students are struggling to contain costs and to create new avenues for aid.

Financial pressures and decreasing public support are leading to higher percentage increases (in cost of tuition) at public institutions (Denning, 2003). "Public confidence has eroded because there is a belief that many colleges are not operating as efficiently as they should" (p. 1). With this rise in the cost of attendance being absorbed via higher tuition costs, access to higher education is a problem for some students. Financial pressures are forcing more students to take loans and to work. According to Farrell (2005), a record percentage of students work while attending college and expect to take on large chunks of debt to pay their tuition. It must be remembered that a number of studies have shown that working more than 20 hours a week increases the likelihood that a student will drop out of college.

College housing programs need to recognize this additional burden and to keep this in mind when setting rates. Students will continue to look at reducing their costs to attend colleges, and if housing programs do not reduce costs and operate efficiently and effectively, then many students will not be able to afford to live on campus. Housing officials must be upfront about the costs of running the program on their campus. As institutions try to keep tuition reasonable, housing programs may be asked to contribute more significantly to institutions' bottom lines through additional administrative costs and subsidies, which will impact the affordability of living on campus compared to the local off-campus market. Housing staff need to be able to demonstrate the true cost of living on campus, be open about budgets, and to help stakeholders understand how money is spent and why. Benchmarking costs with other similar housing programs to show how they compare is crucial to educate the student population and the campus community as a whole.

Housing programs should better define their roles in the educational process of the student so they're not seen as just money generators for an institution. Housing programs need to align their goals with the mission of the institution as well as with the state's agenda for higher education. Without this alignment, it is easier for legislators and others to make erroneous assumptions about the value of the on-campus experience. As state lawmakers decide on the level of appropriations they are willing to provide higher education, they want to know that institutions are spending the money wisely. They want institutions to meet their goals for education and want students to get what they pay for in terms of their educational experiences. This same level of accountability will begin taking place in university support functions that are outside the main teaching mission. Housing professionals need to define what they do to enhance the educational experiences of students and the value the on-campus experience has on students' success. The various stakeholders, including parents and legislators, want to see the value of the money spent. If that cannot be shown, then many questions will arise as to the necessity of the program or service. In an article published in *The Chronicle of Higher Education*, Davies (2003) contends, "the discussions [of the rising cost of college] should center on the services that are being provided in order to help an individual become an economically self-sufficient, productive member of society" (p. 3). Additionally, housing programs need to demonstrate how they add to the local and state economy. Localized studies need to be done to show the impact that the on-campus students have on the local economy.

A challenge that several college housing programs (both at public and private institutions) face is the condition of the facilities. The costs to maintain decades-old residence halls continue to rise. Deferred maintenance and general upkeep, notwithstanding modernization, have forced many institutions to raise rates to cover these costs. Institutions cannot divert money from their academic mission nor can they pass the total cost of these upgrades directly to the students. If they do, then the accessibility and affordability factor comes back into play. Colleges and universities have put off spending money on construction and repairs as public higher education institutions have suffered deep cuts in their state budgets. This is counterproductive to the pressure that colleges are facing for new facilities. Modernizing is important to keep up with the expectations of students, parents, and others (Schmidt, 2005). Housing operations should explore additional sources of revenue to supplement revenue from rent. Housing directors will need to take a more entrepreneurial approach to running programs on college campuses.

One piece of legislation that could provide some relief in this area is House of Representatives 1548 (2005) – The Collegiate Housing and Infrastructure Act of 2005, and House of Representatives 3908 (2005)—Charitable Giving Act of 2005. Since many housing programs on college campuses have Greek housing as part of their residential stock, this act furnishes a mechanism in which money can be spent to provide, improve, operate, or maintain collegiate housing that may involve more than incidental social, recreational, or private purposes. These grants will be deductible for tax purposes as long as all active members of the organization are full-time students. This requirement will force universities to maintain very accurate records and documentation of housing lists and membership.

The outsourcing of services on a college campus may be a way to reduce operating costs and concentrate tuition dollars on the academic mission of the institution and still provide services to students. Some of the most prestigious universities are increasingly contracting out portions of their campus operations. According to Gose (2005), "the fear that once permeated the academy of corporate intrusion have given way to soul searching over whether the typically higher costs of self-operation are worth continuing" (p. 1). Smaller colleges may have the most to gain from outsourcing because they often lack both the financial resources and the staff expertise to handle auxiliary operations on their own. But outsourcing has challenges of its own. When an institution is considering outsourcing, it must have a clear understanding why it wants to pursue this direction. Is it to reduce costs, eliminate personnel problems, upgrade facilities, enhance programs and services, or whatever? Without a clear vision and set of goals that can guide the decision-making process for outsourcing, an institution can incur more costs and problems than originally thought.

Housing programs on campuses are not immune to the outsourcing dilemma. Even though housing has traditionally not been one of the first to be outsourced, it is an area that promotes discussion. With the growth of privatized housing companies, the cost of running self-operations on campus, and the burden many schools are placing on the housing program to help subsidize institutional costs, the outsourcing of the housing program fosters much debate. It is imperative again that housing officials continue to demonstrate their contributions to student learning and to make sure that they are running an efficient program while maintaining a high level of effectiveness.

Security Issues

Companies like Strategic Technology Group of Milford, Massachusetts, have found that campus security departments today are finding it necessary to integrate security systems, upgrade access control systems, and expand closed-circuit television systems (CCTV) in response to "a very tight regulatory environment and horrific liability exposures today" (Fickes, 2004, p. 1). Fickes points to laws with familiar names like the 1998 Clery Act which requires the collection and disclosure of campus crime statistics. The Family Educational Rights and Privacy Act (FERPA) of 1974 focuses on student privacy requirements. The Health Insurance Portability and Accountability Act (HIPAA) of 1996 also focuses on student privacy requirements. The Gramm-Leach-Bliley Act requires updates related to the security of financial data, and the Sarbanes-Oxley Act alters financial reporting requirements. There are also various state laws that have forced college and university security departments to increase their reliance on security technology, which requires expenditure of funds.

Fickes (2004) cites a statement by Adam Thermos, a consultant who specializes in advanced technology applications for security, that "campus security staff find themselves on the front lines. Anything that happens on campus – from date rape, to murder, to IT encroachments – lands at their feet" (p. 1). The laws in place do not require a campus to install numerous cameras in various places around campus, but they do require university administrators to exhibit reasonable care in enhancing the security of the campus environment. Security issues on campus have a major connection with on-campus housing. Students should have the means to travel from class, libraries, and late-night events back to their residence halls safely. It is crucial that housing professionals are able to articulate that even with all of the appropriate "hardware" available and in place to enhance security in the residence halls, student safety depends on individual choices that are made and cannot always be controlled by the university.

Legal Issues

Legal issues concerning higher education have grown significantly in scope and impact in the past five decades. Housing administrators know that housing a microcosm of the nation's population in residence halls and apartments on campus means almost routine involvement in the myriad legal issues confronted by university lawyers. In the May 27, 2005, issue of the *Chronicle of Higher Education*, White cites an article by J. Peter Byrne, first published in *The Yale Law Journal* in 1989, that defined institutional autonomy as "a First Amendment right of the university itself – understood in its corporate capacity – largely to be free from government interference in the performance of core educational functions." White indicates that "today it's fair to say that institutional autonomy is under relentless assault by legislators, government administrators, and others who presume to know better than faculty members and academic administrators how to make financial, managerial, and even pedagogical judgments affecting campus life" (p. 3). Clearly, housing officials need to have a close relationship with the legal counsel on campus for questions ranging from facility issues to programming to contracts.

Freedom of speech impacts the type of programming possible. Bringing a controversial speaker to campus is one way to offer students an opportunity to broaden their intellectual horizons, but this also involves heightened emotions and potential for disorderly conduct that may spill over into life in the residence halls. As an article in *The Chronicle of Higher Education* states, "Colleges are places where people pay and get paid to express themselves, but one person's articulation of a challenging or unpopular idea can be another's wantonly unacceptable provocation" (White, 2005).

Other legal issues that university lawyers deal with today include:

- The parameters of protest and the protection of unpopular speech and debate about social and political issues.
- Attempts by universities to suspend or expel students for racial discrimination in higher education.
- Whether students have the right to associate and form organizations that promulgate unpopular political and social topics.
- The freedom of the campus press.
- Employment discrimination laws.

College administrators vary in how well they work with lawyers. Many officials are knowledgeable about the law and its relation to policy issues. In the future, the practice of higher education law will continue to become more specialized, along with the addition of administrative responsibilities for counsel. One question that institutional leaders need to address is whether the general counsel department is a policy-making entity of the institution. If so, many other issues arise including allowing risk management to dictate programming, both educational and otherwise. Housing officials need to be knowledgeable about potential risks and liability issues to know when to consult their general counsel. If they are not, then the general counsel could fall into a policy-making role that could inhibit the successful operation of a residential program. When acting in a policy-making role, general counsels are likely to err on the side of caution, thus confounding the developmental and educational approach to programming on campus.

Parental Issues

Residential students spend a significant portion of their time at college in their residence hall room or in the rooms of friends. Housing staff inevitably will become involved in conversations with parents of residence hall students who are trying to resolve any number of issues that range from academic problems to social and developmental troubles. In learning more about today's Millennial students, it appears that communication between them and their parents is frequent and positive, even after the students arrive at college. Millennial students seek advice from their parents instead of making independent decisions. Technological advances in cell phones, instant messaging, and e-mail have greatly enhanced connectivity and communication between parents and students. In addition, Millennial students report significant levels of stress and anxiety, especially as compared to previous generations. Parents of Millennial students have been involved in their children's lives from infancy. They have worked hand-in-hand with teachers, beginning in preschool and continuing through high school. The intention of parents has been to support their students' success. Now that their students have entered college, the message from the college administration is that parents are no longer welcome and that "higher education does not allow the same level of involvement" and "parents of Millennial have higher expectations of colleges and universities than their predecessors, expect greater involvement in decisions that impact their students, and demand rapid and favorable institutional responses to their concerns" (Keppler, Mullendore, & Carey, 2005 p. 12).

It is extremely important that student affairs professionals develop a good understanding of how parents are now involving themselves in the lives of their sons and daughters on campuses. *Partnering with the Parents of Today's College Student* (2005) offers an excellent suggestion:

> Create a well-crafted internal university position that can help the staff persuade parents that: (a) their concerns are important, but not uncommon; (b) the institution hears concerns like theirs routinely; and (c) the institution has a track record of developing thoughtful policies and practices that have been successful in meeting the needs of those who came before them and are likely to be successful in also assisting their students. (p. 58)

Housing administrators should initiate the same type of policies as an aid to housing staff who must interact with parents who are upset or angry about a perceived injustice to their son or daughter.

Governmental Issues

The involvement of parents in the lives of their students does not stop with university administrators. Lipka (2005) says, "more and more parents are taking their concerns, frustration, and complaints to state legislators" and "legislators are increasingly intervening in a range of student-life issues" (p. 1). If parents feel their concerns are not taken seriously or dealt with in a timely matter, they want to make it a public issue and involve government officials. Administrators can grow frustrated with responding to proposed legislation that is a result of parental concerns, but communication with lawmakers has become a greater part of their job.

Colleges and universities are spending more time, energy, and money on the legal aspects associated with many issues on campus. The increase of expectations from both students and parents, spurned by higher tuition costs and the consumer orientation of society in general, will continue to affect how housing programs operate in the future (Santora & Kaplan, 2003).

Two options are available in addressing the increasing role of the legal system in higher education. Universities and, more specifically, housing programs can react as issues arise or they can seek to be proactive by reducing potential issues in the first place. Housing directors must be vigilant in identifying potential legal pitfalls in the way they do business and in what issues may impact the community they are trying to develop on campus. To be proactive, using the resources on campus such as risk management, general counsels, and affirmative action offices during the decision-making process may help to alleviate potential problems down the road as housing directors try to move their programs forward. Housing directors need to have the knowledge to identify potential legal implications and know when to seek guidance.

Another area that may potentially influence housing operations on campus could be revisions to the Fair Labor Standards Act (FLSA). Discussions have revolved around what impact FLSA could have on campus employment. It is likely that some jobs on campus currently defined as exempt will now be eligible for overtime pay, which has many institutions concerned about ballooning payrolls (National Association of Student Personnel Administrators [NASPA] "Fair Labor"). Positions such as hall directors and even resident assistants may be affected. The potential cost to a housing program would be astronomical and could even impact the way communities are developed on campus. Housing staff must continually evaluate the job requirements of these positions to ensure that there are no complications with regard to FLSA. Over the years, student positions have been seen as "off limits," but as graduate students push the envelope with regard to assistantships, it could be a matter of time before other student employment positions come under scrutiny. This author has had to explain to his human resources area what the impact of categorizing the resident assistant position into a nonexempt position would have on the residence hall system, both programmatically and financially.

Conclusion

As colleges and universities feel the pressures of external forces, residential housing programs will too. For now and in the future, housing programs need to be proactive in anticipating potential pressures from the outside. If programs wait until the pressures are upon them, it will be too late to react, causing mandates that may impede their mission.

In looking at future enrollment trends, both from an ethnic point of view as well as from a customer point of view, housing programs will need to be in tune with the demographics of current middle-and high-school students. Additionally, research on this group of future college students needs to be part of the literature that housing professionals keep at their nightstands for review. By examining and being cognizant of the trends at the secondary level, housing professionals will be able to plan for and anticipate correctly the needs and desires of incoming students.

With advances in technology, students' wants and expectations change constantly. The professional who is not in tune with that information will not be able to plan accordingly. Remember, students' desires change rapidly, while change in higher education is equated to moving an ocean liner on dry dock. It happens very slowly. Adequate planning with appropriate supporting research will enable housing professionals to meet the ever changing needs and demands of students.

Besides being able to plan from a programmatic and amenities standpoint, tracking demographic changes and the needs of the next generation will allow housing professionals to recruit and train staff to meet not only today's needs, but tomorrow's as well. If housing professionals do not stay abreast of the potential shift in demographics, then there could be certain ramifications. If government feels that the new generation of students is not being accommodated, legislative mandates could force programmatic and facilities changes.

Parents are more vocal and want what they want for their children. Also, if housing professionals are not meeting the new demands and needs of students, then, as with any market-driven business, students will vote with their feet and move off campus or transfer to another institution. Campus housing will need professionals who can anticipate and react accordingly to help meet the university's goal of bringing the institution to the next level.

One of the greatest challenges for meeting the needs of the students is ensuring that facilities are appropriate. This cannot be just from an amenities standpoint, but also from a financial one. As budgets become tighter and institutions are looking at ways to reduce costs or increase revenues, housing programs are very attractive enterprises. Private companies will promise that they can do it better and cheaper, while financial officers will try to persuade the governing boards, including the presidents, that the housing department can generate revenue and should be used to supplement institutional resources. Both of these pressures will require housing professionals to be more efficient and effective in their delivery of services. One of those services is the type of housing facilities they have on hand to meet the market. As states try to reduce costs by not funding capital projects or allowing the sale of bonds for residential facilities, housing professionals are going to be stretched to maximize an opportunity when faced with having to build new facilities or renovate existing ones. The era of facilities having life spans longer than 40 or 50 years is no longer viable because it is very hard to anticipate the future physical as well programmatic needs of students.

Planners need to look at designing facilities that allow for maximum flexibility now and in the future. Planners should look at designing buildings that have a strong structure but should allow for flexible interior space that can be renovated at a lower cost to respond to the changing needs of students. Load-bearing walls, conduit, and HVAC systems, which allow for the most flexibility in the future, should be in the forefront of planners' minds. A building that is built in the traditional way and that requires restructuring to meet new needs is neither cost-effective nor practical anymore. Multi-use facilities will enhance the life of the facilities. Additionally, facilities that can be adapted to meet institutional needs with minimum costs are a must. Demonstrating that a facility can meet both the short- and long-term needs of an institution will be easier to put forth as institutions plan for the future.

Also, legislators, in their desire to protect public interests, want to be able to demonstrate that they are good stewards of the states' resources and will appreciate this forward-thinking. Housing professionals need to be at the table when institutional design decisions are made. These are the professionals who realize how the residential component can affect not just the structures on campus, but also the feel for campus. Housing professionals understand that residential buildings should not be seen just as an afterthought in the planning process but as a vital component of the type of community the institutions want to develop.

How do housing professionals plan for the future? Remaining informed and knowledgeable about the external forces influencing programs and services is essential. Successful housing programs must link program costs to a university's student-learning objectives. Establish goals and objectives that are clearly integral to the learning component of the university experience. Legislators must acknowledge that on-campus housing programs are linked to students' academic and personal success. Housing programs must be seen as an extension of the academic mission and not as just bricks and mortar. Faculty members may be quick to dismiss the budgetary needs of the residence life program as unimportant in relation to the need for money for the classroom. Housing professionals must forge cooperative ties with academics on campus. Use those ties to educate faculty about what you do and how your program affects student success.

Housing professionals must understand the demographics of their service region while not neglecting the students living on campus from outside that service region and what their characteristics may be. They also must consider the local economy, understand and keep abreast of employment trends in their region, and support efforts to increase needs-based financial assistance for those students from depressed (economic) regions.

Jim Grimm, director of university housing at the University of Florida from May 1977 to June 2000, authored an online article in *Reslife.Net (n.d.)* that included thoughts and ideas about the future of the housing profession taken from a book titled *Peak Experiences,* edited by Norb Dunkel and Paul Jahr and published in 2000. Grimm quoted John Schuh, professor of education and director of the higher education program at Iowa State University, who stated that "of one thing we can be sure: the future will be shaped as much by external forces as internal" and "in preparing for the future, the savvy housing officer will develop plans by paying careful attention to publications and reports related to the country's economic health and social trends" (p. 4). It behooves housing professionals to keep up to date on their state legislature and any bills up for vote that may affect the on-campus residential program.

Grimm also included comments from Ken Stoner, then director of housing at the University of Kansas which remind us that "process cannot out weigh outcomes" (p. 6). Stoner shares the following:

> There is an old Arabic proverb that says, "A dog barks in the night, but the caravan moves on!" To be successful, all university administrators, including directors of student housing, must find ways to keep moving toward established goals. One concern for the future is what appears to be an increasing tendency for the caravan to stop in an effort to quiet the barking dogs along the way. We must find mechanisms to keep the caravans of progress moving. Processes are designed to facilitate action, not to prevent action from occurring. (p. 6)

Overall, there are many external pressures that have had and will continue to have an impact on colleges and universities. Housing programs—even self-supporting enterprises—cannot operate in isolation. Housing directors must be aware of the potential land mines out there. As technology increases, policies must be developed and updated to ensure compliance with federal and state guidelines for open records, academic freedom, and use of the Internet. It was hard to imagine 10 to 15 years ago the impact the Internet would have on student learning, and it is even harder to predict what will be available in the future that will have the same type of effect. The government will constantly be involved in exploring legislation and policies that will regulate campuses, including the release and use of student information. Helwick (2004,) says, "the privacy of the individual versus public accountability dilemma will continue to be debated." It is imperative that housing programs use the information available in trying to predict the next great challenge or issue that lies before them if they are going to be successful in moving their programs forward. Preparation and planning are two important tools that can aid professionals in anticipating the future.

References

Bickel, R.D., & Ruger, P.H. (2004, June 25). The ubiquitous college lawyer [Electronic version]. *The Chronicle of Higher Education.* Retrieved April 29, 2005, from http://chronicle.com/prm/weekly/v50/i42/42b00101.htm

Davies, G. (2003, May 2). Colleges bring better lives...but who will pay [Electronic version]. *The Chronicle of Higher Education.* Retrieved April 29, 2005, from http://chronicle.com/prm/weekly/v49/i34/34b02001.htm

Denning, G. (2003, August 15). Is tuition going up too fast, or are colleges caught in an economic bind? [Electronic version]. [Letter to the editor]. *The Chronicle of Higher Education.* Retrieved April 29, 2005, from http://chronicle.com/prm/weekly/v49/i49/49b00402.htm

Farrell, E.F. (2005, February 4). More students plan to work to help pay for college [Electronic version]. *The Chronicle of Higher Education.* Retrieved April 29, 2005, from http://chronicle.com/prm/weekly/v51/i22/22a00101.htm

Fickes, M. (2004, May). More security technology on campus [Electronic version]. *College Planning & Management.* Retrieved July 17, 2005, from http://www.peterli/com/archive/cpm/682.shtm

Gose, B. (2005, January 28). The companies that colleges keep [Electronic version]. *The Chronicle of Higher Education.* Retrieved April 29, 2005, from http://chronicle.com/prm/weekly/v51/i21/21b00101.htm

Grimm, J. (n.d.). *Some collective thoughts on the future direction of the housing profession.* Retrieved July 17, 2005, from Reslife.net Web site: http://www.reslife.net/html/administrative_1200a.html

Hall, K.L. (2003, June 20). The biggest barrier to college isn't race [Electronic version]. *The Chronicle of Higher Education.* Retrieved April 29, 2005, from http://chronicle.com/prm/weekly/v49/i41/41b02001.htm

Helwick, C. (2004, June 25). Pressing legal issues: 10 views of the next 5 years [Electronic version]. *The Chronicle of Higher Education.* Retrieved April 29, 2005, from http://chronicle.com/prm/weekly/v50/i42/42b00401.htm

Hussar, W.J. (2005). *Projections of education statistics to 2014* (NCES 2005-074). Washington, DC: U.S. Department of Education, National Center for Education Statistics, U.S. Government Printing Office.

Institute of International Education. (2005, November 14). U.S. sees slowing decline in international student enrollment in 2004/05 [Electronic version]. *The Open Doors Report.* Retrieved December 1, 2005, from http://www.opendoors.iienetwork.org

Johnson, V. (2003, April 11). The perils of homeland security [Electronic version]. *The Chronicle of Higher Education.* Retrieved April 29, 2005, from http://chronicle.com/weekly/v49/i31/31b00701.htm

Keppler, K. , Mullendore, R.H., & Carey, A. (Eds.). (2005). *Partnering with the parents of today's college students.* Washington, DC: National Association of Student Personnel Administrators.

Lipka, S. (2005, December 16). State legislators as co-pilots [Electronic version]. *The Chronicle of Higher Education.* Retrieved December 15, 2005, from http://chronicle.com/weekly/v52/i17/17a02201.htm

National Association of Student Personnel Administrators Center for Public Policy, Policy Issue Summaries. (n.d.). *Bryan's law*. Retrieved May 9, 2005, from http://www.naspa.org/policy/issues.cfm

National Association of Student Personnel Administrators Center for Public Policy, Policy Issue Summaries. (n.d.). *Campus fire safety*. Retrieved May 9, 2005, from http://www.naspa.org/policy/issues.cfm

National Association of Student Personnel Administrators Center for Public Policy, Policy Issue Summaries. (n.d.). *Fair Labor Standards Act (FLSA) – What you need to know*. Retrieved May 9, 2005, from http://www.naspa.org/policy/issues.cfm

National Association of Student Personnel Administrators Center for Public Policy, Policy Issue Summaries. (n.d.). *Fraternity Charitable Giving Act*. Retrieved May 9, 2005, from http://www.naspa.org/policy/issues.cfm

National Association of Student Personnel Administrators Center for Public Policy, Policy Issue Summaries. (n.d.). *Garret Lee Smith Memorial Act*. Retrieved May 9, 2005, from http://www.naspa.org/policy/issues.cfm

National Association of Student Personnel Administrators Center for Public Policy, Policy Issue Summaries. (n.d.). *Honest in Campus Justice Act*. Retrieved May 9, 2005, from http://www.naspa.org/policy/issues.cfm

National Association of Student Personnel Administrators Center for Public Policy. (2005, March). This week in Washington. *This Week in Public Policy, 58*. Retrieved May 9, 2005, from http://www.naspa.org/policy/thisweek.cfm

Santora, K. C., & Kaplan, W. A. (2003, April 18). Preventive law: How colleges can avoid legal problems [Electronic version]. *The Chronicle of Higher Education*. Retrieved April 29, 2005, from http://chronicle.com/prm/weekly/v49/i32/32b02001.htm

Schmidt, P. (2003, November 28). Academe's Hispanic future [Electronic version]. *The Chronicle of Higher Education*. Retrieved April 29, 2005, from http://chronicle.com/weekly/v50/i14/14a00801.htm

Schmidt, P. (2004, June 11). A public vision for public colleges [Electronic version]. *The Chronicle of Higher Education*. Retrieved April 29, 2005, from http://chronicle.com/weekly/v50/i40/40a01601.htm

Schmidt, P. (2005, January 7). Facilities: Playing catch-up on maintenance [Electronic version]. *The Chronicle of Higher Education*. Retrieved April 29, 2005, from http://chronicle.com/weekly/v51/i18/18a00901.htm

White, L. (2005, May 27). Which legal issues will keep colleges busy in the year 2012? [Electronic version]. *The Chronicle of Higher Education*. Retrieved December 11, 2005, from http://chronicle.com /weekly/v51/i38/38b00101.htm

White, W. (2005, December 16). Students, parents, colleges: Drawing the lines [Electronic version]. *The Chronicle of Higher Education*. Retrieved December 15, 2005, from http://chronicle.com/weekly/v52/i17/17b01601.htm

▫11▫

Financial Pressures on Higher Education and Housing

Ernest R. Goeres, Ph.D.

T he survival of most higher education institutions (HEIs) depends on sustained growth in student recruitment and retention. Along with their consideration of tuition costs, students and parents alike make their college choices based on the safety and attractiveness of the campuses, the facilities, and how both contribute to the overall development of students. Of special interest are residence halls, where college students spend much of their time. It is extremely important for campus student housing to be attractive, safe, and affordable to help institutions recruit and retain students.

To remain viable partners in the education of students, housing and residence life directors must become effective leaders in the largest sense of the word. They must understand the variety of challenges housing directors face, the general financial pressures on colleges and universities, the cumulative financial impact on student accessibility, and students' expectations for residence living and dining.

General Context

Auxiliary service units make up a significant part of any college or university budget. As such, they face the same financial pressures of the larger institution to which they belong. At the same time, auxiliary service units must fulfill institutional expectations if they are to contribute to the overall mission of the college or university. This is especially true of housing and residence life operations, which are expected to generate sufficient revenue to not only cover day-to-day operating expenses, construction and renovation loans, and emergency needs but also pay for scheduled repairs and alterations as well as overhead costs to central administration.

Revenues to meet these obligations are typically raised through student fees. Room and board fees represent a significant portion of students' college expenses. According to the College Board (2005), these fees ranged from $6,222 a year at public HEIs to $7,434 a year at private HEIs in the 2004-05 academic year. In this same year, the College Board (2005) cited average total costs of $13,833 a year for resident students attending four-year public colleges and $29,541 a year for students in private colleges. Farrell (2005), using College Board figures, cites the 2005-06 average total attendance costs for resident students in four-year public institutions and private four-year institutions as $15,566 and $31,916, respectively. These figures are just the tip of a financial iceberg facing all colleges and universities as national and state economies continue to sputter following a major economic free fall in the previous decade.

General Financial Pressures on Colleges and Universities

The extent to which state and national economies are strong or weak has a direct effect on all HEIs, whether public or private. In recent years, there has been a significant decline in state economies, resulting in fiscal year deficits in most states. While the impact on all state agencies and state-funded programs has resulted in reduced funding, public HEIs have taken a disproportionate cut because of a sense by state policy makers, the legislature, and general public that priority should be given to funding other important state programs: public elementary and secondary education health and welfare and corrections and public safety. Many state lawmakers see higher education as a private good or luxury that should be supported by students and donors, rather than as a public good that merits state support. As a result, public HEIs have been forced to offset budget cutbacks through record-setting tuition and fees increases.

At the same time, there is pressure at the state and federal level to limit these increases to the national inflation rate or some other gross domestic product indicator, which likely will be far less than the tuition increase necessary for HEIs to offset the loss of state support. In fact, state support of public HEIs has gradually eroded so much that more than one of these public institutions has considered going private to gain greater independence in terms of setting tuition rates, controlling contractual activities, and developing personnel administration programs. In return for these freedoms, the institutions would sever all ties to the state. Another option would be to do as Maryland's St. Mary's College did in 1992 (Stickelmaier, 2004), when the school negotiated with the state an annual block amount of funds. As publicly funded HEIs gradually move from state-supported through state-assisted to state-located status, this trend may gain momentum. In the meantime, public HEIs will be forced to impose substantial tuition increases to offset decreasing state support.

There is a significant societal cost linked to substantially raising tuition:

decreased opportunities for children from low- and middle-income families to attend college. This is especially true for public land grant and state HEIs that were established, among other reasons, to democratize higher education by providing accessibility to the greater public.

While one might expect that some financial relief to students would come from college and university endowments, this was not to be the case in the beginning of the twenty-first century. A devastating bear market followed the stock market boom of the late 1990s. The results of a 2003 National Association of College and University Business Officers (NACUBO) endowment study show that

> Declining dollars from endowments will compound colleges' and universities' economic woes. The three-year bear market for stocks, which began in March, 2000, also drained parents' and students' savings, so demand for services and financial aid is rising. But fewer funds are available from any source.
>
> Donors are definitely feeling the pinch, too. And state revenues went down with the deflating bubble, making higher education a prime target of statehouse budget cutters. (McNamee, 2004b, pp. 16-17)

The impact of this stock market decline has been particularly hard on independent HEIs and especially so for those small institutions which typically operate within tight financial constraints. Lord (2003), citing an endowment management study, observes

> Institutions that rely significantly on endowment contributions to their operating budgets are facing tough decisions on staffing and program cutbacks. The study indicates that 29 of the 39 largest endowments belong to independent institutions. And, in general, budgets at independent institutions rely more heavily on the endowment contributions than those at tax-supported public institutions, where endowment spending is more likely to be allocated to scholarships and other short-term commitments. At certain independent colleges and universities, endowment spending may constitute up to 20 – 30 percent of the institution's overall budget. (pp. 32-33)

Small, independent institutions were hard hit in the early 2000s, according to Townsley (2005), in a NACUBO study of the impact on small, independent colleges.

> As losses intensified through 2002, the devastating effects began to tally up for small institutions' finances. Between 2000 and 2002, revenues fell 32.5% while expense growth rates remained persistent, for a loss of nearly $2.8 billion in net income. At the same time, the percentage of institutions reporting deficits went through the roof – from 15% in 2000 to half in 2001 to nearly 64% in 2002. (p. 20)

While the stock market has recovered somewhat as of this writing, the net loss to HEIs will be difficult to make up. Dick Anderson, NACUBO senior fellow, used information from Hammond Associates to predict how long it will take for institutions to recover from their losses:

> By using both average asset allocations and spending rules of endowment study participants and Monte Carlo simulations for expected returns of asset classes. . . . it's reasonable to expect that nominal endowment spending will not return to fiscal year 2002 levels until 2017. . . . it will take considerably longer to reach those levels in real (after inflation) terms. (Lord, 2003, p. 33)

A variety of other issues, some continuing, others new, that housing directors must deal with are many, varied, and complex. As Ryan (2003) states

> In years past, utilities, renovation, fire safety, maintenance, and employee benefits were issues on the student housing agenda. Today, those issues remain, joined by new challenges in the student housing financial environment. Terminology such as bandwidth, resnet, wireless, online services, ADA compliance, indoor air quality, sprinkler fitters, design-bid-build, and 24/7 is now relatively common in the student housing vernacular. (p. 59)

In addition, housing directors must deal with other issues such as implementing escrow payments for building and renovation loans, negotiating additional loans for planned expansion of housing facilities, and ensuring that occupancy and student rates are sufficient to pay central administration some percentage or set amount of overhead funds for services provided by the larger college or university. Inasmuch as housing directors are successful in generating a "profit" after meeting these commitments, there is always a danger that, in adverse financial conditions, this profit may become a very attractive "loan" pool to central administration to help balance the larger institutional budget. At the same time, governing boards have been known to put a limit on the percentage of unspent or uncommitted (contingency) funds that budget units may carry into the next budget year. Many administrators perceive this as a penalty for operating in a fiscally responsible manner.

Cumulative Financial Impact on Student Accessibility

What has been the financial impact on students (and their parents)? Today, a greater percentage of family income is needed to cover college costs than has ever been the case in the past. A National Center for Public Policy in Higher Education report, *Losing Ground* (as cited in "Americans are losing, 2002), identifies five national trends that have emerged in the past two decades:

- **Tuition increases have made college less affordable for most American families.** From 1980 to 2000, the percentage of average family income required to pay for tuition rose for all families, except for those with incomes in the top 20%. Low- and middle-income families experienced the largest increase. In 1980, tuition at public four-year colleges consumed 13% of family income for low-income families. By 2000, that figure had increased to 25%.
- **Federal and state financial aid grants have increased but have not kept pace with tuition hikes.** The average Pell grant award at a public four-year institution covered 98% of tuition in 1986 but only 57% in 1999. Both need-based and nonneed-based grants covered 75% of tuition in 1986 and 64% in 1999.
- **At all income levels, more families have been borrowing—and borrowing more—to pay for college.** Since 1980, federal financial aid has shifted from a grant-based to a loan-based program. The rich, as well as the poor, borrow to pay for college, but a higher percentage of poor students borrow, which results in a greater debt burden. The average cumulative debt of seniors in the bottom debt and income quartile grew from $7,629 in 1989 to $12,888 in 1999.
- **The sharpest increases in tuition always take place during times of economic adversity.** This was especially prevalent in the 1990s and early years of 2000.
- **State support has not kept pace with rising tuitions.** Although state appropriations to public institutions increased by 13% between 1980 and 1998, tuition rose a staggering 107%. (pp. 13-14)

This impact is even greater when several children in a family are of college age at the same time. While state and federal grants and loans have helped low- and middle-income students in the past, the impact of this support has been eroded as college enrollments continue to rise while increases in financial support have remained relatively the same when compared to the national rate of economic growth. At the federal level, there has been a shift in the last two decades from grants, which do not have to be repaid, to student loans. Current and former students face higher levels of indebtedness from their reliance on loans to pay for college expenses. Clark (2005, Steals and deals section), in an article about student loan consolidation, notes that

> Nearly two thirds of approximately 15 million undergraduates have federal student debt; the average debt to Uncle Sam upon graduation is $19,400. In addition, 40% of last year's 2.4 million graduate students borrowed an average of $15,500 from the federal government.

Clark goes on to point out that 735,000 families have borrowed an average of nearly $9,000 through the Parent Loan for Undergraduate Students (PLUS) in the past school year. And it appears that federal student loan availability will not improve in the near future. The federal budget request for the 2005-06 federal year, for example, has dramatic reductions in all domestic programs, many of which are education related. More specifically, the budget proposes the elimination of the Perkins Loan Program, designed for first-generation, low-income students. "Alarmed by the growing costs of the loan program," Clark (2005, Immediate payment section) reports, "Congress is considering a proposal to tie the interest rate on consolidated loans closer to the market. No matter what happens in Congress, mounting rates are bad news for tomorrow's college students." He finishes his admonition to parents and students to consolidate their student loans as quickly as possible by stating that, "Next year's crop of freshmen and parents will not only get socked by tuition increases that have generally exceeded inflation but will also have to pay thousands of dollars more on their college loans" (Immediate payment section).

At the same time, states dealing with financial difficulties have had to sharply limit or even reduce scholarship and need-based support programs for worthy students as they attempt to stay fiscally solvent. Those states that have implemented tuition-free scholarships based on academic performance in high school and high standardized college admission test scores (without considering family income or ability to pay) now find that, to provide continued support, it will be necessary to increase the qualifications for these awards to limit the number of eligible students. Other states that have these programs are now modifying them to include family financial support as part of the scholarship award eligibility. By doing so, states hope to limit the availability of such scholarships, further reducing the financial strain on the state's budget. However, all other things being equal, these adjustments will further limit access to college for low- and middle-income families. Hubbell and Lapovsky (2004) state that

> The increase in price at the public institutions is changing the landscape of higher education. The tuition gap in dollar terms between public and independent colleges is narrowing. Current public policies are moving away from increasing access. Other factors are also contributing to reduced access. Federal grants on a per-pupil basis have been flat for several years, which has led to a growth in the amount of tuition for which students and their families are responsible. In addition, the federal government's recent attempts to increase support for higher education through savings incentives and tax credits benefit the middle class, not the poor. (pp. 28-29)

Private HEIs are not without their unique problems as well. Many of the smaller ones (fewer than 1,000 students) continually operate on the brink of financial disaster because of increased operating costs, deferred physical plant maintenance and renovations, changing expectations of students in terms of campus amenities, and extreme competition for students. Because these institutions largely depend on student tuition for their operation and survival, they are under pressure to make the campus environment more attractive through such things as constructing recreation centers, modifying housing and residence halls to more closely reflect the homes from which students are coming, and providing all the technology expectations this new generation of students brings with them.

These expectations are difficult to address when the costs are covered almost solely from student tuition. As a result, private HEIs find that their tuition costs must be substantially increased. That, however, may make it difficult to attract students. These institutions are then forced to raise their tuition discount rates to make it financially feasible for low- and middle-income students to attend. Hubbell and Lapovsky (2004) point out that the current national discount rate for private institutions is between 36% and 42% of tuition and fees. These institutions will continue to have a difficult time balancing institutional needs with appropriate tuition rates and discounts to ensure sufficient enrollments to remain fiscally solvent and viable as higher education institutions. To the extent that the tuition or discount expense ratio is not appropriate, these institutions may well price themselves out of business, further reducing college accessibility to those who prefer education in a private rather than a public college.

Recently, some private institutions have dramatically slashed their published tuition and fee rates in an effort to increase enrollments. A closer look at this practice reveals that they correspondingly reduced their tuition discounts. As a result, students are not any better off financially than if the institution had not adopted such a policy in the first place. Compounding the problem for these institutions is the growing number of freshmen who need and receive institutional aid. In their analysis of a NACUBO survey of independent institutions and their tuition discounting policies in 2002, Hubbell and Lapovsky (2004) point out that the percentage of freshmen receiving institutional aid rose from 63% in 1990 to 81% in the fall of 2002.

The idea of tuition discounting has not gone unnoticed by publicly supported HEIs. One example of this can be seen at Miami University in Oxford, Ohio. Hubbell and Lapovsky (2004) report that

> Miami University just became the first public institution to adopt a full-cost pricing strategy. The university has raised its price to $18,000 for both in-state and out-of-state students for 2004 and will use a variety of aid/discount strategies to subsidize the price to different groups of students. (p. 26)

Archibald and Feldman (2004) add, "Under this plan Miami will return all state-appropriated funds directly to its Ohio resident students in the form of across-the-board grants and specific scholarships. (Archibald & Feldman, 2004).

Another example of discounting—including room and board in addition to tuition for out-of-state students—can be found at Slippery Rock University in Pennsylvania. Freshmen and transfer students who will be attending full time and have a 3.0 GPA receive a 29% discount on tuition and a 27% reduction in room-and-board costs (Hubbell & Lapovsky, 2004).

A recent idea that may gain momentum is for states to shift appropriations from institutions to students in the form of a savings account, scholarship, or voucher as is being proposed by the Colorado Blue Ribbon Panel on Higher Education for the 21st Century. "An amended version of this proposal has been adopted, and starting in the fall of 2005 most of the state appropriation—which formerly went to Colorado colleges and universities—will fund direct grants to students" (Archibald & Feldman, 2004, p. 27).

Past and continuing tuition increases and the associated difficulty in paying for a college education are just two factors that housing and residence life directors will have to deal with in the future. Other challenging issues include catching up with deferred maintenance, attempting to stay ahead of the technology curve, and meeting a new expansive and expensive set of student expectations for college living.

Changing Student Expectations

One major challenge confronting housing directors is the changing expectations of today's students. Most residence halls, built 30 to 40 years ago, were designed to accommodate students who came from homes where children shared rooms and the family shared one bathroom, personal items were far more limited in number and size, and recreational activities took place in public community settings. Students were relatively satisfied sharing limited floor space, sleeping four to a room in bunk-bed arrangements, and using community bathroom and shower arrangements.

Today, students have different ideas for their on-campus living and learning environments because of the homes in which they are raised. High on the lists of today's students as they consider college enrollment are privacy; expanded floor and storage space for computers and printers, stereo systems, refrigerators, and other electrical appliances; occupancy limited to one or two individuals; rooms wired for numerous electrical appliances and computer network connections; semiprivate bathrooms and showers; and recreational facilities and equipment. Modifying existing residence halls so they more closely resemble hotel facilities is expensive, yet necessary to attract and retain students in the boarding operations of the college or university.

Students want "the good life" in their living arrangements. An example of this is found in a new apartment complex being developed in Morgantown, West Virginia, home of West Virginia University. This new development, called "The District," is described by *Dominion Post* writer Gary Gray (2005) as

> more than a dorm or an apartment—it's closer to a mini-resort, with such goodies
> as The District Café, a swimming pool and 14-person heated spa, tanning facility,
> fitness center, a jogging trail and a free shuttle to campus. The District also offers

basketball and volleyball courts and a 24-hour computer lab with high-speed Internet access. (p. 1-A)

Also offered are one-year leases on two-, three-, and four-bedroom apartments and rents by the bedroom. Apartments feature private balconies, furniture and appliance packages, and private bathrooms in every bedroom. The bedrooms are equipped with full-size beds, a bath, shower, and walk-in closet. The living room area comes with a sectional couch and table, and a dining area contains a table and four chairs. The living room increases with size, according to the number of bedrooms. Community assistants, who are part-time students and work approximately 20 hours per week, support the academic success and personal growth of students in The District. Members of local fire departments will patrol the grounds to provide security and safety. A recreation center next to the café will be equipped with treadmills, free weights, and stationary bikes. A large, grassy area will be provided for sunbathing and "blanketing" activities. A shuttle bus will be provided to transport students to the various campuses of the university. The stated philosophy of the corporation providing these facilities is, "There's no comparison! After all—college is supposed to be fun" (Gray, 2005, pp. 1-A, 2-A). All of these services and surrounding amenities will be provided at a competitive cost to students and others who choose to reside there.

Besides the different set of expectations for their living arrangements discussed above, students have more complicated demands when it comes to dining services. For the most part, HEIs are finding that the traditional meal plan with breakfast, lunch, and dinner served at specific times at specific locations no longer meets student needs. Students today also want more flexibility in terms of food options, locations, availability, and physical settings and are willing to pay for these things. Hignite (2003), in describing contemporary student dining expectations, states that campus food services have gone upscale eclectic. She states that traditional students on campus today are a retail-oriented and individual-oriented culture. They demand round-the-clock service and have also been exposed to global cuisine like no other generation. She goes on to point out that successful food service programs have the following characteristics: made-to-order food, with the kitchens out front; provision for special diets, such as kosher, organic, locally grown, or health-centered; base-priced buffets, with extra-cost items, such as steak, lobster, or salmon; attractive food services available not only to meal-plan students but also to commuter students, upperclassmen living off-campus, faculty, parents, and guests; a wide variety of food options; flexible meal and payment plans; different eating venues, such as coffee kiosks, sushi bars, or ice cream stands; fast-food franchises in food-court settings; enhanced and attractive dining areas; convenience stores that stock food basics, such as milk, bread, and microwavable and other popular food items; continuous feeding availability to accommodate the various schedules of students; and dining plans that include the participation of off-campus restaurants.

While the emphasis on meeting students' dining needs is largely based on the consumer needs of traditional students, aged 18 to 22, issues of location, flexibility, cost, and convenience are also important to nontraditional students, many of whom commute to campus for late afternoon and evening classes. They must fit their nourishment needs into a tight schedule of work, parenting, classes, and commuting distances. This will become increasingly important with the current predictions for the continuing rise in the number of part-time, nontraditional student enrollments.

Challenges to the Housing Profession

While living and dining services are the primary concerns of housing professionals, there are other issues they must be prepared to deal with as well: enrollment changes, facilities maintenance and renovation, campus safety and security, student dining, health issues, and whether their programs contribute to positive lifestyles for students. Addressing these issues will be important to both students and parents.

Changing enrollments

Housing directors must be ready to navigate changing enrollment trends. For those HEIs facing increased enrollments, housing directors must deal with providing sufficient accommodations on either a temporary or permanent basis. Part of the issue is to determine whether the enrollment increase is a temporary spike or a more long-term trend. The same can be said for enrollment declines. Either situation requires directors to investigate a variety of options, their associated costs, and the extent to which each option best meets student needs and is cost-effective. Options for anticipated increases range from renting temporary space, working out housing arrangements with private businesses, and contracting for leased facilities to planning for new facilities. In terms of declining enrollments, the important issues become what to do with vacant facilities. In short, accurate enrollment projections are critical in the financial operation of housing units.

When enrollment estimates indicate a significant increase or decline, housing directors should not be rushed into making hasty decisions. Ryan (2003) points out

From a traditional student housing perspective, a surge in enrollment or new emphasis on the first-year experience may cause some members of the campus community to call for more housing on campus without first assessing the long-term demand. Conversely, a plunge in enrollment, empty floors or residence halls, or an overall shortage of campus office space could cause some members of the campus community to advocate for premature conversion of residence halls from student housing to other uses. Occupancy projections require an understanding of college or university strategic directions, demographics, past trends in enrollment and occupancy, and the off-campus market. (p. 61)

Facilities operation and maintenance

Another challenge for housing directors is the ongoing maintenance and renovation of housing facilities, much of which may have been deferred for a number of years. Medlin (2003), in writing about the accumulated deferred maintenance/renewal (ADM/R) in HEIs, sounds this alarm:

> Today, higher education would have to invest more than $500 billion to replace buildings, fixed equipment, and infrastructure. The many ancillary changes taking place within the higher education community during the late 1980s and throughout the 1990s have served to further exacerbate the problem of a swelling ADM/R backlog. Among these changes: rapidly escalating tuition increases; increased square footage of space to operate and maintain; major budget reductions; dozens of new, unfunded mandates from governmental regulations; and increased demand for the use of new technologies in classrooms, laboratories, offices, and dormitories. (p. 36)

While Medlin's figure of $500 billion refers to the needs of higher education in general, one can be sure that a good portion of this amount is associated with student housing facilities, because most were constructed during the 1950s and '60s. Ryan (2003) notes that, along with the normal repairs, alterations, and preventative maintenance issues that housing programs are dealing with, there are numerous and changing federal and state laws and codes that can require significant facilities upgrades: Those associated with the Americans with Disabilities Act and the United States Fire Administration (concerning student housing safety), as well as issues associated with toxic mold, asbestos, and campus security. Finally, an additional challenge for housing and residence life directors will be meeting the growing expectations of students for more amenities in their living arrangements.

Campus safety, security, and accessibility

The security and safety of the campus and its facilities will be an important factor in attracting students and parents to housing and residence life offered by the institution. Housing directors need to have at hand information that will assure both parents and students that campus safety is always at the top of the institution's priorities. What are the crime rates of the institution compared to other colleges or universities? How is security and safety provided to students who live in the residence halls? Are there well posted evacuation plans for the halls? Housing and residence life orientation programs should address safety issues and include plans to deal with emergency situations.

Are there personnel who live in the residence halls; what are their qualifications and training? It will be important to point out that security is maintained in and around the residence halls and that walking and parking areas are well lighted and monitored by security personnel. Are there facilities where students can park their cars during the week when they don't need them to get from one class to another? Students and parents may want to know what arrangements are made to accommodate students who stay on campus during vacation breaks when classes are not in session.

Are there ways to safely transport students between campuses, from town to campus and back and to the nearest airports and bus terminals and back at vacation times? Any arrangements with local transit operations to provide these services, as well as access to shopping centers, cultural events, and outlying areas should be described.

These will all be important selling points when discussing student-related travel security and safety issues. It is paramount that this information be shared with students and parents and that any questions they have about residence hall and campus safety concerns be answered.

Students and parents also may be interested in which campus facilities are accessible to those with physical handicaps. It will be important to point out the accommodations that have been made in terms of parking, restrooms, wheelchair accessibility, and general mobility by the institution on and around the campus.

Student dining

The availability, quality, and ambience of dining will be important to students and parents. How can food services best meet the needs of students? Horwitz (2005) suggests

> The best model to describe the spatially distributed, socially diffused, and food-centered contemporary campus is the ever-present distributed network—with a bite of something at every node. If one reviews the history of campus architecture to see how it gives form to everyday life—whose paths cross at meals, who sits face to face, and what activities go together—that new model reflects a major shift from the long traditions of the past. (p. 1)

Parents also will be particularly concerned about the dietary health of their children. Are food services outsourced or provided by the institution's employees? It will be important to point out the various food plan options for students. Will students have access to dining at any time of the day and on any part of the campus? Students and parents will want to know how healthy the meals are and who plans the menus, as well as the qualifications of those preparing the menus.

Are there food options available to accommodate cultural and ethical preferences and needs? At some institutions, meal plans include the purchase of food at off-campus local eateries. Are meals available during vacation periods for students staying on campus? It may be important to some parents and students to know if organic, locally grown produce and dairy products are used in the meal plans of an institution. These and other dietary health questions will be on the minds of students and parents as they consider enrolling in any institution.

Health and wellness issues

Students, and particularly parents, will be concerned about general health conditions of the campus, as well as the availability of and access to health and hospital services. For example, are students required to have had certain inoculations before they can live in campus housing? It would be good to share any arrangements to meet emergency needs and treatment of major and minor illnesses. Even though student health offices are not a formal component of housing and residence life operations, parents will want to know how these two organizations work together to ensure the health and safety of their children.

Positive lifestyles and academic success

Housing directors should be able to point out how housing and residence life operations contribute to the development of positive lifestyles, academic success, and personal growth of students. How closely does the housing program work with other units on campus to educate students about appropriate living habits?

It will be important to show how the housing operations encourage and support the integration of different cultures, races, religions, and nationalities to broaden students' appreciation of global-wide diversity. How do programs contribute to the personal growth of the students living in residence halls? Many institutions provide a variety of activities that emphasize alternatives to the "bar scene", organize cultural and sporting excursions to broaden students' horizons, highlight community service projects to acquaint students with civic responsibility, and sponsor programs that enhance opportunities for personal and positive student growth. Housing and residence life can be a major partner in these activities.

How does housing and residence life foster the academic success of students? Many institutions provide for the teaching of classes in residence life facilities and close accessibility to faculty mentors. They also make available learning centers, advisors, and computer facilities.

Optimizing operations

In striving to optimize the operations of housing and residence life as outlined above, directors will need to constantly look for ways to enhance the viability of their programs. Although the list could be endless, here is a sampling of ideas directors might consider:

- Outsource for goods and services.
- Host summer conferences for professional groups and high school students.
- Bring Greek operations back on campus (if they're currently off-campus).
- Prioritize room and apartment arrangements.
- Increase retention in housing facilities from year to year by foregoing fee increases.
- Conduct energy audits associated with HVAC systems and utilities costs to determine potential savings.
- Use advisory committees to monitor operations and processes with an eye toward increasing the effectiveness and efficiency of all operations.
- Elicit feedback from students who live and dine in the housing program to ensure their needs are being considered.

Conclusion

Directors must keep in mind the various responsibilities they have to students, parents, and the larger college or university. Students desire the good life while attending college and want to reside in attractive, up-to-date campus facilities with a variety of dining options. Even though parents share many of the same interests about campus living arrangements as their children, they have additional concerns, including safety, health, lifestyles, academic success, personal growth, and preparation for appropriate employment or graduate studies after graduation. As housing directors strive to be a partner in meeting these needs, they must juggle the past, present, and future: considering and implementing new initiatives while building on previous successes.

In terms of housing and dining services, directors must keep in mind that the days of dorms and one-size-fits-all meal plans are becoming an anachronism on most campuses today. Accommodating student needs in housing and dining services as well as meeting their expectations in other areas outlined above—all at competitive and attractive costs—will not only be a recruiting plus, it will probably do more than anything else to ensure the financial health of these operations. As importantly, meeting these needs will be a major factor in the success of an institution's students. Finally, housing directors will have to meet these needs in such a way that both parents and students feel that the associated costs are not only reasonable, but also attractive. To do so will require the enlightened leadership of housing and residence life directors.

References

Americans are losing ground when paying for college. (2002). *Business Officer*, *35*(12), 13-14.

Archibald, R.B., & Feldman, D.H. (2004). Funding students instead of institutions. *Business Officer, 38*(4), 27-32.

Clark, K. (2005, May 30). Payback time—attention, students, grads, and parents: Act now to lock in low rates on your college student loans. *U.S. News & World Report*. Retrieved October 14, 2005, from http://www.usnews.com/ usnews/biztech/articles/050530/loans.htm

College Board. (2005). Average college costs, 2004-5. *The Chronicle of Higher Education Almanac Issue 2005-6, 52*(1), 32.

Farrell, E.F. (2005). Public colleges tame costs of tuition. *The Chronicle of Higher Education, 52*(10). Retrieved November 7, 2005, from http://chronicle.com/ weekly/v52/i10/10a00101.htm

Gray, G. (2005, June 1). The district offers students the good life. *The Dominion Post*, pp. 1-A, 2-A.

Hignite, K. (2003). Food for thought. *Business Officer, 37*(5), 12-22.

Horwitz, J. (2005). Following the food: Where students eat. *The Chronicle of Higher Education, 51*(29). Retrieved August 17, 2005, from http://chronicle.com/weekly/v51/i29/29b02601.htm

Hubbell, L.L., & Lapovsky, L. (2004). Widening the higher education gateway. *Business Officer, 38*(3), 21-29.

Labovsy, L., & Hubbell, L.L. (2003). Tuition discounting continues to grow. Business Officer, 36(9), 22-23.

Lord, M. (2003). Experts on endowment: Coverage of NACUBO's 2003 endowment management forum. *Business Officer, 36*(11), 31-46.

McNamee, M. (2004a). The faculty factor. *Business Officer, 38*(3), 16-19.

McNamee, M. (2004b). Old principles, new rules. *Business Officer, 37*(8), 15-24.

Medlin, E. L. (2003). Deferred maintenance dilemma. *Business Officer, 36*(9), 35-37.

Ryan, M.A., (2003). Contemporary issues in student housing finance. In J.H. Schuh (Ed.), New directions for student services: contemporary financial issues in student affairs. 103. (59-71). San Francisco: Jossey Bass.

Stickelmaier, L. (2004). Trading dollars for independence. *Business Officer, 37*(10), 27-35.

Townsley, M.K. (2005). Recognizing the unrealized: Effective financial strategies for small, independent institutions on the brink require accounting and anticipation. *Business Officer, 38*(9), 19-26.

Accountability in Student Housing and Residential Life

John H. Schuh, Ph.D.

The external demands on housing officers are substantial. While housing officers work in an environment filled with considerable pressure to deliver a high-quality living and learning experience for students, they also have to meet fiscal challenges, keep facilities contemporary, and, in some cases, provide an attractive food service. What makes meeting fiscal challenges particularly difficult is that housing officers have limited control over the rates they charge (Schuh & Shelley, 2001). In short, housing staffs increasingly are being held accountable for their work, as is the case for many dimensions of higher education (Kuh, Kinzie, Schuh, Whitt, & Associates, 2005).

Dimensions of Accountability

At minimum, housing officers need to address four dimensions of accountability: how a housing department supports an institution's mission, the fiscal health of a department, the quality of services provided, and how living in residence halls contributes to student learning. Each of these dimensions will be addressed in detail.

Mission

Institutional missions provide a framework for the various units found in a college or university, and housing is no exception. Barr (2000, p. 25) wrote, "the mission of an institution influences all aspects of the day-by-day institutional life and the future growth and development of the college or university." For a residential institution, where a substantial proportion of students live or have lived on campus, the role of student housing may be central to the life of the campus. At a commuter campus, where a small percentage of students have the experience of living on campus, student housing is likely to be more of a peripheral operation.

Besides shaping the nature of the housing department, the mission will affect the expectations that an institution has for the housing program. For example, the following mission statement makes it clear that living on campus at this college is central to the student's experience: "St. Olaf College, a residential campus in Northfield, Minn., combines a leading liberal arts experience with the dynamic energy of a small university" (About St. Olaf, n.d.).

Much can be learned from mission statements in terms of the relative importance of living on campus and, presumably, the level of accountability campus leaders have for the housing department. That is not to say that leaders of housing departments that are relatively small and not central to an institution's mission will receive a free pass. Rather, the extent to which living on campus is a common experience for students will affect the level of attention the housing department receives and the expectations for its contributions to the student experience. Senior leaders of an institution that does not mention living on campus in its mission statement or emphasize that residence halls are integral to the student experience presumably will have a different perspective on the contribution of the housing department to the total student experience than they would on a campus where nearly all students live on campus.

Fiscal health

In difficult fiscal times, such as the current environment of higher education (Schuh, 2003), the press for fiscal accountability is clear and obvious. Institutions of higher education compete aggressively for students, and one of the dimensions of the competition is managing costs. At many colleges and universities, the cost of tuition and fees is less than that of room and board (Ryan, 2003; Schuh & Shelley, 2001). As institutions try to manage the cost of attendance, fees for room and board are integral elements of the equation.

But there is more to fiscal accountability than simply trying to keep costs competitive with other institutions. The other dimension is whether departmental resources are spent wisely. Housing officers are stewards of the money that students spend for room and board and, in effect, serve as their agents. That means resources must be spent in ways that provide the greatest return to students.

It means that funds devoted to food service, an important part of the residential living experience, should generate the best meals possible (however one determines that). It suggests that rooms are equipped appropriately and that learning can be enhanced through judicious investment of resources. It requires that student experiences be carefully conceived so they contribute to student learning, consistent with the mission and culture of an institution. In short, because the resources are finite, they must be used wisely.

Service

Students also have the right to expect good service. Much of what is provided in a residential environment is a matter of service—buildings kept in good repair, meals served on time, and information provided on an accurate, timely basis. This dimension of accountability cannot be overlooked. Students are used to being served well (see Lowery, 2004), and housing officers should do everything they can to provide a level of service that is consistent with what is advertised and consistent with how their institutions serve students in the other dimensions of their lives.

Learning

Finally, there is the commitment housing officers need to make to ensure that students have the best learning environment possible. The pressure on institutions to provide robust learning experiences has been a part of the higher education landscape for years (e.g., Study Group on the Conditions of Excellence in Higher Education, 1984; Wingspread Group, 1993). This emphasis is unlikely to change in the future. Plenty of ideas are available on how to provide for enriched learning experiences for students (Kuh, Schuh, & Whitt, 1991; Kuh, Kinzie, Schuh & Whitt, 2005), so housing officers can apply existing research and proven concepts to enrich the student learning experience. If anything, the emphasis on robust learning experiences for students will increase in the future. And housing officers will need to provide data that demonstrate the positive effects of the residential experience. (See Pascarella & Terenzini, 2005, for more information about the effect of the residential living experience on students.)

Sources of accountability pressures

Pressures on housing officers and departments come from a variety of sources. Three sets of pressure sources are discussed in this section: students and their parents; faculty and administrators; and additional stakeholders.

Students and parents

The concept of paying attention to what students and their parents expect from the college experience was acknowledged in a formal sense by the document "Reasonable Expectations" published by the National Association of Student Personnel Administrators in 1994 and then in a follow-up document by the Association of American Colleges and Universities in 2002 (National Panel, 2002). More recently, student expectations have been discussed in detail in a work edited by Miller, Bender, and Schuh (2005). Students and their parents have all kinds of expectations for college. Kuh, Gonyea, and Williams (2005) have covered this topic in depth, but most importantly they observe following: "students attending the same college may differ in what they expect from college. These varying expectations are a function of previous academic achievement, family socioeconomic and educational backgrounds, previous educational opportunities, and exposure to information regarding college" (p. 35). The three researchers provided substantial information about the use of the College Student Expectations Questionnaire (CSXQ; Kuh & Pace, 1999) as a means of measuring student expectations for college.

The value in the use of an instrument such as the CSXQ is that it can provide empirical information to use in aligning the student experience with student expectations and in making sure that what institutions report to prospective students about the experiences they can *expect* to have in college is consistent with the experiences students *actually* have.

Parents have certain expectations for the college experience of students, and they have another set related to what college attendance will cost. Mostly, they overestimate the costs of college. Rather than breathing a sigh of relief, college administrators, admissions counselors, and others responsible for communicating the cost of attendance to parents need to do a better job of explaining what it actually costs to go to college (Schuh & Ross, 2005), since students from low-income families are more likely to attend lower-priced institutions (The Institute for Higher Education Policy, 2002) and are very sensitive to price increases.

Faculty and administrators

Institutions of higher education have particularly stressful environments, exacerbated in part by a lack of agreement on institutional goals (Birnbaum, 1988) and ambiguity of power and success (Cohen & March, 1986). Faculty and administrators have expectations for student housing as well. Those on the business side of an institution expect that the housing operation will follow specific operational guidelines (Ryan, 2003; Tellefsen, 1990) while others, including faculty members, will look to student housing as the locus for learning communities and freshmen interest groups (Westfall, 1999). Regardless, housing officers need to clearly articulate the goals of their units and document the extent to which their goals have been achieved.

Additional stakeholders

External pressures come from a variety of sources. For the purposes of this discussion it is important to acknowledge that accountability pressures in student housing can come from two primary sources, including those who are concerned about the cost of attending college (e.g., Boehner & McKeon, n.d.) and those who are concerned about student learning (e.g., Wingspread Group 1993). In each case, the pressures from those external to higher education advocate strongly that higher education must be held accountable for the cost of attendance borne by students and their parents and for the level of student learning that occurs as a result of the student learning experience. Housing administrators cannot ignore these pressures, be they related to costs of attendance or student learning. Most importantly, data developed by assessment and evaluation studies will help housing officers demonstrate efficiency and effectiveness in their responses to these pressures.

Characteristics of Institutions With A Culture of Accountability

Some institutions have evolved to the point where they hold themselves accountable for their work. This matter of accountability, as it leads to continuous improvement, is part of the fabric of institutional life. Kuh, Kinzie, Shuh, and Whitt (2005) identified this institutional characteristic in their study of 20 high-performing colleges and universities. They found certain elements of these institutions that led to ongoing improvement and can be adapted by housing departments that continuously seek to improve. The following paragraphs are based on their work.

Efforts to improve are grounded in missions and values.   Mission and values support constant improvement at these institutions. Members are accountable to each other and their stakeholders. Feedback, such as the written evaluations in classroom experiences by faculty to students and by students to faculty, is provided routinely. Studies are conducted routinely on campus to learn how the quality of the student experience might be improved. In an environment where people offer feedback and information to each other on a routine basis, the evaluative data are not particularly threatening and become useful in terms of providing a basis for improvement.

They question what they do.   Members of these colleges and universities question what they do on a routine basis. This does not mean they are hypercritical of themselves, but that they are not afraid to ask such questions as

- Are we doing as well as we can?
- How might we improve the learning experiences of students?
- What barriers need to be overcome to improve students' experiences?
- How might we improve our efficiency?
- How might we develop partnerships across campus to deliver better experiences for students?

They are confident enough to revisit and rework policies and practices to improve.   When things are not working to the best advantage of students and others associated with an institution, institutional members are open to new and better ways to accomplish their objectives. That might result in reworking the curriculum, but it could also mean that the student experience in the residence halls could be improved if learning communities are the organizing unit (see Levine, 2001).

They are inclined toward innovation.   Just because things have always been done a certain way in the past does not mean that things will be done that way in the future. Innovation is very much a part of the fabric of the institutions. They are willing to take risks, to be unsuccessful, and to try again. For example, just because room assignments have always been done a certain way doesn't mean that a different approach might not be tried in the future. It also might mean that staffing patterns or roles could be recast so as to provide improved services and experiences for students. Residential staff roles might be reconfigured as student demographics change. The point is that staffs at these institutions are willing to try new ideas as long as the ideas are designed to accomplish the goals that the institutions set out for the student experience.

They collect data systematically.   Finally, and this is particularly important for the accountability dimensions of their work, these institutions collect data systematically. The effectiveness of programs is evaluated. The student experience is assessed. Data are available to inform decisions. The collection of information is a routine part of an institution's annual calendar. Rather than thinking about evaluation and assessment as "extra" tasks to be managed, they are part of the routine of offering programs, starting new initiatives, or redirecting efforts. To use a trite phrase, at the end of the day, or in the case of academic institutions at the end of the academic year, they know what has worked, what has not worked, and why.

Why Accountability in Student Housing?

The question of why accountability measures should be germane to student housing is raised from time to time and certainly is legitimate. Developing accountability measures takes time and effort and can distract housing officers from their primary, daily activities. So, a place to begin thinking about accountability is to answer the simple question: Why? Several answers based on Upcraft and Schuh (1996) are provided in this section:

Survival

Housing officers are under tremendous pressure to provide superior service and learning experiences for students at the lowest price possible. Unless they can demonstrate their ability to do so, private housing providers who are able to offer attractive off-campus housing options may supplant them.

The issue of survival is especially complicated when facilities are worn down and in need of updating. Contemporary students expect to have Internet access, cable television, and other amenities they have been used to in their homes. They want flexible meal plans and a minimum of rules to govern their behavior. All of this has to be provided and demonstrated to prospective students and their parents. Without some data that suggest that what is being promised actually is being delivered, the housing department may become vulnerable to competition.

Quality

A second dimension related to accountability is the quality of the student experience. Other than assertions of housing administrators, what evidence is available that shows that students have a high quality experience? Systematic data provide an opportunity to document that, in fact, the student experience is of high quality. This can be done through annual evaluations of the student experience, from their perspectives or through data that substantiate that students who live on campus actually have high quality experiences. An example of a high quality-experience is a specialized program described by Li, McCoy, Shelley, & Whalen (2005) that was linked to student satisfaction.

Affordability

Comparisons with the competition, be that off-campus housing or other institutions that recruit students from the same applicant pool, need to be conducted to document that on-campus living is affordable in the context of the competition. Securing the rates of the off-campus competition typically is not a difficult task, although comparing the costs and amenities of off-campus housing with on-campus housing can be tricky. On-campus housing may require a meal plan, where off-campus apartments very well may not. Off-campus housing rates may not include the costs of utilities or local telephone service, even though on-campus housing may build these services into the basic room rate. And developing a sound understanding of the room and board rates at other institutions can be a challenge, particularly if the facilities are substantially different. For example, comparing a standard residence hall room with an on-campus apartment at another institution may result in the proverbial comparison of apples and oranges. Nevertheless, the affordability dimension of student housing cannot be underestimated, especially when one is trying to position campus housing to be competitive with off-campus housing in terms of costs, amenities and the student's living experience.

Decision-making

Housing administrators make decisions all day long. Some are relatively minor and without dramatic implications, but others have far-reaching consequences. An example of the former may have to do with changing vendors for a particular product when a contract has expired. The latter might have to do with converting a residence hall from serving first-year students to a conference center. Account-ability means using available data to inform decisions rather than relying on instinct, or basing decisions on opinions voiced in the most recent edition of the newspaper; or the most recent regional or national trends. The use of data will help housing officers make the most informed decisions possible. That does not mean that their decisions will be infallible, but that they are more likely to make better decisions by using data than not.

Politics

Colleges and universities have many political characteristics (Birnbaum, 1988). Faculty members seek an emphasis on academics and learning as part of the student housing environment. Students want an emphasis on the social dimensions of the residential experience and parents may look for an emphasis on behavioral control. Balancing these desires, as well as those of the physical plant, the controller, and the bondholders, presents challenges for housing officers. Account-ability suggests that housing officers have a responsibility to all of these groups and others. Data will be helpful in working with these disparate groups.

Accreditation

Accreditation is another element related to why housing staff and their programs ought to be accountable for their work. It is clear that members of accreditation site visit teams are interested in the learning that the results from the student living experience. For institutions to simply report that students are satisfied with campus housing or that they have had an enjoyable experience is not enough. The student learning that results from living on campus is a crucial dimension for members of accreditation teams, and they will ask to see what evidence is available that supports the conclusions drawn by the housing staff.

An accountability model for student housing

Schuh and Upcraft (2001) described a number of different ways that assessment and evaluation could be conducted in student affairs. They provided advice for student affairs staff in terms of how they could conduct routine assessments that would generate data that could be used in evaluating the success of their programs, services, and activities. That model has been modified to identify how it might be applied in the context of accountability for housing officers.

Relational database

The first element of this model is that those responsible for the residence hall system should have good data about who lives in the residence halls. What are the demographics of residents? Are some classes overrepresented or underrepresented in campus housing? Are some students more likely than others to move out before the end of the year? Such important questions can be answered by the database.

From a financial point of view, do certain groups of students have more difficulty paying their bills on time than others; do some residence facilities experience more damage than others; are utility bills in some halls greater or less than expected? And from a student learning point of view, do some student groups learn more from their living experience than others, or are some students more (or less) likely to be retained than others?

A relational database can help develop the answers to many of these questions. And, as it provides answers to some questions, it is likely to raise other questions as well.

Needs assessment

A needs assessment should be conducted in advance of building renovations, a change in food service philosophy, or developing programs, activities, and other experiences for and with residence hall students. At times this can be done through surveys; at other times, student development theory can provide excellent guidance in identifying the needs of college students (Hamrick, Evans, & Schuh, 2002; Evans, 2001). Elsewhere (Schuh & Upcraft, 2001), it is argued that student affairs practitioners should differentiate between students' needs and wants. That is a crucial element of needs assessment. Student needs should be framed by how an institution can provide experiences that will help students learn within the context of its philosophy and the learning objectives that have been identified for students. Framing student needs with those objectives will provide a residential program that will have substance.

Satisfaction assessment

Another approach is to measure student satisfaction with their experiences. This measure must go deeper than simply determining if students had enjoyable experiences. Rather, the assessment can measure if students were satisfied with certain outcomes associated with their learning experiences. If not, why? If students are unable to accomplish their learning objectives, the difference between on-campus and off-campus living for students becomes blurred.

Student culture

Measuring and understanding student culture is another important element of assessment and evaluation. This kind of assessment will help those responsible for oversight of residence halls to gain a sense of what students value in their residential experience and what is unattractive to them. Aligning objectives for the residential experiences with what students value is a means of measuring accountability. Changes may be warranted if it is found that what students value is inconsistent with their experiences.

National standards

The Council for the Advancement of Standards (CAS) has developed a set of national standards for various student affairs units, including student housing (see Miller, 1996). The CAS standards provide an excellent accountability measure. They are an example of what professionals in the field deem appropriate for the operation. To be sure, not all elements of the CAS standards will be meaningful for all housing operations, but this is a particularly useful accountability measure, especially for those who are not housing professionals, since the concept of national standards has been applied to many aspects of contemporary life. The national standards can provide a series of baseline dimensions for a housing department, including such dimensions as mission, human resources, and leadership (Miller, 1997).

Another important set of standards developed for student housing was published in 2005 by the Association of College and University Housing Officers-International (ACUHO-I). Titled "Standards for College and University Student Housing," this document identifies standards for housing operations including business and management, physical plant, education and programming, food service, ethics, and qualifications for professional staff. ACUHO-I holds periodic workshops to provide in-depth training in the application of the standards by housing officers.

Cost effectiveness

Another accountability measure of particular value is the degree to which housing operations are cost effective. Typically, this means making comparative judgments using off-campus housing units or similar institutions as the yardstick in measuring housing costs. To be sure, there are always subtle and not so subtle differences between housing operations, but this measure is a good discussion point with students and other members of the campus community. For example, in some cases the housing operation will pay for security services provided by the campus police department. In other cases, these services are provided without charge. Similarly, the campus may provide without charge other services such as grounds keeping or accounting services, or they may be billed to the housing operation. Regardless, cost effectiveness is an important element in discussions of accountability for student housing.

Outcomes

Measuring student learning outcomes may be the most important element of any accountability program for student housing. Student learning is a primary focus of higher education institutions (along with research and public service). The more that student residential experience contributes to the learning objectives that institutions have identified for their students, the more central living on campus will be to the total student experience. Excellent examples are available for the residential learning experience (Barefoot et al., 2005), and these can be used to stimulate discussion about how the student learning experience can be enhanced.

Assessing outcomes can be a difficult process, but it is an absolutely essential part of accountability for housing officers. A particularly useful resource in measuring outcomes is provided by Terenzini and Upcraft (1996). Among the outcomes that might be measured are leadership skills, appreciation of diversity, or commitment to community service.

Comparable institutions

An increasingly popular accountability measure is the use of benchmarking. Doerfel and Ruben (2002) observed, "The past few years have seen the growth of centers on many campuses devoted to identifying, adopting and adapting effective organizational practices from other institutions and sectors" (p. 14). Student housing is no exception. Detrick and Pica (2001) have described the advantages associated with benchmarking, including how it may challenge long held beliefs, inform decision making, and motivate staff (pp. 56-57).

Benchmarking can be difficult in that identifying institutions for comparison can be a challenge. There are always nuances and subtleties that make comparisons difficult. Nevertheless, from an accountability standpoint, as long as institutions are relatively similar on the most important dimensions (institutional mission and control, capacity of housing program, financing plan), very useful comparisons can be made; and they will help the organization in its efforts to be accountable to its stakeholders.

The accountability challenge

Pressures abound on housing officers, and the work has become even more challenging and complex. One of the challenges housing officers face in contemporary practice is to develop strategies to meet the pressures of accountability. For those who believe that accountability will go the way of management by objectives or other management fads in higher education (see Birnbaum, 2001), my fear is that they will pay a price by taking this approach. Citizens are demanding increasing accountability from institutions, be they governmental, educational, medical, or other forms of public service. My suggestion to the housing officer who does not have an accountability strategy in place is to start somewhere. Build a relational database. Implement a systematic cost-effectiveness program. Measure the effectiveness of residential programs. By starting and learning about the process of assessment and accountability, confidence will come, and more complex projects then can be designed for the future. Accountability is being demanded of all of higher education, and student housing officers have an opportunity to take leadership on this very important issue. The challenge is to get started.

Conclusion

The environment in which housing officers work demands that they be able to produce data that underscore that they are accountable to their various stakeholders, internal and external to their institution of higher education. While this task is not easy, housing officers have no choice but to develop strategies that will satisfy this dimension of their work. Various forms of assessment and evaluation studies will help them achieve this goal.

References

About St. Olaf. Retrieved March 15, 2005, from http://www.stolaf.edu/about/

Association of College and University Housing Officers-International. (2005). *Standards for college and university student housing.* Retrieved May 17, 2005, from http://www.acuho.ohio-state.edu/resource%20center/ethical.html

Barefoot, B.O., Gardner, J.N., Cutright, M., Morris, L.V., Schroeder, C.C., Schwartz, S.W., et al. (2005). *Achieving and sustaining institutional excellence for the first year of college.* San Francisco: Jossey-Bass.

Barr, M.J. (2000). The importance of the institutional mission. In M.J. Barr, M.K. Desler, & Associates (Eds.), *The handbook of student affairs administration* (2nd ed., pp. 25-36). San Francisco: Jossey-Bass.

Birnbaum, R. (1988). *How colleges work.* San Francisco: Jossey-Bass.

Birnbaum, R. (2001). *Management fads in higher education: Where they come from, what they do, why they fail.* San Francisco: Jossey-Bass.

Boehner, J.A., & McKeon, H.P. (n.d.). *The college cost crisis.* Washington, DC: U.S. House of Representatives.

Cohen, M.D., & March, J.G. (1986). Leadership in an organized anarchy. In M.C. Brown, II (Ed.), *Organization and governance in higher education* (5th ed., pp. 16-35). Boston: Pearson.

Detrick, G., & Pica, J.A. (2001). The power of benchmarking. In R.L. Swing (Ed.), *Proving and improving: Strategies for assessing the first college year* (Monograph No. 33, pp. 55-59). Columbia: University of South Carolina, National Resource Center for the First-Year Experience and Students in Transition.

Doerfel, M.L., & Ruben, B.D. (2002). Developing more adaptive, innovative, and interaction organizations. In B.E. Bender & J.H. Schuh (Eds.), *Using benchmarking to inform practice in higher education* (New Directions for Higher Education No. 118, pp. 5-27). San Francisco: Jossey-Bass.

Evans, N.J. (2001). Developmental theory as a basis for assessment. In R.L. Swing (Ed.), *Proving and improving: Strategies for assessing the first college year* (Monograph No. 33, pp. 39-43). Columbia: University of South Carolina, National Resource Center for the First-Year Experience and Students in Transition.

Hamrick, F.A., Evans, N.J., & Schuh, J.H. (2002). *Foundations of student affairs practice.* San Francisco: Jossey-Bass.

The Institute for Higher Education Policy. (2002). *The policy of choice.* Washington, DC: Author.

Kuh, G.D., Gonyea, R.M., & Williams, J.M. (2005). What students expect from college and what they get. In T.E. Miller, B.E. Bender, J.H. Schuh, & Associates. *Promoting reasonable expectations: Aligning student and institutional views of the college experience* (pp. 34-64). San Francisco: Jossey-Bass.

Kuh, G.D., Kinzie, J., Schuh, J.H., Whitt, E.J., & Associates. (2005). *Student success in college: Creating conditions that matter.* San Francisco: Jossey-Bass.

Kuh, G.D., Schuh, J.H., Whitt, E.J., & Associates. (1991). *Involving colleges.* San Francisco: Jossey-Bass.

Levine, J.H. (2001). Assessing learning communities. In R.L. Swing (Ed.), *Proving and improving: Strategies for assessing the first college year* (Monograph No. 33, pp. 99-101). Columbia, SC: University of South Carolina, National Resource Center for the First-Year Experience and Students in Transition.

Li, Y., McCoy, E., Shelley, II, M.C., & Whalen, D.F. (2005). Contributors to student satisfaction with special program (fresh start) residence halls. *Journal of College Student Development, 46,* 176-192.

Lowery, J.W. (2004). Student affairs for a new generation. In M.D. Coomes & R. DeBard (Eds.), *Serving the Millennial generation* (New Directions for Student Services No. 106, pp. 87-99). San Francisco: Jossey-Bass.

Miller, T.E., Bender, B.E., & Schuh, J.H. (Eds.). (2005). *Promoting reasonable expectations.* San Francisco: Jossey-Bass.

Miller, T.K. (1996). Measuring effectiveness against professional standards. In M.L. Upcraft, J.H. Schuh, & Associates, *Assessment in student affairs* (pp. 252-272). San Francisco: Jossey-Bass.

Miller, T.K. (Ed.). (1997). *The book of professional standards for higher education.* Washington, DC: Council for the Advancement of Standards in Higher Education.

National Association of Student Personnel Administrators. (1994). *Reasonable expectations*. Washington, DC: Author.

National Panel. (2002). *Greater expectations: A new vision for learning as a nation goes to college*. Washington, DC: Association of American Colleges and Universities.

Pascarella, E.T., & Terenzini, P.T. (2005). *How college affects students* (Vol. 2). San Francisco: Jossey-Bass.

Ryan, M.A. (2003). Contemporary issues in student housing finance. In J.H. Schuh (Ed.), *Contemporary financial issues in student affairs* (New Directions for Student Services Sourcebook No. 103, pp. 59-71). San Francisco: Jossey-Bass.

Schuh, J.H. (2003). The financial environment of student affairs. In J.H. Schuh (Ed.), *Contemporary financial issues in student affairs* (New Directions for Student Services Sourcebook No. 103, pp. 3-16). San Francisco: Jossey-Bass.

Schuh, J.H., & Ross, L.E. (2005). Student expectations about paying for college: Are they reasonable? In T.E. Miller, B.E. Bender, J.H. Schuh, & Associates. *Promoting reasonable expectations: Aligning student and institutional views of the college experience* (pp. 102-121). San Francisco: Jossey-Bass.

Schuh, J.H., & Shelley, M.C., II. (2001). External factors affecting room and board rates: How much influence does the housing director have? *The Journal of College and University Student Housing, 30*(1), 41-47.

Schuh, J.H., & Upcraft, M.L. (2001). *Assessment practice in student affairs*. San Francisco: Jossey-Bass.

Study Group on the Conditions of Excellence in Higher Education. (1984). *Involvement in learning: Realizing the potential of American higher education*. Washington, DC: U.S. Department of Education.

Tellefsen, T.E. (1990). *Improving college management: An integrated systems approach*. San Francisco: Jossey-Bass.

Terenzini, P.T., & Upcraft, M.L. (1996). Assessing program and service outcomes. In M.L. Upcraft, J.H, Schuh, & Associates, *Assessment in student affairs* (pp. 217-239). San Francisco: Jossey-Bass.

Upcraft, M.L., & Schuh, J.H. (1996). *Assessment in student affairs*. San Francisco: Jossey-Bass.

Westfall, S.B. (1999). Partnerships to connect in- and out-of-class experiences. In J.H. Schuh & L.J. Whitt (Eds.), *Creating successful partnerships between academic and student affairs* (New Directions for Student Services Sourcebook No. 87, pp. 51-61). San Francisco: Jossey-Bass.

Wingspread Group on Higher Education. (1993). *An American imperative: Higher expectations for higher education*. Racine, WI: Johnson Foundations.

Concluding Thoughts: Strategies for Practitioners

Beth M. McCuskey, Ed.D.

What does the future hold for the campus housing profession? Of course, no one can say with total certainty. But within these pages are the collected insights from colleagues and professionals who are involved in the research and practice of student housing. Within these discussions, some common themes emerged. By examining those themes and then adapting them for their own practice, housing professionals can begin to form the foundation that will be required to succeed in the future.

Understand Campus Climate and Personal Administrative Philosophy

First, it is critical to understand one's campus climate in light of the administrative philosophy. The programmatic philosophy is important in determining approaches to residence life operations as well as issues such as the role of entry-level staff in the context of the institutional mission, the role of residents as learners, or the role of students as consumers. Given the many roles that housing officers juggle, they will likely have to consider each of these and many others.

There may be times when philosophical conflicts arise. As such, it's critical for housing officers to understand their own values and how they relate to the institutional mission and to the administrative values of key decision makers on campus. A housing officer who concentrates more on the financial bottom line may be exasperated by a new boss who expects to see data that demonstrates the impact of residential operations on the cognitive development of residents. When philosophies collide, it may be prudent to assess whether differences can be complementary or whether a new job is in order.

Similarly, understanding the philosophical leanings of campus administrators can help when seeking support for programs. Aligning with individuals with similar values may help to generate wider backing. Additionally, knowing what values are important to leaders can help in framing proposals for their consideration. Finally, housing officers should be open to considering other perspectives and how they may apply to their work.

Stay in Tune With the Changing Student Population

The demographics of the United States are changing rapidly. These changes speak to the racial-ethnic composition changes on campuses, enrollment numbers, and more. These changing demographics will play an enormous role in the delivery of programs and services. Are programs structured to meet the needs of a more diverse audience? Is space available to house the large numbers of students predicted to attend campuses? Similarly, what happens to this space if the numbers of matriculates decline after the predicted boom? How do greater numbers of students affect the culture of student life on campuses? All of these questions suggest the need for housing officers to closely monitor demographic shifts and discuss the implications of these shifts upon their programs.

Demographics are not the only area of consideration when exploring student trends. The cultural shifts that occur as generations change have huge implications for residential programs. Research findings put forth divergent views of the emerging current generation of college students. For example, it remains to be seen whether tomorrow's students are "team-oriented" or "self-interested." Whatever the result, there is no doubt about the value of attempting to stay attuned with today's middle- and high-school students to help forecast the trends housing officers will face during the next few years. Overall, attention must be paid to these generational shifts if programs are to remain relevant.

Involve Parents as Partners

Will parents be partners or problems on the college campus of the future? There has been much discussion on the Millennial students' reliance on their parents. Thinking of parents in this supportive role—or even as a "customer" group—is a relatively new phenomenon in the housing profession.

Housing practitioners are finding it difficult to balance their interpretation of the Family Educational Rights and Privacy Act of 1974 (FERPA), which limits parents' access to the educational records of their adult students, with increasing pressures by parents to discuss the needs of their students. Institutions must consider designing programs and services for parents. The effort required to meet their demands, though, is compounded by college administrators' own beliefs about what the collegiate experience should be. There is often sentiment that students cannot learn and grow effectively if their parents are standing by to intervene on their behalf.

Consider the responses when a case study recently was presented to a group of resident assistants involving the suicide death of a traditional-age college student. One of the questions that emerged from the case study was whether the institution should have done more to share information with the student's parents as an intervention strategy. The expectations were for a lively debate among the RAs about the role of parents in the lives of their college students. Instead, the group was incredulous that the parents weren't included as a partner in helping the student. Only one RA (out of about 70) took the position that the student was an adult and that her parents should not have been notified when her behavior became concerning. The point is that it's not just the parents who expect to be involved. The students expect them to be.

Parental involvement in programs is a current issue that has future implications. It behooves practitioners to have conversations on their campuses to discuss these issues and to have a consistent approach to dealing with parental concerns. This requires housing officers to step back from their own parental relationships during college and reflect on the current cultural changes that are underway on campuses.

Develop Broad-Based Expertise

The list of functional roles played by senior housing officers and their staff is lengthy. Among those are educator, technology administrator, human resource manager, facility manager, legal interpreter, and contract manager, to name just a few. Each campus is unique in how these duties may be allocated, but there is little question that residence life staff must have a broad understanding of a variety of different issues.

The "Jack/Jill of all Trades" moniker certainly could have been crafted with housing professionals in mind. It's not uncommon for an appointment calendar to list meetings about student learning, the budget, a major building renovation, enrollment management, students in crisis, and students with behavioral issues. Add to this the desire for housing professionals to be learning specialists and multiculturally competent, and one wonders how is it possible to develop an understanding in so many different areas?

First, it's important to recognize that no one can possibly know it all. Good resources, however, can fill the void. Practitioners in the position to affect the structure of a housing organization should hire staff members who complement their strengths. Housing officers not in that position should develop working relationships with colleagues on campus who can help them understand the fine points of facilities management or technology, for example.

Develop a library of excellent resources and commit to keeping that library current. Reading outside of the traditional higher education publications also can serve as a means of gaining insight into new issues. Attending a conference presentation on a topic that doesn't carry immediate appeal can also broaden horizons.

Finally, and most importantly, practitioners must stretch themselves. Picking a project outside of one's comfort zone is a good way to learn more about another aspect of the profession. Volunteering to lead a project in another area of campus or asking to be on a committee in an area that gives one a different perspective on a topic can lead to new insights.

The variety of chapters presented in this book serves as a reminder of the complexity within the housing profession. Through committing to continued learning, practitioners can prepare themselves to lead their organizations into the future.

Plan to Make the Best Use of the Money

Financial acumen is necessary when managing a large housing department. The revenue potential of housing departments is large and quickly determined by a calculation of housing capacity times housing rates. Of course, this only accounts for potential room and rent fees. Many housing departments earn millions of dollars in additional revenues from sources such as summer conferences, space rentals, and technology fees. A large base of expenditures subsequently offsets this large revenue stream. Thus, understanding the money means knowing where it's coming from and where it's going.

This is far easier said than done. Revenue streams are affected by occupancy, timely payment, competition, and changing preferences. Full occupancy at the beginning of the year is a good thing, but high levels of attrition throughout the year can affect the bottom line. Similarly, ineffective collection strategies can leave thousands of dollars unpaid at the end of the year. Student preferences also play into the revenue equation. Consider the captive market campuses had on long-distance telephone revenues in the late 1990s and how these streams have nearly dried up because of the emergence of phone cards and cell phone usage. Understanding what affects campus revenues is the first part of the equation.

Expenditures are arguably even more difficult to analyze, in part because there are generally more expenditure categories than revenue sources in a typical housing budget. Major categories of operational expenditures include salaries and benefits, utilities, debt service, and equipment replacement. Many housing departments also pay an assessment (sometimes also termed *overhead* or *administrative* fee) to central administration to offset centralized costs that are incurred by supporting the housing operation. Of course, there are a myriad of other expenditure categories ranging from supplies to staff travel.

Understanding exactly how expenses are generated and apportioned to the department is critical. For example, do salaries solely support departmental staff, or is this budget supporting staff in other university departments? Are departmental staffing patterns reasonable and are salaries consistent with institutional benchmarks, or is there an opportunity to save money by changing the nature of staffing? Are utilities metered or allocated based on some formula, and is the housing department getting the best utility rates available? Is the administrative assessment based on cost studies or calculated on some other basis? One caveat: Digging into expenditures may provide the opportunity to uncover additional resources, but also may expose other political issues. Housing officers should think through what ground they will tread upon before they head in that direction.

It's not enough to merely understand the revenues and expenditures that are generated and incurred by a department. Understanding the cash flow and cash balances is also critical. If a housing department is considered an auxiliary, it will generally have reserve accounts associated with it. These accounts may be used to cover an operational deficit, to purchase equipment, or to fund renovation projects. Other reserves may be required as part of the department's bond obligations. The key is to have a sense of how the cash position changes over time and how much cash is reasonable or required to be maintained in reserve. Having a plan for the cash is also key, whether it will be used to fund new construction or to replace old furnishings. Getting administrative backing for these plans also helps to ensure that the funds will be used to support student housing-related initiatives rather than to serve simply as an institutional money maker.

Collaborate

While there are many roles inherent within the housing profession, attempting to fulfill all of them as a stand-alone department is redundant at best. It is important to build relationships across campus and, when appropriate, with off-campus service providers to facilitate work.

An important first step in forging these alliances is for housing professionals to consider themselves equal to their colleagues in the business and academic realms of campus. Partnerships must first be about partners.

Partnerships are valuable in addressing needs related to information technology. Housing departments might consider strategic partnerships with either the campus IT office or an outside provider if they do not have an IT department. Similarly, a housing department may face a situation best met by partnering with an external company to develop student housing on campuses. When it comes to questions of facilities, housing practitioners must make sure they are at the table to discuss related issues across campus. Residential facilities are quite different from academic buildings, and helping colleagues appreciate the unique nature of student housing may pay dividends in reduced project costs. Finally, new academic approaches have increased the importance of collaborating with academic affairs colleagues. These sorts of partnerships are essential components of the blurring lines between the curriculum and the cocurriculum.

Collaborating may be a way to share resources, information, and ideas or to create seamless experiences for residents. It may be done formally (as when a contract is developed with a service provider) or informally (such as a group that meets over coffee occasionally to discuss student concerns). Collaborating also can serve as a mechanism to build relationships and to build support for programs.

Each campus has unique norms that play into how collaborative relationships become established. On some campuses, for example, vendors are partners, even before they get a bid award. They might be asked for their ideas before issuing a request for quotations. Other campuses restrict communication to vendors to the purchasing office until after a bid is awarded.

Different norms exist on campuses related to on-campus collaboration as well. In some cases, it is very easy to invite a colleague to coffee to discuss a project. In other cultures, such meetings must be arranged with great care. These differences do exist, and it's important for housing practitioners to recognize the cultures on their own campuses. By making the effort to build partnerships on campus, housing officers are poising their programs to serve the needs of residents well into the future.

Understand the Big Picture: Think Strategically

Housing departments do not operate in a vacuum. They are part of a much larger system and, as such, housing administrators must understand how the larger system affects the department. For example, as part of the campus community, housing departments are held to similar standards of operational performance as other units. But when serving in an auxiliary role, they are also held to a certain level of financial performance. An institution that is state-funded may be allocated funding to grant a 3% raise to all staff. As an auxiliary, the housing department also must grant those raises but must find those funds through higher fees or through reducing services. In a tight housing market, this could have occupancy implications. Understanding how to balance the auxiliary role with the department's role in the housing market is one example of the interplay departments have with larger systems.

Aligning the departmental mission with the institutional mission is another example of strategic thinking. Whether this is to support the academic culture of campus or to demonstrate financial prudence, housing administrators who wear an institutional hat as opposed to a departmental one are more likely to gain support from key administrators when it's necessary.

Getting blindsided can be an administrator's worst nightmare. One way to minimize the unforeseen is to pay attention to emerging trends. Are high school graduates peaking in the state next year? It may not be the time to propose building a new residence hall. What's happening nationally or internationally that could affect operations? There are a number of external forces that play upon housing operations. Staying in tune with those forces helps to avoid getting hit with the unexpected.

Big picture thinking also involves developing an understanding of the current state of affairs. Managing from the gut is not an effective strategy. How can practitioners evaluate whether or how to change without grounding their evaluations in hard data? There are several assessment strategies that can pave the way for departments to build data sets to assist with decision making. Developing a data-based understanding of one's own department combined with a general sense of the trends in the external environment helps housing officers to be better prepared for what the future might hold.

Stay Adaptable

All of the subjects discussed in this book have one thing in common: change. The future will not just be a reflection of today, and that is why campus housing departments must not only be able to adjust to change, but also be *willing* to adapt.

It's ironic that despite this changing environment, so much work is dedicated to the built-to-last bricks and mortar of institutions. While housing professionals experience continual pressure from students for the latest and the greatest, they also are making facility and corresponding financial decisions that can last decades. One strategy is to build contingency plans into facility master plans. Staging projects over several years buys time to ascertain the effect of new or renovated facilities on occupancy, enabling opportunities to change directions for the next phase if necessary. Constructing flexible buildings is another way to build adaptability into a facility master plan.

Building assessment strategies into departmental program planning efforts also enables a department to either tweak programs or to change directions. By requiring an assessment plan as part of any new program proposal, housing administrators can ensure that they have a quick way to gauge the effectiveness of a program whenever they need the data.

To be comprehensive, program assessment must include both formative and summative strategies. Formative assessment includes questions that gauge the success of programs along the way. An assessment plan for RA training, for example, might include formative questions such as the RAs' satisfaction with the training and their understanding of individual training modules. Formative assessment allows for a change in direction if needed. If RAs aren't satisfied with their training, how can it be changed? If they don't understand one of the modules, how can it be redelivered so they gain additional insight?

Summative assessment is comprehensive in nature and accommodates evaluation at the end. This type of assessment is linked to the original goals of a program. If one goal of RA training is to enable staff to build community, a summative question might include an assessment of the community that was developed on the floors. Resident satisfaction and institutional or departmental retention results also may be measures that indicate effective RAs (and thus the effectiveness of their training). While it becomes a little more work on the front end, building formative and summative assessment strategies into program plans enables practitioners to determine whether their programs are doing what they were designed to do.

These examples demonstrate it's no longer just enough to plan. The higher education environment is changing so quickly it is critical for plans to be responsive to change. This means being adaptable and making plans that include factors such as decision points, contingency plans, and assessment opportunities. Planning for change will continue to be a priority for the profession well into the future.

Determine What Is Important and Keep Track of It

Housing officers perform a variety of competing roles. Should funds be spent on facilities equipment or on programs? Should square footage be allocated for community use, or does every square inch need to be used to generate revenue? Additionally, changes in administration can sometimes force a change in what is deemed important. Thus, it's critical to understand what is motivating key administrators on campus. Being grounded in one's own professional philosophy and ensuring that this is aligned with the philosophy of one's campus is the first step in determining what is important.

Once one knows where administrators are coming from, it can be determined what data is most relevant. Does the budget need to be reviewed quarterly with the vice president for finance? If so, make sure that it's presented in a way that is easily explainable. Does the dean of students wish to review the housing department's discipline statistics? Make sure that the housing judicial database is accurate and reflects current cases. Building accurate data systems around topics that are important on campus helps to pave the way to demonstrate the effectiveness of an operation.

Data also can be used to drive planning purposes as a more proactive approach to management. One can explore retention trends, assess satisfaction, and develop an understanding of the student culture as ways to monitor the current state of affairs in the housing department. By taking the initiative to understand operations more fully, practitioners position themselves to take the lead in orchestrating change that will have a positive effect for students. Rather than merely generating data for administrators, one is now making informed decisions to move the housing organization into the future.

Data serves as the foundation for effectiveness and for change. Housing officers can use it to demonstrate their own managerial effectiveness when they align their data generation with the focus of campus administrators. Practitoners also can monitor various aspects of their departments as mechanisms to promote new directions. Without good data management, professionals are left to their own instincts, which is not an appropriate way to survive in a technologically advanced environment.

Invest in the Staff

When reflecting on the breadth of the operations that are managed, the nature of the students that come to campus, and the influences of the environments housing practitioners operate within, the complexity of a housing department's responsibilities becomes clear. Successfully accomplishing the required work under these conditions requires the dedication of staff, as well as the department's dedication to them.

Developing effective staff members who will work, and often live, on the front line with residents is one of the key functions of work within the housing profession. Attracting and retaining staff is also a major consideration and one that has been particularly concerning in recent years. But staffing also goes beyond the live-in positions and may include custodial and maintenance positions, clerical roles, accounting functions, and other professionals. Maintaining alignment with the department's vision among the breadth of staff members employed by a large housing department can be difficult.

Opportunities for staff members to enjoy each other socially can enhance working relationships. Departmental potlucks, awards ceremonies, or staff meetings can help to define the culture of the overall department as opposed to that of the smaller work group. Involving all staff in planning efforts—whether it's through a series of focus groups or as members of a planning committee—also can help to secure a broader appreciation of the department. Merely explaining how decisions are made can also help staff members think outside of their work group and understand the broader balancing act that administrators engage in.

Providing the staff who do not live in the residence halls an opportunity to work directly with students is another way to emphasize the broader goals of residence life work. Whether it's collaborating with the residence hall association on a fund raiser or involving students in the departmental committee structure, the connection between staff and students helps to solidify the greater educational purpose.

Training and professional development opportunities must also be provided as a way to help employees learn and grow. For professional staff, this might be easy: subscription resources or funding to attend conferences may provide necessary development opportunities. For clerical and service staff, defining creative opportunities outside of traditional online classes or OSHA training is in order. Consider taking staff to visit another campus to see how work is arranged there. Perhaps a professional staff member can develop a student development workshop for custodial staff. The possibilities are endless. The key is to take the time and effort to invest in the people who serve our students.

Conclusion

The authors of this book have shared their experiences and reflections and identified themes that should be prevalent in the future of the collegiate housing profession. It is certainly not an exhaustive list of ideas, but the book has been written with the hope that it will spur further reflection by its readers to generate action on our campuses.

This book should serve as a resource to stimulate creative thinking or as a topic for a reading group. With insights from many of the profession's most creative thinkers about the trends that influence our work, it was not written to sit on a shelf, but to spur further thought and action.

The authors of this book have taken the time to think beyond today and reflect upon tomorrow. Through researching trends—some directly related to our work, others more remote—they have captured the essence of the dynamics that confront our profession. This book is not a panacea for a lack of our own due diligence. To stay ahead of the curve, we must remain in tune with the changes in our work, the changing nature of our students, and the environments that confront us. Only then will we be best prepared to lay the proper foundation and begin to address the future of collegiate housing.

About the Editors

Beth McCuskey

Beth M. McCuskey is the director of residence life and dining services at the University of Wyoming in Laramie. Prior to this role, she held administrative appointments in the Housing and Residence Life Department at West Virginia University. She currently serves as the president of the Association of Intermountain Housing Officers (AIMHO) and as chair of the Association of College and University Housing Officers-International (ACUHO-I) Academic Initiatives Committee. She is also a member of the ACUHO-I Audit Committee and the *Talking Stick* Advisory Committee and serves as an ACUHO-I Foundation Trustee.

McCuskey received her education at West Virginia University, earning a B.S. in Economics, an M.A. in education administration, an M.S. in industrial relations and an Ed.D. in education leadership. Her doctorate, completed in 2003, focused on the future of the university housing profession and serves as the foundation for this book.

Norbert Dunkel

Norbert W. Dunkel is the director of housing and residence education at the University of Florida in Gainesville. He has held various administrative positions at the University of Florida, South Dakota State University, and the University of Northern Iowa. He cofounded the Association of College and University Housing Officers–International (ACUHO-I) National Housing Training Institute and served as its codirector from 1990–2000. He has served on the ACUHO-I executive board as publications coordinator and was elected the association's vice-president in 2006.

Dunkel has authored more than 40 articles and chapters and served as an associate editor for *The College Student Affairs Journal* and as editor of *The Journal of College and University Student Housing*. He has also edited or authored eight books and monographs, including coauthoring with Jon Coleman the book *50 Years of Residence Hall Leadership: NACURH, Inc.* in 2004. Norb also coedited a monograph in 2003 with Jim Grimm, *Campus Housing Construction.*

Dunkel received the ACUHO-I Presidential Service Award in 2005. In 2004, he received the NACURH Ken Stoner Distinguished Service Award and the 2004 James C. Grimm ACUHO-I Leadership and Service Award. In 2001, he received the ACUHO-I Research and Publication Award.

About the Authors

Chapter 1: Programmatic Philosophies in Residence Life

Phyllis McCluskey-Titus is assistant professor and program coordinator for the College Student Personnel Administration master's degree program at Illinois State University, Normal. Prior to accepting her faculty position, Phyllis held housing positions at Florida State University, Tallahassee; Indiana University of Pennsylvania, Indiana, Pennsylvania; Syracuse University, New York; and Western Illinois University, Macomb. Phyllis earned her bachelor's degree in history, her master's degree in college student personnel from Western Illinois University, and her doctorate in higher education administration from Florida State University.

Chapter 2: Understanding Students Today and Tomorrow .

Cynthia Anderson is the associate director of residence life and teaches graduate courses in counseling and student affairs as an adjunct faculty member in educational psychology at Northern Arizona University. Anderson has served her regional association (AIMHO) as the chair and faculty member for the AIMHO College and as program chair for the annual conference. Before her current role, Anderson served as the assistant dean of students and codirector of the master's program in student affairs. Anderson has degrees from Oregon State University (B.S. in elementary education, 1980), Colorado State University (M.Ed. in college student personnel, 1983) and Northern Arizona University (Ed.D. in educational leadership).

Richard Payne has been a housing professional for more than 25 years and has served as the director of residence life at Northern Arizona University for the past

12 years. Payne has been involved in ACUHO-I since the late 1970s and has served in numerous capacities, both regionally and nationally. In 1992 he received the Sage Award from the Association of Inter-mountain Housing Officers for his long-standing contributions and leadership within the profession. Payne holds a B.S. in education from University of North Texas, an M.Ed. in counseling from University of North Texas, and an Ed.D. in educational leadership from Northern Arizona University.

Chapter 3: Diversity and Multiculturalism on College Campuses

Dr. Mary F. Howard-Hamilton is a professor in the department of educational leadership, administration, and foundations in the higher education program at Indiana State University. She received her B.A. and M.A. degrees from the University of Iowa and an Ed.D. from North Carolina State University. Howard-Hamilton was a higher education administrator for 15 years and worked at five institutions fulfilling higher education administrative duties including orientation, developmental education, judicial affairs, multicultural affairs, commuter life, and residence life. As a researcher, Howard-Hamilton has published more than 75 articles and book chapters. Her areas of expertise are multicultural issues in higher education, student development theories, feminist theory and therapy, and consultation. Her first book – *The Convergence of Race, Ethnicity, and Gender: Multiple Identities in Counseling* – was coauthored with Dr. Tracy Robinson. Howard-Hamilton also has edited two New Directions in Student Services monographs on *Student Services for Athletes* and *African American Women in Higher Education*.

Susan D. Johnson is a doctoral candidate in the higher education and student affairs program at Indiana University. A native Floridian, she graduated from the University of Florida in Gainesville, earning a bachelor's degree in psychology along with master's degrees in social psychology and in student personnel. Before returning to graduate school as a full-time student, she spent 5 years as the coordinator of student organizations at the University of North Dakota. She is currently a project associate at the Center for Postsecondary Research, where she works with the National Survey of Student Engagement (NSSE). Her research interests include ethnic and gender identity development, issues of access and equity in higher education, and institutional research as it relates to strategic planning at universities and colleges.

Chapter 4: Academic Integration and Campus Transformation

William Zeller is assistant vice chancellor of student housing at the University of California, Irvine. He was formerly the director of university housing at the University of Michigan, Ann Arbor, and has held similar positions at Washington State University, Pullman, and Southeast Missouri State University, Cape Girardeau. He earned his bachelor's degree from Northern Illinois University, his master's in college student personnel administration from Western Illinois University and his doctorate in higher education administration from Iowa State University.

He is the author of more than 25 articles and book chapters with particular concentration on the first-year experience and living-learning programs. He has most recently served as a collaborator for the ACUHO-I sponsored National Study of Living Learning Programs. He has served as a consultant to many campuses in the development of new residential learning communities and facility design. He also has held several leadership positions in ACUHO-I, including chair of the Academic Initiatives Committee and the International Committee.

Chapter 5: Human Resources in Residence Life

Holley A. Belch is an associate professor in the student affairs in higher education department at Indiana University of Pennsylvania. Previously, she had been a faculty member at Southern Illinois University at Carbondale. She has held various administrative positions in student affairs at Arizona State University, Babson College (Massachusetts), and Siena College (New York).

Dr. Belch has received several grants from the Association of College and University Housing Officers International (ACUHO-I) for her research focusing on the issues and concerns of entry-level live-in professional staff in residence life. Her work has been published in leading journals, and she has authored several chapters in both the NASPA Monograph series and the New Directions for Student Services series. She has been a guest editor for a New Directions for Student Services sourcebook on students with disabilities and has served on the editorial boards of the *Journal of College Student Development*, the *NASPA Journal*, and the ACPA Books and Media Board.

Gary Kimble is the senior associate director of residence life at the University of Southern Mississippi. He has been involved in the housing profession for the past 28 years and has served the state, regional, and international association. He has served as a conference presenter at 20 previous ACUHO-I annual conferences as well as having served as a member of the ACUHO-I Executive Board. He has served the SEAHO region as president and host chair and was instrumental in the creation of the Southern Placement Exchange.

Chapter 6: Technological Change and Residential Operations

Azfar Mian is the associate director of administrative services in the Department of Housing and Residence Education at the University of Florida, Gainesville. In his role he maintains the offices of assignments, village housing (graduate and family housing), network services, and information technology for the department. He is the coauthor of the article, "The Lowdown on Illegal Downloading," published in the ACUHO-I *Talking Stick*, 22(6). In his tenure at University of Florida and Kent State University in Ohio, he has automated numerous manual processes and developed strategies to increase customer satisfaction, productivity, and efficiency. He has served as an IT consultant and has been involved in academic initiatives work. His recent work has focused on extending IT support across the Division of Student Affairs at the University of Florida.

Chapter 7: Managing Construction and Renovation in Residential Facilities

Mark D. Hill is the assistant director of housing for facilities management at the University of Florida, Gainesville. He currently sits on the campus-wide construction standards steering committee, the Campus Construction Managers and Professional Services Selection Committee, the Information Technology Advising Network Infrastructure Sub-Committee, and the Environmental Health and Safety Codes Enforcement Appeals Committee, among others. He has been involved in more than $85 million in new construction and $180 million in renovation projects during his tenure at the University of Florida. He previously coauthored a chapter in the book *Campus Housing Construction*, published by ACUHO-I (2003).

Fred Fotis has been chief housing officer at the University of South Dakota, Vermillion; the College of William & Mary, Williamsburg, Virginia; the Pennsylvania State University, State College; and the University of British Columbia, Vancouver. At these institutions he has been responsible for $300 million in new construction and $150 million in renovation projects. Fred currently serves as treasurer of the ACUHO-I Research and Education Foundation.

Chapter 8: Privatized and Off-Campus Housing Relationships

Jim G. Short is president of Century Campus Housing (CCHM). CCHM manages a portfolio of approximately 20,000 on-campus student beds on 31 campuses. He has been with CCHM since 1993. Prior to CCHM, Short worked for a variety of real-estate-related companies, a medical technology company, and a public accounting firm. He graduated from the University of Arkansas with a bachelor's in accounting. Currently Short is a certified public accountant, a certified property manager, and a licensed real estate broker in five states.

Christi R. Chisler is director of university services for housing, dining, and card services at George Mason University, Fairfax, Virginia. She also serves as the university ombudsman for nonacademic issues. Chisler has been at GMU for 11 years in that capacity and in other administrative positions. Prior to her career in higher education administration, Chisler was a management consultant for 11 years in the construction industry, working with developers, contractors, architects, and engineers. She received her master's in public administration from American University, Washington, D.C.

Chapter 9: The Changing Nature of Housing Operations

Alan Hargrave is the associate dean for student affairs and director of housing and residence life at Ball State University in Indiana. He holds bachelor's and master's degrees from Eastern Illinois University and a doctoral degree from Ball State University, where he serves on the faculty of the student affairs administration master's program. He has served as GLBT representative, Central District representative, and president of the Association of College and University Housing Officers-International and maintains active involvement in the association.

Chapter 10: External Pressures to Higher Education and Housing

James F. Conneely is vice president for student affairs at Eastern Kentucky University. Before going to Eastern Kentucky, Conneely spent 10 years at the University of Arkansas as assistant vice chancellor for student affairs and director of residence life and dining services. He also has 7 years at Emory University both as an assistant director for residential facilities and associate director for residential services. Conneely's most recent publications include editing a book on careers in university housing and coauthoring a chapter in the New Directions in Student Services series titled "Consumers, Adversaries, and Partners: Working with Families of Undergraduates."

Claire Good is the associate vice president for student affairs and dean of students at Eastern Kentucky University. She received her doctorate in counselor education from the University of Arkansas in 2002. Good spent the first 15 years of her career in student affairs, working in various positions from resident hall director to interim director of university housing at Northwestern State University in Louisiana, the University of Arkansas at Monticello, and at the flagship campus of the University of Arkansas in Fayetteville. Good has been at Eastern Kentucky University since September 2003.

Chapter 11: Financial Pressures to Higher Education and Housing

Ernest R. Goeres is professor of educational leadership studies in the College of Human Resources and Education at West Virginia University, where he previously served as assistant, associate, and interim deans.

Chapter 12: Accountability in Student Housing and Residence Life

John H. Schuh is distinguished professor of educational leadership and policy studies at Iowa State University. Previously, he has held administrative and faculty assignments at Wichita State University, Indiana University (Bloomington) and Arizona State University. Schuh has been studying the college student experience for 35 years.